A Psalms Devotional
God's Comfort and Direction for Us
Second Edition

250 Daily Devotionals

By David Meengs

A Psalms Devotional
God's Comfort and Direction for Us
Second Edition

By David Meengs
English

Copyright 2019
Second edition, first printing 2021
Biblical Counseling Worldwide

All Scripture quotations are from the NIV unless otherwise mentioned.

ISBN – 978-0-9849619-5-5

Published and distributed by:

Biblical Counseling Worldwide
P. O. Box 547
Caledonia, MI 49316
USA

Printed in the USA By Sheridan Publishing

Dedication

This book on the psalms is dedicated to those who are in physical, mental and spiritual prisons.

"Remember those in prison as if you were their fellow prisoners, and those who are mistreated as if you yourselves were suffering."
Hebrews 13:3

A Psalms Devotional

God's Comfort and Direction for Us
Second Edition

250 Daily Devotionals

"For everything that was written in the past was written to teach us, so that through endurance and the encouragement of the Scriptures we might have hope." Romans 15:4

Thank You

There have been many efforts to get this devotional book out. I just wanted to acknowledge those who have helped. Mary, my dear wife of 49 years has spent many hours over the past three years going over this material. She has corrected mistakes and has given good advice when something was not said as well as it could have been. Thanks to Rebecca Van Laan who worked on the cover and to Mandie Wierenga who did the final edit of this work. What a big help and comfort they both are, as we go to print. There are others who have helped who have asked to remain unknown. Our thanks to them!

Above all, we want to thank our God who has established a relationship with us so that we might be devoted to Him. He has blessed us and encouraged us. May His Name be lifted up! The very last verse in the Psalms sums it up for us all. *"Let everything that has breath praise the LORD. Praise the LORD!"* Psalm 150:6.

The Author

David Meengs

Text	Title of the Devotion
Psalm 23:3a	God restores His children
Psalm 23:3a	God restores our soul
Psalm 23:3b	God guides us, *"for His names sake"*
Psalm 23:4a	He is with us, *"through the valley"*
Psalm 23:4b	Fear is not faith!
Psalm 23:4c	God disciples us
Psalm 23:4c	God comforts us
Psalm 23:5a	God prepares a table for us
Psalm 23:5b	God delivers us
Psalm 23:5c	God anoints us
Psalm 23:6a	Faith doesn't doubt the goodness of God
Psalm 23:6b	God gives eternal life to us
Psalm 24:1-2	This is my Fathers world
Psalm 24:3-5	Who may go to Heaven?
Psalm 25:11	A great lesson in prayer
Psalm 25:16-18	The lonely must turn to God
Psalm 26:1-3	*"Vindicate me, O LORD"*
Psalm 27:1	*"The LORD is my light"*
Psalm 27:4	*"Gaze upon the beauty of the LORD"*
Psalm 27:12-14	*"Wait for the LORD"*
Psalm 28:7	*"Give thanks to Him in song"*
Psalm 29:3-4	*"The voice of the LORD"*
Psalm 30:4-5	Our attitude is everything
Psalm 30:11-12a	*"That my heart may sing"*
Psalm 31:5	Do we trust our soul to God?
Psalm 31:9	*"Be merciful to me, O LORD"*
Psalm 31:15-16	*"My times are in Your hand"*
Psalm 32:3-4	Confession, to overcome depression
Psalm 32:4-5	Confession, the cleansing of the soul
Psalm 32:5	I will confess my own sins
Psalm 32:5	Our sin has physical consequences
Psalm 33:1-3	*"Sing joyfully to the LORD"*
Psalm 33:8	God, the perfect designer
Psalm 33:11	God doesn't change, what a blessing!

Text	Title of the Devotion
Psalm 51:5	Why do we sin?
Psalm 51:10a	*"Create in me a pure heart, O God"*
Psalm 51:11	The work and evidence of the Holy Spirit
Psalm 51:12	When we lose the joy of Your salvation
Psalm 51:13	Restored, to restore others
Psalm 51:17	God loves a *"broken and contrite heart"*
Psalm 52:1	Who in "the church" is boasting of evil?
Psalm 53:5	God despises our foolish and evil enemies
Psalm 54:2	*"Hear my prayer O God"*
Psalm 55:22	*"Cast your cares on the LORD"*
Psalm 56:8	*"List my tears on Your scroll"*
Psalm 57:2-3	*"To God who fulfills His purpose for me"*
Psalm 58:10-11	*"Surely the righteous still are rewarded"*
Psalm 59:16	I will sing of Your strength and love
Psalm 60:12	The battle is the Lord's
Psalm 61:1-2	*"Lead me to the Rock that is higher than I"*
Psalm 62:1-2	Resting in God *"alone"*
Psalm 62:11-12	*"You will reward each person"*
Psalm 63:3-4	*"I will praise You as long as I live"*
Psalm 64:6-8	God strikes down those who mock Him
Psalm 65:4	*"You choose, and cause to approach You"*
Psalm 65:9	God's gift, NOT "mother nature's"!
Psalm 66:18	When God doesn't hear our prayers
Psalm 66:19-20	God is worthy of our praise
Psalm 67:5-7	Praising God brings us His blessings
Psalm 68:35	God gives power and strength to His own
Psalm 69:30	How well do I communicate praise to God?
Psalm 70:5	Prayer, a gift to *"poor and needy"* sinners
Psalm 71:18	Strengthen us to teach the next generation
Psalm 72:12-14	How much does injustice bother you?
Psalm 72:19	*"Amen and Amen"*
Psalm 73:2	*"My feet had almost slipped"*
Psalm 73:2b-5	When self-pity almost buried Asaph
Psalm 73:1-2, 23-25	True faith believes in three tenses

Text	Title of the Devotion
Psalm 74:19	LORD, see our affliction
Psalm 75:4-5	'I Did it My Way'
Psalm 76:10	God's wrath against men brings Him praise
Psalm 77:2	Suffering, our souls alarm clock
Psalm 77:3b-4	Bible characters were depressed
Psalm 78:40	Our rebellious sins grieve the heart of God
Psalm 78:52-53 AMP	*"But God"*
Psalm 79:9 & 11	*"The groans of the prisoners come before You"*
Psalm 80:19	*"Restore us, O LORD God Almighty"*
Psalm 81:13-14	If only we would listen to God
Psalm 82:3-4	*"Rescue the weak and needy"*
Psalm 83:1-4	Israel's enemies are God's enemies
Psalm 84:11	Thinking God's thoughts brings *"honor"*
Psalm 85:10 ASV	Grace and truth, the balance we need
Psalm 86:1-2	A needy believer petitions a merciful God
Psalm 86:16-17	When God's mercy and goodness meet
Psalm 87:1 & 6	Is our spiritual house Rock solid?
Psalm 88:10-12	The misery of a severe trial
Psalm 89:1-2	A life-long commitment to evangelism
Psalm 89:14	The justice of God is our salvation
Psalm 90:10-12	*"Teach us to number our days"*
Psalm 91:2-4a	My God, *"is my refuge and my fortress"*
Psalm 91:4b	God's faithfulness, our *"shield"*
Psalm 91:5 & 11	We have God's guardian angels!
Psalm 91:14-16	Seven *"I will"* promises of God
Psalm 92:12-15	Flourishing and bearing fruit in old age
Psalm 93:1-2	*"You are from all eternity"*
Psalm 94:3;5;7	The wicked say, *"The LORD does not see"*
Psalm 95:1-2	Called to worship God
Psalm 95:7b-8a	Called to worship, not to make excuses
Psalm 96:9	Worship the holiness of God
Psalm 96:13b	He will judge the peoples, *"in His truth"*
Psalm 97:10	*"Let those who love the LORD hate evil"*
Psalm 98:9	*"Sing,"* the holy Judge is coming

Text	Title of the Devotion
Psalm 99:1	*"The LORD reigns, let the nations tremble"*
Psalm 99:5	*"Worship at His footstool; He is holy"*
Psalm 100:1-2	*"Worship the LORD with gladness."*
Psalm 101:1-4	Living a holy life, Part 1
Psalm 101:2a	Living a holy life, Part 2
Psalm 101:3	What is wrong with quitters?
Psalm 102:1-2	In distress again, I cry to God!
Psalm 103:1-2	*"Forget not all His benefits"*
Psalm 103:2,5	My God keeps me young!
Psalm 103:13-14	God's divine pity
Psalm 103:17-18	God's forever love to our grandchildren
Psalm 104:1	Talking to your soul
Psalm 105:1-4	Our covenant responsibility to God
Psalm 105:13-15	Do not touch My anointed ones
Psalm 106:35-37	Sons and daughters, sacrificed to demons
Psalm 107:10-13	A addicts only hope
Psalm 107:23-26	When our courage melts away, then what?
Psalm 108:12-13	*"With God we will gain the victory"*
Psalm 108:12-13	*"With God"* demons become beggars!
Psalm 109:30-31	Looking to God when unjustly accused
Psalm 110:1-2	The reason there is a New Testament
Psalm 111:10	Fear of the LORD, the beginning of wisdom
Psalm 112:1a & 7	Like Father, like son!
Psalm 113:5	*"Who is like the LORD our God?"*
Psalm 114:5-6	Why does the creation obey God?
Psalm 115:8-9	Idols deceive us!
Psalm 115:11	No help from idols; big help from God
Psalm 116:1-2	*"He has turned His ear to me"*
Psalm 116:7-9	Rest in the Lord, *"once more"*
Psalm 116:15	We die in order to live forever!
Psalm 117:1-2	Radical Christianity from a radical Savior
Psalm 118:4	Do I believe His love endures forever?
Psalm 118:8	Self-confidence or God-confidence?
Psalm 119:1-2	Introduction to the longest Bible chapter

Text	Title of the Devotion
Psalm 119:9	A young man can keep his way pure!
Psalm 119:11	Are our devotions a delight?
Psalm 119:33-34	Obedience, God's responsibility or ours?
Psalm 119:67	Affliction, God's way of teaching us
Psalm 119:116-117	*"Do not let my hopes be dashed"*
Psalm 119:165	God's secret to peace
Psalm 120:6-7 NKJV	When others treat us badly, then what?
Psalm 121:2-4	More than a traveling Psalm
Psalm 122:6-9	Peace, security and prosperity in the church
Psalm 123:1-2	We are totally dependent on God
Psalm 124:8	Our help is in the name of the LORD
Psalm 125:1	Difficult trials are the food of faith
Psalm 126:5-6	*"Go"*
Psalm 126:6	Sow the seeds, return with joy
Psalm 127:1-2a	Over commitment brings down the house
Psalm 128:1	When God is your walking friend
Psalm 129:2-3	The church family, abusive or loving?
Psalm 130:7	Hope in the LORD's *"full redemption"*
Psalm 131:1-2a	Have I *"stilled"* my soul?
Psalm 132:15	Blessings to those who trust in the LORD
Psalm 133:1	Relationships, the spice of life
Psalm 134:3	God's benediction, receive it with joy
Psalm 135:5	Self-confidence or God-confidence
Psalm 136:1	God's mercy to us is personal
Psalm 137:1	Why do we hurt the ones we love?
Psalm 138:8	*"The LORD will fulfill His purpose for me"*
Psalm 139:1-3	Searching for a Biblical spouse
Psalm 139:7-10	God is always everywhere present
Psalm 139:23-24	Search my heart, Lord
Psalm 140:4	Moving with the wicked is ugly
Psalm 141:1	Moving with God is beautiful
Psalm 142:1-2	David's cave experience
Psalm 142:3-4	When my spirit grows faint, God knows
Psalm 142:5-6	In our desperation, may our faith look up!

Psalm 1:1-2

"Blessed is the man who does not walk in the counsel of the wicked or stand in the way of sinners or sit in the seat of mockers. But his delight is in the law of the LORD, and on His law he meditates day and night."

God's way to a *"blessed"* life

We all want a *"blessed"* life, but at times our lives do not seem very blessed. The psalms direct us to a real *"blessed"* life! Psalm 1 is a great introduction to the psalms, to a heart to heart relationship with God. It is noteworthy that the content of Psalm 1, is the same message Jesus used to introduce Himself to His new disciples in Matthew 5:3-12. There also, the word *"blessed"* is used nine times. Blessed is not a single blessing, but blessings, a benediction from our faithful God!

There are two ways to live life: man's way, and God's way. Blessed is the man who lives God's way. But if a person is intent on living man's way, the pattern is shown in the first verse. See the progression of man's unblessedness. First we *"walk"* in the counsel of the wicked. What they have to say sounds interesting! Captivated, we now *"stand"* in the way of sinners. We are becoming comfortable with sin that is beginning to rock us to sleep. Finally, we *"sit"* comfortably with those who mock truth, order and decency. We are no longer sensitive to the wrongness of sin but an advocate of it. Sin has become our habit and we are now a slave to it. That is man's problem!

A man who chooses to live God's way is interested in doing what is right according to God. He will not always be able to do what is right but will ask God for help. He will study and take pleasure in what is right instead of what is wrong. He will say "I'm sorry" when he fails. He asks for forgiveness when he sins. But his delight is in a close, not a distant, relationship with God. Such a person will be blessed because God is leading him. God will make him flourish.

So do we want a blessed life, living God's way? Or, do we want a cursed life by "doing life" man's way? God help us to live His way. *"For it is God who works in you to will and to act according to His good purpose,"* Philippians 2:13.

Prayer: Lord, we appreciate Your introduction to the Psalms and a closer walk with You. Open our eyes and give us the strength to live for You. In Jesus' name we pray. Amen.

Psalm 2:1-2

"Why do the nations conspire and the peoples plot in vain? The kings of the earth take their stand and the rulers gather together against the LORD and against His Anointed One."

What is your world-view?

This educational psalm pleads for us to think as God does! The psalm ends by teaching us there is just one World Leader. He knows the truth about the world and its condition. That King is Jesus! He lived. He died and was buried. He was resurrected and is now ascended in Heaven. He presently sits at the right hand of God. He is in charge of this world and the next. See how this psalm shows it is His world.

"The nations conspire and the peoples plot in vain." This means that some national leaders and individuals quickly have wrong world-views. They often do not know why they are in the world and why they are in power. Their agenda is vain, for it conflicts with what is true according to God. It is vain, because as God tells us here and in Acts 17:26-28, we are here to find Him and to know Him. A world-view *"against the LORD and against His Anointed One,"* is rebellion.

In Psalm 2, we have different voices. The first voice is of leaders and people who are defiant towards God, which we have seen. Now secondly, we have the voice of God to man. He is *"the One enthroned in Heaven laughs. The LORD scoffs at them."* God sees the foolishness of the defiant. How can we, who are a speck of dust, who live in chaos, try to tell the Creator God, that He is not needed? That is a giant pride problem!

The third voice of God, to Jesus, speaks in verses seven to nine. *"He said to Me, 'You are My Son...Ask of Me and I will make the nations Your inheritance, the ends of the earth Your possession."* God gave everything to His Son. God said of Jesus, *"You will rule them with an iron scepter; You will dash them to pieces like pottery."* If Jesus is not for someone, they are broken pottery, good for nothing, unable to be repaired. How vain it is to plot our "own" course in life.

Prayer: Lord, we see the foolishness of thinking that we don't need You. Lord God, bring some sense into our minds so we "get it" before it's too late! In Jesus,' our Savior's name, we pray. Amen.

Psalm 2:11-12

"Serve the LORD with fear and rejoice with trembling. Kiss the Son, lest He be angry and you be destroyed in your way, for His wrath can flare up in a moment. Blessed are all who take refuge in Him."

"Kiss the Son"

We have seen the beginning of Psalm 2 that some men are against God. Some work so hard to try define who God is. But the opposite is true. It is God who defines who we are and what our relationship to Him must be. God also tells us, *"The heart is deceitful above all things and beyond cure. Who can understand it? I the LORD search the heart and examine the mind, to reward a man according to his conduct, according to what his deeds deserve,"* Jeremiah 17:9-10.

The voice of the Holy Spirit speaks in Psalm 2. He has an inspired message for us *"all."* Serve God, not sin! *"Therefore, you kings, be wise; be warned; you rulers of the earth?"* God holds every ruler on this earth accountable. *"Serve the LORD with fear and rejoice with trembling."* It is man's habit to serve himself first. He may even serve others at times. But God's order of love and service is to serve Him first. If we do, then we will have the heart to serve others and not be so ungodly selfish!

"Kiss the Son." How can God be any clearer? We must respect the Son of God. He who gets the Son, gets God. He who rejects the Son, rejects God the Father and God the Holy Spirit also! The ugly sin of rejecting the Holy Spirit is the only sin that is without pardon! The reason is that the Holy Spirit points us to Jesus Christ. Here the Holy Spirit says, *"kiss the Son."* Our life for all eternity will be determined by whether or not we *"kiss the Son."* We can't blame God in the Judgment if we do not respond to the truth. Thus we must kiss the Son.

The wise Mark Twain said, "The most important days in your life are the day you are born and the day you find out why." God tells us, don't miss the main point of life. *"Kiss the Son."*

Prayer: Eternal and Holy Lord, what a great message You give us in Psalm 2. In the midst of all the useless noise in this worldly world, may we be still and know that You are God. May we reach for You with all of our heart. We do not want to be destroyed. We want to be with You now and for all eternity. In Jesus' name we pray. Amen.

Psalm 3:1-2

"O LORD, how many are my foes! How many rise up against me! Many are saying of me, 'God will not deliver him.'"

Get out of God's sandbox!

Satan's demons are masters at doubt and discouragement. Our text is what we say to ourselves, in response to those who hurt us. I just met a suffering veteran and told him to get out of God's sandbox.

I first met this man in the jail "Psyc. Pod," where the very mentally unstable are put. The truth was, he was also spiritually unstable. A serious drinking problem finally put him behind bars. His home life was bad, and he drank to try block it out. He was without God in his life. God used the depression book I wrote, to get through to him. He grew in his faith and was able to leave the "Psyc. Pod." I saw him many times.

Months later, I met him again, in the city. It was good to see him again. He began to sob, as he tried to catch me up in his life on the "outside." Through tears he told me how his wife left him for another man, and she was heavily drinking. She refused to come back to him. I told him, "You need to get out of God's sandbox."

I pointed at a small two column chart on the wall. I said, "That left column is, "Be Faithful." That is your responsibility. The larger column is labeled, "Results," and is God's sandbox, His responsibility. You are crossing the line. You are too focused on the results of your new faithfulness. You are not drinking, yet, Satan's demons are pushing you to do just that. Get out of God's sandbox before you do!

You are not strong enough to change your wife and bring her back. That is God responsibility, His sandbox. You smile when your wife does something good. You frown when she does something bad. Up and down you go, without peace. Who is the Prince of Peace, your wife or God? You must faithfully do everything for God's approval, first. Then, wait on the Lord. Wait for Him to change her, and you will be at peace. Your good God is trying to teach you that. Be faithful, pray, put your hope in Him. Smile as you trust in Him.

Prayer: Loving Lord, help us to understand that all we have to do is be faithful and then, leave the results to You, who alone are able to do miracles. In Jesus' name we pray. Amen.

Psalm 3:8

"From the LORD comes deliverance. May Your blessing be on Your people."

David's testimony on God's protection

David had many serious trials. Years after they were over with, David looked back in worship. He made some key points, to guide us through our difficult times. David highlights three main points that we, in faith, need to seriously act on.

<u>Pray your heart out</u>! David was not a silent prayer warrior. "O LORD, how many are my foes! How many rise up against me!" Psalm 3:1. David knew there were many against him. Surely, there were even more threats than David knew about, but God dealt with them too. David knew and could say in praise to God, *"But You are a shield around me, O LORD, You bestow glory on me and lift up my head,"* Psalm 3:3. David openly admitted, *"To the LORD I cry aloud."* The fervency of the heart is good, and God notices. David prayed his heart out.

<u>Expect God's answers</u>! *"He answers me from His holy hill,"* Psalm 3:4b. In Heaven, God is "tuned in" to His precious children. Our God, with His acute sense of justice for the oppressed, has the ability and desire to pour out His mercy. When God hears, He answers. At times the answer may be "No" or "Not yet," but He always answers. Expect God's sure answers.

<u>Experience God's safety</u>! David wrote, *"I will not fear the tens of thousands drawn up against me on every side,"* Psalm 3:6. The reason is in our text, *"From the LORD comes deliverance."* He who owns all, controls all, for He sees all who are His. He, who has all power and all wisdom, is able to deliver His own children. Does it really matter how strong our enemy is? Intellectually, we do need to ask this question. We know the answer. God is stronger than all. Now by faith, we need to believe it. For greater is He who is in us than he who is in the world!

Prayer: Lord give us the faith to believe fully in You. For we know that whatever comes our way, You will provide *"deliverance."* Though there will be trials, they will only serve to drive us closer to You! We praise You. In Jesus' name we pray. Amen.

Psalm 4:4

"In your anger do not sin; when you are on your beds, search your hearts and remain silent."

David to unbelievers: Stop your sinful anger!

David begins the psalm by praying to God for relief from his many persecutors. In verses two through five, David talks to unbelievers who are trying to harm him! David asks them, *"Why do you try to 'shame' me? Why do you love your delusional thinking? Don't you know, 'the LORD has set apart the godly for Himself."* You can't really hurt me, so stop trying! *"The LORD will hear me when I call."* Those God elects to salvation, He also elects to hear their cries for mercy! Wow!

David tells his unbelieving enemy, *"Think on your bed at night about what you are doing. 'Stand in awe and sin not,'"* KJV. The NIV says, *"In your anger do not sin."* David said this to unbelievers! However, they can't stop their anger without a new heart from God. Paul quoted David in Ephesians 4:26. Notice that Paul said this to believers! Why then, do many believers try justify their anger from this verse. To believers, Paul adds, *"Get rid of all bitterness, rage and anger, brawling and slander, along with every form of malice,"* Ephesians 4:31. This is the very Gospel itself. Christians have a new heart filled with the needed grace and power of God. They can replace their anger. Christians must *"Be kind and compassionate to one another, forgiving each other, just as in Christ God forgave you,"* Ephesians 4:32

James agrees. In 1:16-18, he points out how God gave us the gift of salvation. Therefore, he concludes: *"My dear brothers take note of this: everyone should be quick to listen, slow to speak and slow to become angry, for man's anger does not bring about the righteous life that God desires,"* James 1:19-20. If you disagree, then why was Moses severely disciplined for striking the rock in anger in Numbers 20:10? Was his anger at wayward Israel "righteous"? No. God considered the sin so great that He did not let him enter Canaan!

If unbelievers are responsible for their sinful anger, then believers are doubly responsible to show grace actions, instead of angry ones.

Prayer: Lord, we see the Gospel message. Give us changed hearts, softened by Your grace. Help us act like Jesus! Lord impress this on us so that we stop our sin of anger. In Jesus' name we pray. Amen.

Psalm 4:4-5

"In your anger do not sin; when you are on your beds, search your hearts and remain silent." Offer right sacrifices and trust in the LORD."

Trusting in God, overcomes anger

Yesterday's message is so important for us to see the seriousness of our anger, that we repeat this verse. Did we ever consider that our anger is not trusting in God? Imagine that a brother and sister are fighting and hurting words are exchanged. If looks could kill, two murders just occurred. God and Satan are watching this drama. Satan smiles in his front row seat. This is his kind of fight, and we have foolishly provided the entertainment.

Our anger is very wrong. It doesn't trust God to fix a relationship problem. Our anger says that we will handle it ourselves. But did God not say, "leave room for God's wrath, *'For it is Mine to avenge; I will repay,' says the Lord,"* Romans 12:19b?

Overcoming anger includes thoughtful listening to others. When we are willing to listen it says, "I love you, and care about what you think and about what is going on in your life." When we do speak, be careful how we speak! *"A gentle answer turns away wrath, but a harsh word stirs up anger,"* Proverbs 15:1. People of all ages long to be understood. Our anger fixes nothing, but our listening does. After a long argument, sometimes days later, we begin to ask questions as we finally begin to listen. It is then that we solve problems and establish relationships. Listening increases our commitment to one another and builds relationships. James counsels us, "My dear brothers, take note of this: *"Everyone should be quick to listen, slow to speak and slow to become angry,"* James 1:19.

We want our homes to be a safe and comfortable place. Listening instead of anger teaches our children good theology! Our relationship problems can be overcome by a change of heart, ours first!

Prayer: Lord, our anger has pushed many people away and has prevented good relationships. You even tell us that we cannot love You of we don't love others. Lord forgive our sinful anger. In Jesus' name we pray. Amen.

Psalm 5:2-3

"Listen to my cry for help, my King and my God, for to You I pray. In the morning, O LORD, You hear my voice; in the morning I lay my request before You and wait in expectation."

Praying, *"in the morning"*

What if your best friend was with you all day and you did not talk to him until evening? All day you talked to many others and your good friend was there, always present. Still, you never had a word to say to your friend who for years was there for you! There were problems both big and small and your friend was wiser than all, but you sought the advice of others instead.

Can you imagine how much God is offended when we do not lay our request before Him in the morning? After all, no detail is too small for God to care about. His omniscient eyes saw everything in our past. Every present and future concern is fully known to Him, without any surprises. In His wisdom, He knows what is best for us. His power can bring about exactly what we need. He has a storehouse of blessings that is beyond description. Add to that, His sovereignty completely rules over us and everything He created. By not going to God in prayer in the morning, we ignore the Fatherly concern He has for us and the praise He deserves.

The Lord loves to care for us, His children, especially when we are in a difficult situation. How can we possibly *"wait in expectation"* for God to answer our prayers, if we do not even discuss our day with Him? If we do not specifically pray, how would we know if God answered our prayers? Then, how would we thank Him? To not pray in the morning is to waste the best part of the day.

Let us then, be like Daniel who not only prayed in the morning, but also noon and night! *"The LORD is good to those who hope in Him, to the one who seeks Him; it is good to wait quietly for the salvation of the LORD,"* Lamentations 3: 25-26.

Prayer: Lord, forgive our lack of true devotion to You. How foolish we are when we do not sincerely start the day in prayer. Conform us to Your will, dear Lord. In Jesus' name we pray. Amen.

Psalm 6:8-10

"Away from me, all you who do evil, for the LORD has heard my weeping. The LORD has heard my cry for mercy; the LORD accepts my prayer. All my enemies will be ashamed and dismayed; they will turn back in sudden disgrace."

My enemies, *"will turn back in sudden disgrace."*
David is fully aware of the difference between a forgiven sinner and an unforgiven enemy of God. That's why he confidently says that God accepts *"my cry"* and *"my prayer."* His enemies that formerly accused him, are now turned back *"in sudden disgrace."* Notice how a believer has <u>grace</u> and an enemy has <u>disgrace</u>. Who is this Author of both? How privileged that God knows us and how to reach out to us.

When we are in pain with an inner broken heart and when we are oppressed from outward circumstances, we need to meditate on the amazing grace of God to believers. David begins the psalm passionately praying, *"Be merciful to me, LORD, for I am faint; O LORD heal me for my bones are in agony. My soul is in anguish. How long, O LORD, how long?"* Psalm 6:2-3. David is weeping, in agony, in pain. What beautiful music this is to God's ears when needy sinners turn to Him for help. God wants to ignite our passion for Him! We too must cry to God as David does, looking earnestly for God who accepts our prayer cry. He is our help and strength.

David has been experiencing a loving rebuke from God to wake him up and mature his walk with God some more. God never wastes the pain He allows His children to have. Pain and misery brings us to our knees, but the mercy of God lifts us back up! It is God's great pleasure to give us mercy. He loves to do it, just in time! We get God's mercy in our time of need, not our time of want! David knows, his time of need is near, as he cannot take much more.

God's mercy here is His covenant giving of His inexhaustible supply to those of us who do not deserve it. At the same time, our enemies get what they deserve. *"All my enemies will be ashamed and dismayed; they will turn back in sudden disgrace."*

Prayer: Lord, as Christians, we wonderfully experience the fullness of Your gracious mercy. May our hearts be filled with gratitude, making us more useful for Your kingdom! In Jesus' name we pray. Amen.

Psalm 7:9-11

"O righteous God, who searches minds and hearts, bring to an end the violence of the wicked and make the righteous secure. My shield is God Most High, who saves the upright in heart. God is a righteous judge, a God who expresses His wrath every day."

The *"righteous"* wrath of *"God Most High"*

The wrath of God is almost a forgotten doctrine. It is rare that a preacher wants to preach on the wrath of God. It is more popular to teach about the love of God. However, the Bible speaks more about God's wrath than His love. We cannot understand salvation apart from the wrath of God. True, Christ saves us from our sin, but more accurately, Jesus saves us from the wrath of God.

God's wrath is not a flaw in His character and has nothing to do with uncontrollable rage or bitterness. God is slow to anger. God's wrath is connected to His holiness and to His perfect justice as the judge of all the earth. His holy wrath is against sin and sinners that are not covered by the blood of Christ.

Part of our problem is that we do not think we deserve God's wrath! The truth is, we are all born sinners, and are increasing in sin each day. *"As it is written: 'There is no one righteous, not even one,'"* Romans 3:10. God's holiness and justice demands that He punish sin. God's love, provides Jesus to give us atonement, to turn His wrath away from those who are being saved.

The wrath of God is not just a future reality, in sending unbelievers to Hell. God, *"expresses His wrath every day,"* are David's exact words in our text. *"The wrath of God is being revealed from Heaven against all the godlessness and wickedness of men who suppress the truth by their wickedness,"* Romans 1:18. As God's children, His wrath will, *"make the righteous secure."* Why or how? God's wrath is no longer against us! For this reason, why should we be angry or bitter at anyone? For a believer, God's wrath is a blessing and our comfort!

Prayer: Righteous Lord, we thank You for providing Jesus, Your perfect Lamb, as the atonement for our sin! May we flee to Christ every day! For You not only save us, You are also our daily protector! Thank You Lord! In Jesus' name we pray. Amen.

Psalm 8:1

"O LORD, our LORD, how majestic is Your name in all the earth! You have set Your glory above the heavens."

Your name Lord, how majestic!

Great songs have been made of this verse! For there is only one God, not many gods! Five S reasons show how God's name is majestic.

1. God's name is *"majestic"* for our **salvation.**

"Salvation is found in no one else, for there is no other name under Heaven given to men by which we must be saved," Acts 4:12. *"Yet to all who received Him, to those who believed in His name, He gave the right to become children of God,"* John 1:12.

2. God's name is *"majestic"* for our **sanctification.**

Living a sanctified life is purposeful living. *"Whatever you do, whether in Word or deed, do it all in the name of the Lord Jesus, giving thanks to God the Father through Him,"* Colossians 3:17. *"Where two or three come together in My name, there am I with them,"* Matthew 18:20.

3. God's name is *"majestic"* concerning our **security.**

"The name of the LORD is a strong tower; the righteous run to it and are safe," Proverbs 18:10. There is always and only safety in God, both in this life and in the next. Who else is a *"strong tower"*? None!

4. God's name is *"majestic"* in all our **suffering.**

"The apostles left the Sanhedrin, rejoicing because they had been counted worthy of suffering disgrace for the Name," Acts 5:41. Suffering disgrace for doing wrong is nothing, yet suffering disgrace for His *"Name"* is everything!

5. God's name is *"majestic"* in our **supplications.**

We not only must pray in the name of Jesus, but He teaches us how to pray! Jesus said to us personally, *"This then is how you should pray: 'Our Father in Heaven, hallowed be Your name,'"* Matthew 6:9. *"Therefore God exalted Him to the highest place and gave Him the name that is above every name, that at the name of Jesus every knee should bow, in Heaven and on Earth and under the Earth,"* Philippians 2:9-10.

Prayer: *"O Lord, our Lord, how majestic is Your name in all the earth!"* You are so worthy of our worship and we give it to You! In Jesus' name we pray. Amen.

Psalm 9:9-10

"The LORD is a refuge for the oppressed, a stronghold in time of trouble. Those who know Your name will trust in You, for You, LORD, have never forsaken those who seek You."

The Lord is a refuge for the oppressed

David has been rescued, again. His heart is full of praise to God. David knows, God makes what is impossible for us, a normal love transaction for Him. That's why David says, *"I will be glad and rejoice in You; I will sing praise to Your name, O Most High,"* Psalm 9:2. It is our responsibility to thank God for His grace to us. Satan wants to take us to the grave with sadness. God wants us to praise His great salvation and deliverance! David gets very praise specific, in what God has done. *"My enemies turn back; they stumble and perish before You. For You have upheld my cause,"* Psalm 9:3-4a. It is God's presence that defeats the enemy, every time!

Personally, I was told a certain terrorist in India tried to harm me. But God protected me from even being touched! God alone makes *"my enemies turn back."* God has done this often that I know of, and I trust, more times when I was unaware. It was God who *"upheld my cause."* Why? Because it's His cause, and I belong to Him, body and soul! For many years I was reluctant to talk about the amazing *"refuge"* God provides. I thought it was a private matter, for my faith and trust in Him. It was, but David is insistent; *"I will tell of all Your wonders."* Is David bragging about his deliverance? No! He wants us to know, God is, *"a stronghold in time of trouble. Those who know Your name will trust in You, for You, LORD, have never forsaken those who seek You."*

Satan hates it that God seeks out refugees, which is the Gospel itself. *"Those who know Your name will trust in You, for You, LORD, have never forsaken those who seek You."* There is only one refuge in time of trouble. All other ground is sinking sand! David pleads with God, for the sake of His Own Name! *"Have mercy and lift me up from the gates of death, that I may declare Your praises."* Yes!

Prayer: Refugee seeking Lord, You delivered David often, for Your name's sake and for David's also. You who were his help, are ours! By Your grace, we take refuge in You. In Jesus' name we pray. Amen.

Psalm 10:2, 6, 11

"In his arrogance the wicked man hunts down the weak, who are caught in the schemes he devises." "He says to himself, 'Nothing will shake me; I'll always be happy and never have trouble.'" "He says to himself, 'God has forgotten; He covers His face and never sees.'"

How a wicked man thinks

David asks a difficult question that we also think about. He asks God, *"'Why do You hide Yourself in time of trouble?' Don't You see what the wicked are trying to do to me?"* The question needs an answer. But then, David kind of answers it himself as he reviews how a wicked person thinks, speaks and works to do evil. This tenth Psalm is often called the Psalm of the Antichrist.

The wicked do care about spiritual things! Along with Satan, their father, they hate God and everything God loves. The wicked are proud and arrogant. He *"hunts down the weak."* His agenda is selfish as he *"schemes."* He plans trouble for others and then does trouble! *"In all his thoughts, there is no room for God,"* Psalm 10:4b.

The wicked person *"says to himself, 'Nothing will shake me; I'll always be happy and never have trouble.'"* The wicked are that blind to the danger they are in, for there is a truth-knowing Lawgiver, who cannot turn His back on that which is evil.

The wicked, *"says to himself, 'God has forgotten; He covers His face and never sees.'"* The wicked are much like a dumb ostrich that puts his head in the sand and sees no trouble. Wicked Haman thought his devious schemes would bring him honor. He did not see that his own wicked scheming would come back on himself. He did not consider that God cannot and will not be mocked, not ever!

God tests us as Christians, waiting to see how we will react to those who are wicked. We must never cover our face to the ways of the wicked. All it takes for evil to prevail is for good people to do nothing. We must hate evil, but not evil doers. We must let our light shine into their dark world. We have the truth that sets people free from darkness. Go into all the world and teach the Gospel.

Prayer: Lord, we thank You for helping us see how an evil person thinks. Deliver us from the scheming of the wicked. Help us to shine light and to present Your truth to many. In Jesus' name we pray. Amen.

Psalm 10:17-18

"You hear, O LORD, the desire of the afflicted; You encourage them, and You listen to their cry, defending the fatherless and the oppressed, in order that man, who is of the earth, may terrify no more."

The Lord fights our terrorists

This psalm is so true and encouraging! Even as a wicked man schemes and plots, it is God's plans that prevail. David prays just two words in response to the truth in our text. *"Arise, LORD!"* David calls on God for His mercy to outsmart and over power the trouble the wicked intend. David saw God's mercy early in life with the lion, the bear and the giant. David knew the size of these enemies. But more importantly, David experienced the larger size of his God! Therefore he cries out boldly in prayer, *"Arise, LORD! Lift up Your hand, O God. Do not forget the helpless,"* Psalm 10:12. What a lesson for us!

We have five points in two verses. First, God hears *"the desire of the afflicted."* Desires are often unspoken, yet God hears them since He knows our heart. God's perfect sense of justice, makes Him listen to us, on all occasions. And when God listens, He already has help on the way, *"in our time of need,"* as Hebrews 4:16b teaches.

Second, God encourages the afflicted! We can't live well without hope! Our God is a Master encourager who fully promises us in 1 Corinthians 10:13, we will not have afflictions, more than we can bear. As believers, our trials will only serve to strengthen us.

Third, God listens to the cry of the afflicted! A lifeguard for 20 years was asked, *"How do you hear a cry for help in all this noise?"* He said, my ear is tuned in to a cry for help! God is a Lifeguard with ears a million times stronger. He is expectantly listening for us.

Fourth, God defends the oppressed! God has a heart for the orphan, the widow and the oppressed. The helpless are not really helpless. They can call out to God who is a real Help!

Fifth, God stops the wicked who terrify others. The life of a bully is a short one. The old saying, *"He who lives by the sword, dies by it,"* is so true. God's sword of justice is sharp and quick.

Prayer: Compassionate Lord, You teach us to put our trust in You, who are always bigger than all our trials! We thank You for being our strength and shield. In Jesus' name we pray. Amen.

Psalm 11:1-3

"In the LORD I take refuge. How then can you say to me: 'Flee like a bird to your mountain'? For look, the wicked bend their bows; they set their arrows against the strings to shoot from the shadows at the upright in heart. When the foundations are being destroyed, what can the righteous do?'"

The Church's, 'One Foundation'

David is feeling the torment from those who want him out of the way. He is in conflict, should he run? Or, should he wait on God to protect him? David's struggle is ours as our soul battles to trust in the goodness of God in times of affliction. We want to trust God but there still is a part of "weak faith" in us that wants to get away from it all. We have before us, the best advice, inspired by God Himself.

David sees real danger. The enemy is ready to shoot! The bow is strung. The arrow is in place. The bow is bent. Their intent is clear. Common human sense says, "Run!" But faith speaks, "Pray and look for God to act." A trusting faith knows that God is bigger than our every problem. A mature faith has experienced that God is not just our refuge, He is also our strength. David here is battling to put off his self-inflicted worry. So must we. Worry ends, where faith begins.

God, in His wisdom, allows another great trial to test David's faith. In the very same trial, Satan, is working to tempt David to abandon his faith in God. Satan is whispering, "Your God cannot protect you." "Your strength in God is over." Satan knows our text is true. *"When the foundations are being destroyed, what can the righteous do?"*

David's faith is not over but is instead awakened! By faith David reasons, *"The LORD is in His holy temple; The LORD is on His heavenly throne,"* Psalm 11:4a. The Lord is observing it all! *"The LORD examines the righteous, but the wicked and those who love violence His soul hates,"* Psalm 11:5. This is a present hatred as well as a future one. But note, vengeance belongs to God, not to us. We are to love sinners but hate the sin.

Prayer: Dear preserving and protecting Lord, how our soul battles with the evil one's temptations. How lovingly You build our faith one trial at a time. Forgive our worry, and build our trust. May Your Spirit help us to keep our eyes on You. In Jesus' name we pray. Amen.

Psalm 12:2-4

"Everyone lies to his neighbor; their flattering lips speak with deception. May the LORD cut off all flattering lips and every boastful tongue that says, 'We will triumph with our tongues; we own our lips-who is our master?'"

Liar, liar, pants on fire

In David's day the times were really bad. Saul was in power and Israel is again wicked. David cannot find anyone he can trust. David cries to God in the first verse, *"Help, LORD, for the godly are no more; the faithful have vanished among men."* Then David speaks about a nation full of faithless liars. David is surrounded by liars and he is fed up with all the deception. Liars never consider how disruptive their unending lies are. They do not realize or care how much extra work and expense their lying is to others.

It is the height of self-confidence and self-exaltation when a person will lie and then swear it is the truth. It is a lie to cheat someone and then say you are honest. It is a lie to know the truth and then say you do not know what happened. It is a lie to say you like what someone did, when you did not care for it. Liars selfishly manipulate their words thinking they are bettering themselves. They have no fear of God, which is why David calls them godless. A liar is a god unto himself, not considering there is a God who made his lips.

Can you imagine, managing a bunch of liars? You must make your decisions again and again because the truth is not known. Satan is the father of liars, for he was a liar from the beginning. His destination is the fires of Hell. The kids' rhyme, "Liar, liar, pants on fire" has a ring of truth in it. Unless a liar gets a new heart, the fires will be an unending torment for them. The truth is: *"The good man brings good things out of the good stored up in his heart, and the evil man brings evil things out of the evil stored up in his heart. For out of the overflow of his heart his mouth speaks,"* Luke 6:45. Lying is evil.

Prayer: Holy and loving Lord, You made our lips to praise You and to be a blessing to others. All liars mock You and break Your loving command to, *"not bear false witness."* Lord, heal us and our nation for Your name's sake! In Jesus' name we pray. Amen.

Psalm 13:1-2

"How long, O LORD? Will You forget me forever? How long will You hide Your face from me? How long must I wrestle with my thoughts and every day have sorrow in my heart? How long will my enemy triumph over me?"

When God is silent

David lacked comfort and encouragement. He asked God five serious questions. We do not know the reason for David's discomfort. But one thing we do know, when God is silent, He is up to something! We know that God uses His silence to test us, to see what we will do. Will we remain faithful? Will we trust His heart when we do not understand His Almighty hand? We can see that David is very bold in asking God questions, yet by verse five he passed the stress test in saying: *"But I trust in Your unfailing love; and my heart rejoices in Your salvation."* Thinking on the joy of His salvation really helped David and it will help us!

When God is silent, Satan is busy lying to us. He is whispering, "Do not trust in God, He has forgotten you." "God is not able to care for you and come to your aid." "He has many other things that are more important than you." Remember how Satan tempted Eve to doubt God. Satan wants to cool our relationship with God, yet God wants to warm us up to Him.

By God's grace alone, our hearts desire Him! We cannot live a joyful life without His close presence and favor. Every hour we need His fellowship; without it we are undone. Our Christian friends are a great comfort to us, but God is closer than a friend. His Spirit speaks to our spirit. When God seems silent, we must cry out to the Holy Spirit to intervene for us. When God seems silent, we must be sure that our daily schedule brings praise and honor to His name. When God is silent, may we then "Trust and obey, for there is no other way to be happy in Jesus, than to trust and obey."

Prayer: Faithful Lord, we are so grateful that You teach us to come boldly to You in prayer, seeking Your mercy. May we by faith rejoice in Your salvation like David did, for no one can snatch us out of Your loving hands. Lord, we worship You for Your eternal faithfulness. In Jesus' name we pray. Amen.

Psalm 14:1a

"The fool says in his heart, 'There is no God.'"

The Psalm of the Atheist

In King David's day there were atheists, those who did not believe in the existence of God, as described here. The first word in the Hebrew Bible is Elohim, a name for God. Genesis one starts, *"God in the beginning."* An atheist does not believe there was a God in the beginning and there is no God now. They do not believe there is a Judge of all the Earth; nor do they believe in a providential God. When Richard Wurmbrand witnessed to an Atheist Communist, he would try to get them to understand that there is a God who provides vegetables, fruits, eggs, meat to eat and good water, exactly everything we need.

Satan believes in far more truth about God, than an atheist does. Satan believes in the Trinity; in God the Father, in Jesus Christ the Son and in the Holy Spirit. Satan is well aware of The Judgment that is coming. Two of his demons asked Jesus, *"Have You come here to torture us before the appointed time?"* Matthew 8:29b.

An atheist hates God's good laws to govern a society. God who sees and knows everything says, *"They are corrupt, their deeds are vile; there is no one who does good,"* Psalm 14:1b. God asks in Psalm 14:4, *"Will evildoers never learn-those who devour My people as men eat bread and do not call on the LORD?"* An atheist has no respect for God or for His people. They chew on Christians like they are a hunk of bread. An atheist tries to, *"frustrate the plans of the poor."* How evil it is to step on those who are already down. Jesus, lovingly lifted up the poor. Out of respect for Christ, we also help the poor.

The truth is: an atheist really hates God. If they hate God, then they really do believe that God exists! It is our prayer that they will cry out to God for mercy before it is too late. The truth also is: in Hell there will be no atheist. Everyone there will be fully convinced of the holiness of God, as they experience His unending holy wrath.

Prayer: Holy and loving Lord, You are the hope of all who cry out to You for help. This psalm comforts us with the fact that You are *"present in the company of the righteous."* Even though *"evildoers frustrate the plans of the poor,"* You are our refuge! We worship You. In Jesus' name we pray. Amen.

31

Psalm 15:1

"LORD, who may dwell in Your sanctuary? Who may live on Your holy hill?"

Who may dwell in Heaven?

David asks a most solemn question! Who will be allowed into Heaven? In the verses that follow, there is no mention of God's grace. Why? If the grace of God is in us, we will live God's way, for then we have a relationship with God. We then also have the power of God's Spirit. Because of His holy presence, we do certain holy things!

"He whose walk is blameless and who does what is righteous." Christians will not do the things the world does. The lifestyle of God's child shows. Christians love "the truth" and tell the truth because God is truth. Liars are children of Satan, their father. God's children will not say false things about others to tear them up. Lovers of God, love others. It does not matter if "others" are evil, the person is still loved, even as their deeds are hated. Christians act merciful because God is merciful. That means Christians are nice to those who do not deserve it. That is what mercy is, and exactly what God did for us in salvation. He expects us to do the same and rewards us when we do!

Those who are Heaven bound will also give honor to those who fear the Lord, to those who are of the same household of faith. God's children give encouragement and help where it is needed. Heaven's children will lend money to those in need without "usury," excessive interest. Holy Spirit driven people search for where they can be a blessing, and do it with a grateful heart.

In a few short verses, God shows us that those who go to Heaven will have visible fruit in their lives, just like a good fruit tree. It is obvious that a good tree has to have roots to grow fruit. Rooted in the Lord Jesus Christ, Christians bear good fruit. The fruit does not save a Christian, but it flourishes because of an attachment to Christ.

Prayer: Faithful Lord, how beautifully the Psalm ends. *"He who does these things will never be shaken."* No one can shake the fruit off a person rooted in God their Rock. Lord, fill us with Your Spirit to bear more fruit. In Jesus' name we pray. Amen.

Psalm 16:7-8

"I will praise the LORD, who counsels me; even at night my heart instructs me. I have set the LORD always before me. Because He is at my right hand, I will not be shaken."

We have the most Wonderful Counselor!

What a huge difference there is between the world's counsel and the counsel of God. Since God made us, it only stands to reason that He knows how we should live. He made us, body and soul and counsels us on how our minds should direct our bodies. *"His divine power has given us everything we need for life and godliness through our knowledge of Him who called us by His own glory and goodness." "Through these, He has given us His very great and precious promises, so that through them you may participate in the divine nature and escape the corruption in the world caused by evil desires,"* 2 Peter 1:3-4. God's laws and character examples and the principles taught in the Old and New Testaments are totally, everything we need. Our mental responses must be based on God's revealed will. There are at least four parts to God's Biblical counsel.

1. God helps us to understand our problems from His view. *"There is a way that seems right to a man, but in the end it leads to death,"* Proverbs 14:12. God's way of living is the opposite of man's way. Man says that we need to love self more to come out of our problems. God says that we need to deny self.

2. God gives Biblical hope. *"God is faithful; He will not let you be tempted beyond what you can bear,"* 1 Corinthians 10:13a. This is a promise for every believer, based on the faithfulness of God. The world tries to get us to "cope" in our trials, God gives hope.

3. God helps us change Biblically. The world's change is most often, from one bad habit to another. God counsels us to put off our old destructive habits like anger or bitterness and replace them with forgiveness. He makes us put on a new pattern of living.

4. God guides us to practice Biblical living. He gives us His Spirit to convict us when we live wrong and His same Spirit fills us with joy when we live His way. His Spirit makes us a doer of the Word.

Prayer: O Lord, we praise You for Your flawless life-changing counsel. You are awesome! Accept our praise. In Jesus' name we pray. Amen.

Psalm 17:1-3

"Hear, O LORD, my righteous plea; listen to my cry. Give ear to my prayer-it does not rise from deceitful lips. May my vindication come from You; may Your eyes see what is right. Though You probe my heart and examine me at night, though You test me, You will find nothing; I have resolved that my mouth may not sin."

"May my vindication come from You"

What a great example we have before us. This is how to act when "people" do wicked things to us. Many advocate "righteous anger" as a Biblical response to an evil person. They even quote King David's writings as a proof that their anger is righteous and good. But based on this psalm and the rest of the Bible, God is the One who has the right to correct the evil person. Even though David is tempted by the demonic to be angry, he does not retaliate himself. His words are carefully chosen for us to understand a critical truth.

"May my vindication come from You." So often in this psalm, David wisely cries to God! He appeals to God's omniscient eye that sees everything. He pleads for the holy justice of God to rescue him. He begs for the covenant promises of God's faithful providence. *"Show me the wonder of Your great love."* With great affection David asks God, *"Keep me as the apple of Your eye."*

David's refuge here is in God, not in his strong army, not is his own sharp sword! David's faith looks to and depends on God, even though his enemies are coming after him and he is already "surrounded." He cries, *"Rise up, O LORD, confront them, bring them down; rescue me from the wicked by Your sword."*

What confidence David has in God! David fully believes in the all-powerful attribute of God. He goes to sleep in faith, not in fear! David closes the psalm looking to God, the same way he began. *"And I - in righteousness I will see Your face; when I awake, I will be satisfied with seeing Your likeness."* This too must be our prayer.

Prayer: Loving and protecting Lord, like David, we are surrounded by enemies. We too pray, *"May my vindication come from You."* In Jesus' powerful name we pray. Amen.

Psalm 17:15

"And I - in righteousness I will see Your face; when I awake, I will be satisfied with seeing Your likeness."

Touching the face of God

Did you ever watch a little baby try to communicate with a parent that is holding them. The baby touches the face, especially the eyes and the mouth. The baby knows that those senses are speaking to them, trying to establish a relationship with them. So they focus intently on the face, probing into the one that is interested in them. This is a very beautiful picture of how the Christian must seek God's face.

Here in this Psalm, David's heart is to know God and for God to know him. See how clearly that is expressed when David said, *"Keep me as the apple of Your eye; hide me in the shadow of Your wings,"* Psalm 17:8. David wants to be very close to God. That must be the ultimate longing of our hearts too! We will not find rest, until we rest in Him. David ends the Psalm with the words of our text.

We know that no one has ever seen God the father, because God is a Spirit. Yet these words are said in a way we can understand what our longing for God must be. We were created to know God and to seek Him. Paul instructed idol-worshiping people that God did not live in temples as they believed, but that His dwelling was in the hearts of men, in our spirits. God specifically put each one of us on this earth for one specific reason. *"God did this so that men would seek Him and perhaps reach out for Him and find Him,"* Acts 17:27a.

Prayer: Beautiful Lord, we have not sought Your face for our spiritual good and for Your glory. We often wander from the shelter of Your wings, where we can touch You and learn to know You better. Lord, we so quickly cuddle up to the things of this world and then wonder why our relationship with You is not what it should be. Lord forgive us once again, for we want to touch Your face, to know You better, and to serve You more faithfully. Lord touch us in this because we are weak. In Christ's name we pray. Amen.

Psalm 18:6, 16-17

"In my distress I called to the LORD; I cried to my God for help. From His temple He heard my voice; my cry came before Him, into His ears. He reached down from on high and took hold of me; He drew me out of deep waters. He rescued me from my powerful enemy; from my foes, who were too strong for me."

David's enemy blesses him!

King Saul had an intense jealousy and hatred of David. How will David respond to this threat? How will we respond to those who try to harm us? This is one of life's most difficult tests. In fact, it is a major exam! Our response will greatly determine our spiritual, physical, mental and social well-being. Our enemies can be used by Satan and his demons to make us ugly and miserable. Or, our enemies can be used by God to make us more beautiful. David's right response to the wicked Saul, both protected him and helped him grow up spiritually. Our right response will protect us also. Let's see what David did.

David did not retaliate and take matters into his own hands. He calls Saul, *"my master," "the LORD's anointed'"* and *"my father."* Through this long and difficult trial, God taught David to be gracious instead of vengeful, forgiving instead of bitter, loving instead of angry! David follows Jesus' example in 1 Peter 2:20-21. David *"said to Saul, 'Why do you listen when men say, 'David is bent on harming you'? This day you have seen with your own eyes how the LORD delivered you into my hands in the cave. Some urged me to kill you, but I spared you; I said, 'I will not lift my hands against my master, because he is the LORD's anointed. See my father,"* 1 Samuel 24:9-11a.

Satan's demonic helpers wanted David to respond with anger and bitterness, and try to eliminate Saul. David learned what we must also learn, there is no peace in a bitter response to someone hating us! In the end, God used David's difficult test to teach him and us. As David looked to God, his faith grew. He learned to trust in God and God used David's enemy to make him more beautiful spiritually!

Prayer: Beautiful Lord, our difficult trials are so profitable as You teach us to trust You. Your care and protection is awesome to experience. We praise and worship You. In Jesus' name we pray. Amen.

Psalm 19:1-4a

"The heavens declare the glory of God; and the skies proclaim the work of His hands. Day after day they pour forth speech; night after night they display knowledge. There is no speech or language where their voice is not heard. Their voice goes out into all the earth, their words to the ends of the world."

The sun, moon and stars say: Worship God

The *"heavens"* speak every language and dialect on earth, as the Bible is a history book of the universe God beautifully created. *"The skies proclaim"* so much about the character of God. We see endless sky and boundless space, all pointing to our infinite God. We have been given hundreds of stars that are brilliant and also to chart our course. We see beautiful sunsets, painted by the Greatest Artist ever! The whole creation points to our infinite, omnipotent, omniscient, wise, personal and glorious God! It was God who put all of these lights in the heavens. The cause was God. The effect, is what we see. The heavens teach us to worship the cause, which is God. Why do so many worship the effect, the sun, moon and stars?

In verses 5-6, we see the testimony of the sun, God's greatest gift in His physical creation. Through the sun, God provides energy to sustain life here on earth. The solar heat the sun gives, commands the physical world to obey! Our God who is in absolute command of our physical world, is completely in charge of our spiritual world! Nothing is hid from the heat of the sun. Nothing is hid from the Son of God either. The sun and the Son expose the darkness in our physical and spiritual world.

The earth is small when compared to the solar system. How small the seven billion people are who live here on earth. We are like a speck of dust physically. But spiritually, through a relationship with the Son of God, we shine like stars in the Heavens!

Prayer: Beautiful and wise creator God, how gracious and merciful You are. When we consider Your heavens, the work of Your fingers, the moon and the stars, which You have set in place, what is man that You are mindful of him, the son of man that You care for him? How great You are. In Jesus' name we pray. Amen.

Psalm 19:14

"May the words of my mouth and the meditation of my heart be pleasing in Your sight, O LORD my rock and my Redeemer."

Communication, "talk your walk!"

In "religion" discussions, we hear a lot about walking the talk. We must "talk our walk" also. Our verse is a prayer for God-honoring communication in our daily living. When we have serious problems in our families, there is a lack of respectful communication!

A man had an anger problem. His home life was a war zone. He knew good theology. He understood the doctrines of grace, in his head. We worked on his anger, from James 1:20 and other passages. His anger became less, but his family life remained a mess. His family said he was still angry, but he didn't think so. The truth was, he was keeping his anger inside, which was bitterness. It impacted how he spoke to his family. He needed an example.

His daughter wanted to go to a concert. He forbid her to go and would not allow any discussion. He basically gave her a sermon on why it was wrong. He was right is what he said; very wrong in how he said it. His daughter's ears were plugged after his first "know it all" words. This man could have respectfully asked his daughter, "If you go to this outdoor concert and drugs and booze are evident, would you leave?" "If guys and girls had their hands on each other, where they should not be, what would you do?" He could have patiently waited for her answers. Instead, he pushed her away.

We must learn from Jesus who asked questions! *"Whom do you say that I am?"* Jesus already knew. It is kind to ask questions instead of becoming angry. It is said of Jesus, a bruised reed He did not break and smoking flax He did not snuff out. We must learn our own communication skills from the perfect Man, Jesus.

When we bitterly meditate on our family's faults, we are pushing away our family who needs a relationship. The question is: How can we build them up. It will not be by pointing out all their faults to a lack of noticing their good points. May God help us.

Prayer: Dear Lord, help us to improve our communication skills in our daily lives. May the words of our mouths and the meditation of our hearts be pleasing in Your sight. In Jesus' name we pray. Amen.

Psalm 19:14 NKJV

"Let the words of my mouth and the meditation of my heart be acceptable in Your sight, O LORD, my strength and my Redeemer."

True worship asks God to accept us!

As we begin our Sunday corporate worship, the minister rightly calls us into the presence of the Lord using verses like our text. In worship, we go right into the throne room of Heaven. Our text is a beautiful call to worship our God. Here we humbly ask the Lord, *"Let the words of my mouth and the meditations of my heart to be acceptable in Your sight."* That is true Biblical worship.

In the Old Testament, it was God the covenant giver, who needed to accept the sacrifices and offerings of the people. When the people hardened their hearts towards God, He warned them. *"They have loved to wander; they have not restrained their feet. Therefore the LORD does not accept them; He will remember their iniquity now, and punish their sins,"* Jeremiah 14:10 NKJV.

In the New Testament, salvation was still God's purpose and plan. In Ephesians 1:5, He *"predestined us to be adopted,"* which is God accepting us. Peter knew clearly who had to accept whom. He said to the Christians, *"You also, as living stones, are being built up a spiritual house, a holy priesthood, to offer up spiritual sacrifices acceptable to God through Jesus Christ,"* 1 Peter 2:5 NKJV. Praise God, He accepts our worship of Him through Jesus Christ who is *"my strength and my Redeemer."*

Why then, do we so often hear the question, "Did you accept Christ as the Savior and Lord of your life?" Is such a question really Biblical? Is it accurate theologically? Perhaps in a secondary sense it is true. But we cannot find even one verse that clearly says we must accept God or Jesus. It is when God knows and accepts us, that we are bound for Heaven.

Prayer: Gracious Lord, please accept our praise, strengthen us to worship and serve You as Paul encourages Timothy to do. *"That we may lead a quiet and peaceable life in all godliness and reverence. For this is good and acceptable in the sight of God our Savior."* In Jesus' holy name we pray. Amen.

Psalm 20:1- 4

"May the LORD answer you when you are in distress; may the name of the God of Jacob protect you. May He send you help from the sanctuary and grant you support from Zion. May He remember all your sacrifices and accept all your burnt offerings. May He give you the desire of your heart and make all your plans succeed."

May God, *"make all your plans succeed"*

What a powerful benediction prayer, authored by God, through David, for you and me! See the upraised hands of David giving us this personal blessing! Drink in the *"you"* and *"your"* words in the first four verses. They really are for you, and it is the will of God. What a tremendous comfort it is to see and experience the loving smile of God to us needy believers.

There are many examples of believers like David, who had times of great distress. There will always be, difficult faith tests. As David experienced deliverances by God, He learned to trust in God more fully. David here appeals for us to trust in God also. He knew by experience that the God who never failed him, will never fail you. Therefore, this prayer of blessing is for you.

"May He give you the desire of your heart and make all your plans succeed." David is a wise ruler who encourages his people to pray. King David is also a type of Christ encouraging us to pray.

"May He give you the desire of your heart." A true servant of God can pray this kind of prayer because his or her heart is one with God! And so it is, God's battles are our battles. God's victories are ours. We fight evil together. We celebrate together and it is all for the glory and praise of His name. God is our strength and shield, our present help in time of trouble.

Prayer: Beautiful Lord, we praise You for making all of our plans succeed. You are as Paul said, *"able to do immeasurably more than we ask or imagine, according to Your power that is at work within us. To You be the glory in the church and in Christ Jesus throughout all generations, for ever and ever! Amen."*

Psalm 21:6-7

"Surely You have granted him (David) eternal blessings and made him glad with the joy of Your presence. For the king trusts in the LORD; through the unfailing love of the Most High he will not be shaken."

King David's hope in God, is ours!

In this psalm, David praises God for the joy of God's presence. David is also thankful for God's strength and for His salvation! See the faith of David here, for God is no different today than He was years ago. God's *"presence"* along with all His divine attributes are not in any way weakened. God is not somehow growing old and feeble. He is still completely able to save and deliver us, His loving children.

It is our faith in our Abba Father that is weak! When a big trial is set upon us, we doubt the ability and desire of God to help us. It is then that God, in His infinite mercy, shows us that He is trustworthy and our faith grows for the next trial that will soon come. That was David's experience also, and why he said in the verse before our text, *"Through the victories You gave, his* (us as believers) *glory is great; You have bestowed on him* (believers) *splendor and majesty,"* Psalm 21:5.

God is the author and finisher of our faith! Note the words in our text that highlight the mercy of God to those He adopts as His own! *"You have granted."* You, *"made him glad."* Every true believer trusts in the Lord, *"through the unfailing love of the Most High."* Not just our salvation, but our faith itself, is a gift from God! Meditating on God's gift of Himself in worship is the *"joy in Your presence."* That is what David writes so lovingly about.

How often we lack the joy of the Lord. Too often, we lose sight of His eternal grace and unending favor. No wonder God needs to send so many trials. He wants to get our mind more clearly on His amazing, preserving grace to us. God will surely build the loving trust of every believer. The question is: How many more great deliverances in trials must we experience before we can say with the psalmist, *"Through the unfailing love of the Most High"* I *"will not be shaken"*?

Prayer: Lord, You are amazing! We cannot thank You enough for the joy of Your presence in us. To think that the Creator of the whole world loves us now and for all eternity, puts us on our knees in worship. Lord accept our worship. In Jesus' name we pray. Amen.

Psalm 22:16-18

"Dogs have surrounded Me; a band of evil men has surrounded Me, they have pierced My hands and My feet. I can count all My bones; people stare and gloat over Me. They divide My garments among them and cast lots for My clothing."

Jesus shows us how to cry out to God

All of Psalm 22 points to the intense suffering of Jesus. The appeal of the Psalm is to God; *"Do not be far from me, for trouble is near and there is no one to help,"* Psalm 22:11. Like Jesus, our difficult trials are far beyond the help of man. To cry to man and not to God is to accuse Him of not being able to help! God is our refuge and strength. Let us not cry to man lest we offend the Father, Son and Spirit. It is God's honor and pleasure to help us.

Jesus' most piercing cry was a loud scream at the very height of His suffering. He cried out, *"My God, My God, why have You forsaken Me?"* Psalm 22:1a. He was experiencing the torments of Hell for us! The comfort we have is that Jesus' cry was the scream of the damned, so we will not need to experience Hell's pain. God forsook Jesus in those three hours of darkness, so we might not be forsaken by God.

The comfortable, self-righteous, religious leaders cared nothing for Jesus' righteous suffering. In fact, it was they who put the burden on Christ. *"Dogs"* surrounded Jesus. Lowdown, cheating scoundrels accused perfect Jesus of being a troublemaker.

Jesus' manner of death on the cross is given here. He was pierced. It was our sin also that pierced Him. His bones were not broken but were out of joint, to mend us back to Himself! You could count His bones. Why? Because He was naked on that cross. The people had already divided His garments! WHY? The shame of nakedness was our consequence of sin starting with Adam. Jesus bore our shame. He bore our sinful nature, to unite us back to God. What a beautiful Savior!

Prayer: Dear humble Lord and Savior, we can hardly understand the shame and humiliation that You went through in coming to this world to save us. You were clothed with rags, so that You could give us robes of righteousness. What an amazing Savior You are! We worship You now and for all eternity. In Jesus' name we pray. Amen.

Psalm 23:1a

"The LORD is my Shepherd."

Introduction to Psalm 23

David wrote this particular psalm for our comfort and for the worship of our Shepherd. Psalm 23 is perhaps the most favorite of all the psalms, rich in its pictures of how God by His grace leads us. Our hope and faith as Christians, are in our God, in our "Good Shepherd." May we learn more of who He is, so we can follow Him in true faith and duty.

The psalm begins by saying that God, the maker of Heaven and Earth, is *"my"* personal owner. He is concerned about *"my"* welfare, exactly what a good shepherd does. In this psalm, David speaks as a sheep, proud to belong to its divine owner! He is amazed that as a child of God, he has God's deepest affections.

Sheep are not able to take care of themselves. They are about the dumbest and most stubborn of all animals. And we are all like sheep. It's no wonder then, that we need Jesus, who is, *"the Author and Perfecter of our faith."* How terrible it is that so many do not know the love and attention the Good Shepherd gives to all His sheep! How tragic that so many follow the false shepherd, Satan, who will never care for their soul, but instead, will work to destroy it.

Think carefully on the individual words as this psalm begins. Don't read this psalm too fast! *"The LORD,"* the Maker of all Heaven and Earth, the King of the universe, is *"my"* God, and *"my* Shepherd." He watches over me and cares for me. The One who has the best eyes in the world, the most power, unbelievable wisdom and the biggest storehouse of blessings in the universe, *"is"* my Lord. This God *"is,"* meaning, present tense, today and always, *"is"* mine, He owns me, and I own Him.

Prayer: Loving Lord, forgive us for not meditating enough on the fact that You are presently and forever our personal and loving God. Absolutely nothing about us ever escapes Your divine attention! Your power is able to reach the weakest lamb. Your grace is sufficient for the most unworthy soul. We are so thankful that we belong to You, both body and soul! In Christ's name we pray. Amen.

Psalm 23:1

"I shall not be in want"

God provides for His children

Our hope and faith as Christians, is in our Good Shepherd. God, "my" personal owner, is very concerned about "my" present and forever welfare. David loves his divine owner. His heart is content in his love affair with God. David fully realizes how weak he is without God's amazing protection. David knows that the devil is stronger than he is. He knows that from experience that God has the best eyes, the most power, unbelievable wisdom and the biggest storehouse of blessings in the universe. The Lord God, belongs to him and he belongs to God.

"I shall not be in want" in Psalm 23:1b, is all about contentment. A content animal is a very healthy animal. A content person is healthy physically as well as spiritually. We often lack contentment because we actually have many other gods. When we look elsewhere, we are not content with our Shepherd, and God is insulted because of it. He is a jealous God, proud of His reputation of being the very best. If we will own Him as such, He will own us. Jesus said, *"I have come that they may have life, and that they may have it more abundantly,"* John 10:10b NKJV.

Verse two says, *"He makes me to lie down in green pastures."* See the loving grace of our Shepherd in this word *"makes."* It is not what the Christian does to lie down content, it is what God does! There are 4 ways our Shepherd *"makes"* us *"lie down."* First, He takes away our fears! Sheep will not lie down when afraid. The shepherd spots the danger, defeats it, then comforts the sheep. The shepherd's presence calms the sheep, exactly what God does for each of us. Our powerful Shepherd protects us!

Sheep do not lie down if they are fighting one another. Animals and birds fight for "pecking order." So do we! We want to be first! When two Christians fight, neither is lying down. So the Shepherd will discipline the bossy sheep. The sheep who tries to be first is now last in the affections of the shepherd.

Prayer: Shepherd Lord, how wonderful it is that You are not just a shepherd but You are <u>The Shepherd</u>. How wonderfully You provide for our every need. We worship You. In Jesus' name we pray. Amen.

44

Psalm 23:2a

"He makes me lie down in green pastures."

God protects His children

See the grace and goodness of our *"Shepherd"* in the words *"makes me."* It is not what the Christian does to lie down in a peaceful sleep, content in life; it is what God does. The words *"makes me"* should cause us to fix our eyes on our God in awe and drive our prayer life. There are four main ways our Shepherd *"makes me lie down,"* because sheep have four problems that will not let them *"lie down."*

1. Sheep will not *"lie down"* if they are afraid.
The slightest sound, a glimpse of a snake, dog, wolf, or any other animal causes sheep to run in fear. The shepherd spots the danger, beats the snake, chases away the dog, shoots the varmint, and then draws near to his precious sheep. The shepherd's very presence calms the sheep. This is exactly what God does for us. Before Jesus left this world He said to us, *"In this world you will have trouble. But take heart! I have overcome the world."* Remember that our Shepherd is: *"The Prince of Peace."* The way He calms our fears is nothing short of a miracle, and we love Him dearly for it. Israel saw the size of the 9 foot tall Goliath and trembled! David saw the much larger size of His God and rejoiced. Like Israel, we often think our Goliath (trial) is bigger than our God, and we sinfully fear. Then our tender Shepherd comes along and shows us again and again that He can be trusted. Then He *"makes me lie down"* in peace.

2. Sheep will not *"lie down"* if they are fighting one another.
Animals and birds fight for "pecking order." All want to be number one. Sheep butt heads. When they are fighting, neither are lying down. So the shepherd disciplines the bossy sheep, so much so, that the sheep who tried to be first is now last in the affections of the shepherd. Surely, this is what Jesus meant when He said, *"the last will be first, and the first will be last,"* Matthew 20:16. Jesus' own disciples were fighting for position, and so do we. Praise God, our Shepherd makes us stop fighting and then, we *"lie down."*

Prayer: Loving Lord, we have wasted so much time in our worthless fighting. We are like sheep! Forgive us Lord and make us build up others for Your name's sake. In Jesus' name we pray. Amen.

Psalm 23:2a

"He makes me lie down in green pastures."

God cares for His children

3. Sheep cannot *"lie down"* if something is bugging them.

No animal can *"lie down"* or rest if flies and other bugs are after them. In the hot summer the flies get bad, so the sheep move to a place of shade or where there is a breeze, to escape the bugs. The alert shepherd will also protect his sheep by treating them for insects. God, "The Good Shepherd," does these same things for His children. When people "bug" us too much, we pray to God and He changes us. God often changes the person who is hurting us also. Even if the "bugging" does not stop, God through His Holy Spirit, gives us grace and mercy to accept our situation with joy, knowing that He could remove it if it was His will. In the end, God *"makes"* us to *"lie down"* and rest, as nothing is "bugging" us any longer.

4. Sheep will not *"lie down"* until they are free from hunger.

A hungry sheep is restless. Sheep need lots of good food. If they have it in abundance, they will quickly *"lie down"* and chew their cud. They will then quickly gain weight, the goal of the shepherd. However, the "green pastures" the sheep need, do not just grow up on their own. Farmers spend much time cultivating the ground, planting the right seed, even watering the ground if possible. This is hard work on the shepherd's part! It is a picture of how tirelessly and diligently our Shepherd cares for us. *"For we know that in all things God works for the good of those who love Him, who have been called according to His purpose,"* Romans 8:28. God has a great love for His sheep!

Our Good Shepherd mainly satisfies our spiritual hungering. His Word is just the right food. Good grass is exactly the right food for the sheep. When we stay grazing in the Word of God, He satisfies us, making us *"lie down in green pastures."* Are we grazing in the Word?

Prayer: Beautiful Lord, what a caring Shepherd You are. Your Word is always fresh and filling. We will never, in a thousand lifetimes, be able to eat of all the abundance. Lord, how good You are to us, Your believers. You *"make"* us lie down and rest in You! May we learn to fully trust You, who works so hard for us! We thank You for being a "Good Shepherd." In Jesus' name we pray. Amen.

Psalm 23:2b

"He leads me beside quiet waters."

God leads us to quiet waters

All creatures need good, clean water. One of the quickest ways for sheep to get sick is to drink polluted water. And they will quickly do that, if the shepherd does not lead them to good water. Even on the way to good water, some sheep will drink water that has parasites and other crud in it. Then they get sick and stop eating. What a clear picture of how we also drink from polluted streams! We stop on our Christian journey to get a drink of lust, useless TV and many other distractions. And then we get sick from it all. Why don't we just follow our Shepherd, who leads us to the pure mountain stream? St. Augustine said, "O God! Thou made us for Thyself and our souls are restless, searching, until they find their rest in Thee." Why don't we follow our beautiful Shepherd more earnestly? The reason is, we are slow to learn and disobedient sheep. It is God who leads us to the quiet waters, for we could never find it on our own.

In our own wisdom we go to the *"rushing waters"* and drown. Or, we go to the calm waters that are stagnant. It is God, who is our Good Shepherd, who leads us to the safe, clean and refreshing stream that tumbles quietly along. Only God and His Spirit can satisfy our souls. *"He leads me beside quiet waters."* Proud sheep must be led! You can't drive sheep by being behind them, for they scatter in confusion.

Jesus said, *"Blessed are those who hunger and thirst for righteousness, for they will be filled,"* Matthew 5:6. The problem we also have is, it is only God that can even make us hungry and thirsty! That is why, *"He leads me beside quiet waters."* The Holy Spirit leads us to Christ. And Christ unites us to God the Father. Christ sends us back to the Holy Spirit to dwell in us. Our God in Trinity quiets our souls. We can only thank our great Shepherd for making us hungry and thirsty. How faithfully God leads us to Himself and continues to care for us.

Prayer: Amazing Lord, Your grace gets more amazing every day. You indeed are the author and finisher of our faith, our all in all. Lord, accept our worship and praise for leading us to the quiet waters. Keep us by that beautiful refreshing pool. In Christ's name we pray. Amen!

Psalm 23:3a

"He restores my soul."

God restores His children

Sheep get lost and wander mindlessly. Then they cannot figure how to get back to the shepherd and back to the flock. This truth is also real in the Christian "sheep" camp also. We often try to ignore the fact that we wander because it is embarrassing. It is not just a non-Christian that needs to be restored! The point in this psalm is that sheep, or believers, need restoration. Sooner or later, usually sooner, every Christian will fall because we gave into some temptation. After falling, we need the tender love of God to get us up again. David speaks often about how he had fallen, and how God then lifted him up, restoring him. A good example of David's need of restoration is when he chides himself three times for being *"cast down"* in Psalm 42. *"Why are you downcast, O my soul? Why so disturbed within me? Put your hope in God, for I will yet praise Him, my Savior and my God,"* Psalm 42:5. What is true of David is true of us! We become *"cast down"* and depressed.

Philip Keller, a shepherd, explains how a sheep becomes *"cast down."* It rolls over and becomes upside down, feet up, beating the air. A *"cast"* sheep is unable to *"restore"* itself to a standing position, nor is it able to protect itself! The shepherd is the only one who can help the sheep, and get it back up again! Knowing that a sheep is easily cast down, a shepherd carefully watches to see if any of his sheep are missing. A shepherd will even count his sheep to see if they are all present. If missing, the shepherd will quickly go searching, just as Jesus left the 99 to search for the one. This wandering, "cast" sheep is a believer, not an unbeliever! This is not a Bible truth to emphasize evangelism, but one to encourage loving discipleship with believers that need restoration! The next verses of Matthew 18 prove that the *"lost sheep"* could not find the Shepherd, so the Shepherd lovingly found the sheep.

Prayer: Dear Lord, we see the love and dedication You have for us poor, wandering sheep! May this reality, cause us to love You more. You not only put us back on our feet, You make us walk again, and again, and yet again if necessary. We praise You and pray in the name of Jesus, the Shepherd of our souls! Amen.

Psalm 23:3a

"He restores my soul."

God restores our soul

"Cast down" sheep have three problems that need restoration.

First, sheep that look for the softest spot to lie down are more easily "cast down." If there is a slight dip in the ground, they can easily go from lying on their side, to being flipped onto their back, and then are not able to get up. How many of us are busy trying to "get comfortable," doing what we want to do, instead of what we should do, and then become cast down? Perhaps the biggest god in the Christian camp today is "the god of comfort." This god does more to keep us soft spiritually than any other god! It may be the worse god of all, because it is the one god we do not fear.

Second, sheep that have too much wool are easily "cast down." Long wool gathers mud and manure. This extra weight on the bottom of a sheep does much to keep it from getting up again. Wool in the Bible was often a sign of sin. A priest could not wear wool. Too much sin and we get weighed down. Do you know what the shepherd does to the sheep that becomes cast down because of heavy wool? They shear that sheep! It is very uncomfortable for the sheep as they get a few cuts from that shearing. God too, shears us for our good! He cuts the sin out, and then restores us to righteous living!

Third, sheep that are too fat are easily "cast down." A fat sheep is often a lazy and a weak sheep. A shepherd puts sheep that are too fat on poorer grass. Some of us need poorer grass! Our Lord wants us in shape, sharp and active for Him. God has called us to be warriors, not couch potatoes. The Great Commission says, "Go," a lazy person says, "No." Besides our love for food, we love clothes and pleasures of many kinds. A Christian's body is the temple of the living God. Our bodies contain our soul' and God lives there. God wants our individual temples to be clean and orderly, living as a soldier of the Cross.

Prayer: Dear Shepherd of our souls, what a comfort to see how You look out for us cast down sheep! You run to us and then gently put us back on our feet again. You forgive our sins and restore us. You are a beautiful Shepherd. In Jesus' name we pray. Amen.

Psalm 23:3b

"He guides me in paths of righteousness for His name's sake."

God guides us, *"for His name's sake"*

A big part of God's restoration process, is His guiding us, *"in paths of righteousness."* Cattle of all kinds will use the same *"paths"* when moving through the pasture. They will wear a track into the grass that soon becomes a washout. By nature, sheep do not go down the *"right"* paths either. They spread their manure along these same paths, then eat the unhealthy grass, and get sick from the parasites. A healthy pasture not only has better grass, it is free from bugs also. A good farmer makes sure the old pasture gets a rest and the animals get fresh grass. Otherwise, both the sheep and the ground suffer from poor health.

When sheep and cattle are put into a new pasture they will jump for joy. When Christians follow God's way of living in new ways, they too jump for joy! It is actually God's Spirit that gives the Christian this new joy. But more than that, God in Trinity makes the Christian focus on the new way of living, and by that process is changed. The Biblical process of change is laid out for us in Ephesians 4:22-24. We first must put off the old habits or *"paths."* We then replace them, and walk in the new *"paths of righteousness."* Through the help of the Spirit, we complete the change process when we focus intently on the new *"paths of righteousness."* We never *"get healthy"* by going down the old path. We won't get healthy even looking at it! Concentrating on the old corrupt way of living, prevents change! So like sheep, we need a new pattern, a new path! Praise God, He *"makes"* us go down the right, new path. *"He guides me in paths of righteousness."*

"For His name's sake," God guides us! God always guides us for our good, as Romans 8:28 teaches. But God also guides us for His own glory, "for His name's sake." God wants us to be trophies of His grace. He wants our lives to reflect our Divine Owner. Are we living holy lives to respect, honor, and worship God?

Prayer: Most loving Lord, we thank You for Your abundant grace to us. We, Your precious sheep, are so unworthy. May we stay close to You, loving You with all our hearts! In Jesus' name we pray. Amen.

Psalm 23:4a

"Even though I walk through the valley of the shadow of death."

He is with us, *"through the valley"*

When the summer heat comes, the low land grass is no longer tender and good for the sheep. So the shepherd leads the sheep to higher ground, to the green *"table"* spoken of in the next verse. But on the way up, the shepherd has to take the green valleys to the mountain top. In these valleys there is good grazing, but there are also many snakes, hazards, and places for the sheep to fall. *"Through the valley,"* is the only way up the mountain, symbolic of our journey to Heaven.

"Though I walk," shows the believer, hand in hand with God, enjoying His presence, calmly and purposely finishing life's journey. *"Through the valley,"* are needed words of hope for the Christian. Our Good *"Shepherd,"* will never leave us in that *"valley"* which is filled with danger and despair. He will lead us *"through"* it. We must not look so intently on life's difficulties and respond with fear. God will surely get us all *"through the valley."* Jesus said, *"Do not let your hearts be troubled. Trust in God; trust also in Me. In My Father's house are many rooms; if it were not so, I would have told you. I am going there to prepare a place for you,"* John 14:1-2. Jesus is leading us *"through the valley,"* to that beautiful *"place"* prepared for us, by Him.

"The valley of the shadow of death," shows that for a Christian, dying is merely a *"shadow."* Can a shadow harm us? Can the shadow of a knife or gun hurt us? No, and neither can death hurt us, if Christ is our Shepherd! He has conquered death. The grave could not hold Him because He had no personal sin. We, Jesus' precious forgiven sheep, bought by His own blood, are now without sin. He paid our sin debt for a huge price. He is in the process of taking one of His prized possessions to Heaven. Our body will sleep for some time, but our soul will never die. We will pass from life on this earth, to life everlasting with the great *"Shepherd"* of our souls. How great is our God!

Prayer: Dear Shepherd of our soul, what a comfort that You know the way to Heaven. You are the Way, the Truth, and the Life. When our life is hid in You, we are safe, loved, and privileged. Lord, train our eyes to gaze upon You in awe! For the One who will never leave or forsake us is our forever Shepherd. In Your name we pray. Amen.

Psalm 23:4b

"I will fear no evil, for You are with me."

Fear is not faith!

Sheep quickly fear. If the wind merely blows a tumbleweed or a plastic bag across the pasture, a sheep can run from it in a panic. Could this rolling weed hurt the sheep? No, so what caused the sheep to fear then? The sheep thought it might hurt them. There is the heart of the matter! The rolling weed itself did not cause the fear. It was the fearful heart of the sheep that did. And what is true of sheep, is true of us. Even as God's child, we have many <u>temptations</u> to fear, like a loss of money, health, spouse and the list goes on. Yet the <u>cause</u> of the fear is within us, even in our hearts! What is it that finally quiets us? Our Good Shepherd comes and calms our trembling heart. *"I will fear no evil, for You are with me."* We know from 1 John 4:18 that *"perfect love drives out fear."* Jesus is perfect love. Plus, we live out perfect love when we love God first and then others secondly, before our own selfish interests. That right order of the Ten Commandments shows us what perfect love is. We no longer fear because the Lord who is "perfect love" is *"with me."*

My problem is not that I don't trust God, but even as a Christian, I don't trust Him fully! My spirit of self-sufficiency is still very proud. My selfish nature can still love other "things" more than God. So God in His infinite wisdom, sends yet another difficult trial my way. I learn once again how weak I really am. I learn for the hundredth time that I need God more than anything. And so He builds my faith in Him a little more with each trial. God, in His grace, is leading us all to experience this trial again and again. It is good that the Shepherd knows how to build our faith, because if our selfish heart had to do it, that just would not happen. *"For it is God who works in you both to will and to do for His good pleasure,"* Philippians 2:13. What a beautiful thought that God pours His perfect love into us. What a beautiful experience. *"I will fear no evil, for You are with me,"*

Prayer: Loving Lord, You not only killed David's lions and bears, You kill mine. Lord, You who eliminated David's Goliath, eliminate mine. You who are perfect in love, perfect in power, perfect in wisdom, are my personal Shepherd. Because You guide me *"I will fear no evil, for You are with me."* Lord Jesus, in Your beautiful name we pray! Amen.

Psalm 23:4c

"Your rod and Your staff, they comfort me."

God disciples us

The wooden *"rod"* and *"staff"* were the main tools that a shepherd used to care for the sheep. The Psalmist David was very familiar with these tools, as are shepherds yet today.

1. The rod was a symbol of power and authority. The shepherd was very good at throwing the rod or using it as a club to protect the sheep from snakes, dogs, lions and bears. The rod of Moses was used as a symbol of God's authority over Pharaoh and the gods of Egypt. Sheep are comforted by the rod, as were the children of Israel. The rod of Moses was even put in the Ark of the Covenant.

2. The rod was used to examine the sheep. The shepherd used the rod to move the wool to see if the sheep's skin was healthy. David knew this when writing, *"Search me, O God, and know my heart; test me and know my anxious thoughts. See if there is any offensive way in me, and lead me in the way everlasting,"* Psalm 139:23-24. No one can pull the wool over God's eyes. His omniscient eye sees everything!

3. The rod was used to discipline the sheep. It is amazing how a shepherd can throw the rod at a sheep that wanders away from him. I remember a new dog we once had. I was picking vegetables and he was wandering by the road. I called, but he wouldn't come. So, I threw a stone at him and hit him. Thereafter, he came when called! The dog got the rod, and with it, got the message. In much the same way, *"God disciplines us for our good, that we may share in His holiness. No discipline seems pleasant at the time, but painful. Later on, however, it produces a harvest of righteousness and peace for those who have been trained by it,"* Hebrews 12:10b-11. God says, *"He who spares the rod hates his son, but he who loves him is careful to discipline him,"* Proverbs 13:24. Like sheep, we and our children are foolish. We need the rod then, and loving care must always deliver it.

Prayer: Lord, You tell us in Proverbs that *"Folly is bound up in the heart of a child, but the rod of discipline will drive it far from him."* Truly, *"Your rod and Your staff, they comfort me."* How privileged we are to have a "Shepherd" of our souls. In Jesus' name we pray. Amen.

Psalm 23:4c

"Your rod and Your staff, they comfort me."

God comforts us

A staff is a long and strong stick with a hook on one end, designed to help the sheep. The *"staff,"* more than anything, identifies a shepherd as a shepherd. The *"staff"* is a picture of the concern the shepherd has for the sheep. The *"staff"* is a tool of love in the hands of the shepherd. God's *"staff"* is His Spirit always with us, helping us in life's journey as a Christian.

1. The shepherd uses the *"staff"* to reach up and pull tree limbs and bushes down so the sheep can eat. God gives us our daily bread!

2. The shepherd uses the *"staff"* to bring a newborn lamb close to the mother. If a shepherd touches the lamb the mother could reject it because of the smell of his hand. God in covenant, works in us and our children to bring us together with one heart and purpose.

3. The shepherd uses the *"staff"* to bring a shy sheep closer to Him, or lift a fallen sheep. So too, *"The Lord will rescue me from every evil attack and will bring me safely to His Heavenly kingdom,"* 2 Timothy 4:18.

4. The shepherd uses the *"staff"* to search for danger. There are snakes hiding under brush and logs that can hurt the sheep. There are also small caves. The shepherd uses his long *"staff"* to probe for various enemies. God's Word is often called the Shepherd's *"staff,"* for it searches out dangers in our lives and it brings us *"comfort."*

5. The shepherd uses the end of the *"staff"* to guide the sheep down the right path, or to make them change direction. The *"staff"* gives the shepherd an eight foot arm to direct the sheep. The *"staff"* quickly makes personal contact with the sheep, giving encouragement and love. In much the same way, our Lord leads us in the paths of righteousness, making us holy. When Jesus left this world He told His disciples, *"when He, the Spirit of truth, has come, He will guide you into all truth,"* John 16:13a NKJV.

Prayer: Most gracious Lord, what a loving concern You have for our spiritual condition! You feed us, care for us, comfort us and protect us perfectly. No one else could ever lead us to an eternity with You. We worship You for being our wonderful Shepherd. In Jesus' name we pray. Amen.

Psalm 23:5a

"You prepare a table before me."

God prepares a table for us

In the spring, the shepherd goes ahead of the sheep to the flat, high cool areas called a *"table,"* or mesa. There, the grass grows well in the hot summer. Shepherds *"prepare"* waterholes, put up salt blocks, and remove poisonous weeds. We must fall in love with the word, *"prepare."* A pastor must *"prepare"* to feed the congregation, just as farmers *"prepare"* to feed their animals. A farmer puts up a fence to keep the animals from wandering from the pasture. The animals do not realize how much this fence protects them from outside dangers. God puts up many fences to *"prepare a table before me."*

1. God prepares the *"table"* of His Word to protect us. Sin is tempting and looks fun, just like the grass on the other side of the fence, tempts the animals. We are worse than animals who don't understand the danger when they try to get out. As a boy, I helped the neighbor get the cows from the pasture. One day four cows were missing. We found them dead, hit by a train that ran on the other side of the fence. If only the cows knew that they were free and safe, within the pasture that was prepared for them. They rejected the *"green pastures,"* for an early death. A cow can smell the electric fence to see if the current is on. If there is no immediate shock in the fence wire, they will put their heads through and start eating. Soon they stretch the wire and end up on the other side. We do the very same thing! We smell the fence by playing with sin and watching rotten TV. Praise God for His Holy Spirit that shocks us when we stick our neck through the fence!

2. God prepares two "tables" of the Law for us. The first table is to love God, and the second is to love others. When we feed in these pastures, we will be filled with peace and be most blessed.

3. God prepares a *"table"* of communion for us also. What a huge blessing it is to see and experience this picture of the Gospel and commune with God and fellow Christians. Together, remember and celebrate Christ's perfect sacrifice for our sins.

Prayer: Dear Merciful Lord, our great provider, You put us in many green pastures. Help us to appreciate them and praise You for them. In Christ's name we pray. Amen.

Psalm 23:5b

"In the presence of my enemies."

God delivers us

The fact that God prepares a table with everything that a Christian needs is a miracle in itself. But the fact that God does so *"in the presence of my enemies,"* takes our breath away! David is shouting to us that conditions do not need to be perfect for God to give us what we need. Even when circumstances seem impossible, God can do anything. Let us not put so much of our hope in "conditions" changing, but in our God.

Think of David's situation. Saul, king of the most powerful country in the world, could not find David, even with the best of his soldiers. And Saul knew about where David was. However, hundreds of men who were in desperate need, they were able to find David! So too, we find Christ when our *"enemies"* can't see to locate Him. God supplied all of David's needs, and his small army too. Our Good Shepherd supplies our every need. God can even feed us from the tables of our enemies if He so chooses. That is how much our God cares for us!

We have before us a huge personal faith test. Will we trust God when we are surrounded by those who want to hurt us? We are then, forced to make a *"faith decision."* Will we fearfully look at the size of our enemies and tremble? Or, will we wisely, in faith, look at the size of our God and rejoice? It is my experience that we at first, see the size of our enemies and tremble. Then we pray to God, and He opens our eyes to the fact that He is in complete control. In this way, God matures our faith, *"in the presence of my enemies."*

There's another way God *"prepares a table before me in the presence of my enemies."* In Christ, God has already defeated our enemies at the Cross! The penalty and the power that sin has over us is broken and destroyed. Our number one enemy, Satan, still has some power! But compared to God's power, Satan's power is nothing but weakness.

Our God in Trinity gives us a table of blessings in the presence of our enemies. He has made a covenant promise to us that He will never leave us or forsake us, especially when our enemies are in our face!

Prayer: O Lord, our great Deliverer, we praise and thank You for giving us a table right in the presence of our enemies. So great is Your power. We worship You. In Jesus' name we pray. Amen.

Psalm 23:5c

"You anoint my head with oil; my cup overflows."

God anoints us

In the summertime, flies and bugs come in abundance. When *"bugged,"* the sheep will not gain weight or lie down in contentment. Today a shepherd will commonly run the sheep through tanks or pools of chemicals that will protect the sheep's skin from various ailments, including the bugs. But of course, the sheep will not put his head into the brew, or he would drown. So, many shepherds still put a special oil mixed with other medicine on the sheep's head to protect the sheep from bugs, scabs, and other skin problems.

Just as a shepherd anoints the sheep, God anoints our *"head with oil."* The Holy Spirit, *"anoints"* us at the time of salvation. *"The fruit of the Spirit is love, joy, peace, patience, kindness, goodness, faithfulness, gentleness, and self-control,"* Galatians 5:22-23a. The fruit of His presence becomes noticeable! Some say they are going to "get the anointing." We don't get more of God. He graciously gets more of us. The anointing is given! It is a gift. God *"anoints my head with oil."*

Has any sheep ever walked up to a shepherd and said, "I am coming to you to get anointed?" No, the loving shepherd sees what the animal needs and assists them. The shepherd mercifully anoints them! What sheep ever went to the market and purchased oil for its own head? It is our Good Shepherd, who sees our need and then supplies it for His own glory and for our good.

Jesus was anointed by God and as believers, He gives us an anointing. Disciple John said, *"As for you, the anointing you received from Him remains in you,"* 1 John 2:27a. God's anointing remains in us, to direct and empower us in life's journey. God's anointing comes with an assignment by Him to assist us. It is His power in us that qualifies us, giving us the wisdom and strength to move for Him.

Prayer: Dear Lord Jesus Christ, our Shepherd, You have so graciously anointed us with oil. You have freed us from sin and every defect. You have filled us with Your Spirit and changed us from being fearful to peaceful, from lost to found, from hopeless to hopeful. Then You give us a job to do for You, with the strength and wisdom to do it. Thank You for Your great love. In Christ's name we pray. Amen.

Psalm 23:6a

"Surely goodness and mercy shall follow me all the days of my life."

Faith does not doubt the goodness of God

What an absolute truth and promise flowing from the faithfulness and character of our Good Shepherd! Think of what the goodness of God means for every believer. Because God is self-existent, His *"goodness"* had no beginning. Because God is eternal, His *"goodness"* will have no end. Because God is infinite, His *"goodness"* has no limit. Because God is all wisdom His *"goodness"* will be perfect for every situation. Because God is all powerful, He can give His *"goodness"* anytime and anyplace that we need it. Because God is omniscient, His *"goodness"* is never blind to our need. Because God is forever holy, His *"goodness"* is always perfectly pure. Because God will never leave us or forsake us, His *"goodness"* will never leave us.

God's *"goodness"* is everything that we need! Especially take note: In our trials, the evil demonic forces of Satan chase us, tempting us to doubt the *"goodness"* of God. But God promises us individually, His *"goodness will follow me all the days of my life."*

"Mercy," is God's continual forgiveness of my sins. My sins are forgiven *"all the days of my life!"* Meditate on how God takes such a loving interest in us personally!

There must also be a second part to God's *"goodness"* and His *"mercy"* that *"shall follow me."* Since Biblical love is a sacrificial action for others, God expects us to give out our own *"goodness and mercy,"* to others. It is a must! *"Religion that God our Father accepts as pure and faultless is this: to look after orphans and widows in their distress and to keep oneself from being polluted by the world,"* James 1:27.

A person of the *"world"* is selfish and thinks only of getting good, not giving good. We want others to be good and merciful to us, but we do not want to do the same to others. By leaving a trail of *"goodness"* behind us, we show that the love of Christ is in us. Someone once said, "preach to all people, if necessary use words."

Prayer: God of all *"goodness,"* You are awesome. How good it is to meditate on Your *"goodness and mercy"* that will follow us *"all the days"* of our life. We praise You for Your divine goodness. In Christ's pefectly good name we pray. Amen.

Psalm 23:6b

"I will dwell in the house of the LORD forever."

God gives eternal life to us

We have seen the dedication of the Shepherd to us, His sheep. Now we see the contentment the sheep have for their wonderful Shepherd. Sheep are content to belong to the flock. A question then begs us. Are we content to love and be loved by our fellow church members? Even dumb sheep know that they are part of a caring flock! They move together and lie down in peace together. If we are not content in the "church flock," is there something wrong with us, or is our church the problem?

In Psalm 37, a lack of contentment came about by being *"envious"* of others. Are we filled with a longing for what others have? Our Shepherd tells us, *"Trust in the LORD and do good; dwell in the land and enjoy safe pasture. Delight yourself in the LORD and He will give you the desires of your heart. Commit your way to the Lord; trust in Him and He will do this. He will make your righteousness shine like the dawn, the justice of your cause like the noonday sun. Be still before the LORD and wait patiently for Him,"* Psalm 37:3-7a.

God knows what we need, so He tells us to delight in Him. If we move to the center of His will for our life, we will find that our days will become more satisfying and worthwhile. Why does it take us so long to learn these lessons? Probably because by nature we do not have the heart to trust in God, or commit our ways to Him. But thanks be to God. Our Shepherd poured out His life for us. Our Shepherd had pity on us and loved us so much, and moves us to trust Him more! This is the condition of the sheep in Psalm 23. The Shepherd is in love with the sheep. The sheep respond by loving the Shepherd.

Prayer: Dear Shepherd of our souls. Our only comfort in life and in death is that we are not our own, but belong body and soul to You, our faithful Savior and Shepherd. May Your name be lifted up forever. You are so worthy of praise. The fact that You care so completely for us rebellious sheep, takes our breath away. We know that we love You only because You first loved us. We not only love You today, but will love You for all eternity. In Your name we pray. Amen.

Psalm 24:1-2

"The earth is the LORD's, and everything in it, the world, and all who live in it; for He founded it upon the seas and established it upon the waters."

This is my Father's world

With all the turmoil that is going on in the world today, this world is becoming harder to live in. Suffering is increasing. We know there will not only be more earthquakes, but *"great earthquakes,"* Luke 21:11. We know there will not only be false prophets, but there will be *"many false prophets,"* Matthew 24:11. Persecution will continue to be more intense.

We could get worried and fear these coming difficult events if we do not remember: This is my Father's world! *"The earth is the LORD's, and everything in it."* Our God is in total control of what is going on today. Not only that, God will always be in total control of the world's calendar of events. Better yet, God is my Father, my Heavenly Father! He will always be my Father! He calls me by name. He gave me the name Christian and adopted me to be His son or daughter. Yes, this is my Father's world. To help us meditate Biblically on some of the ways that this is my Father's world, we will use two verses of a beautiful song of faith.

This is my Father's world, and to my listening ears
All nature sings, and round me rings the music of the spheres.
This is my Father's world! I rest me in the thought,
Of rocks and trees, of skies and seas,
His hand the wonders wrought.

This is my Father's world, O let me ne'er forget
That <u>though the wrong seems oft so strong God is the ruler yet</u>.
This is my Father's world! The battle is not done;
Jesus who died shall be satisfied, and earth and Heaven be one.

Prayer: Sovereign Lord, may we rest in the fact that it is You, our personal, loving Heavenly Father's world! As a good Father, You will always have Your eye on us. May this cause us to keep our eyes on You in love, in hope, and in true faith. In Jesus' name we pray. Amen.

Psalm 24:3-5

"Who may ascend the hill of the LORD? Who may stand in His holy place? He who has clean hands and a pure heart, who does not lift his soul up to an idol or swear by what is false. He will receive blessing from the LORD and vindication from God his Savior."

Who may go to Heaven?

The question before us is a practical one. The answer is given in an unusual way. Listed first are those who have *"clean hands."* God knows what is the truth, for nothing is hidden from His eyes. There is a second requirement that is normally listed first. A *"pure heart"* is needed, one that has been washed by the blood of the Lamb.

The Bible has much to say about the condition of the heart. One of the clearest is: *"But the things that come out of the mouth come from the heart, and these make a man unclean. For out of the heart come evil thoughts, murder, adultery, sexual immorality, theft, false testimony, slander,"* Matthew 15:18-19. The point is, *"a pure heart"* leads to *"clean hands."* It is impossible to have clean hands without first having a *"pure heart."* The condition of our heart leads to what we do, which is our thoughts, words and actions.

We need to take this one step further. The condition of our heart not only leads to what we do, but what we do leads to how we feel. Do not miss these three points! In Biblical counseling or in Biblical discipleship, these three are main foundational truths. Let us look at these three points in reverse order.

People generally seek counseling because their feelings or emotions are in a mess. They often say, "I only want to feel better." Well, guess what? To feel better, we first need *"clean hands"* which is to do better. Yet no one can do better, until they first have a *"pure heart."* Our feelings or emotions show whether our hands are clean or not. I will often ask, "What did you do that is making you so sad?" God gives us *"clean hands and pure heart"* that make us sing for joy.

Prayer: O perfect and holy Lord, in Jeremiah 17:10 You tell us: *"I the LORD, search the heart and examine the mind, to reward a man according to what his deeds deserve."* Lord clean our dirty hands for Your glory and for our good. In Jesus' name we pray. Amen.

Psalm 25:11

*"For the sake of Your name, O LORD, forgive my iniquity,
though it is great."*

A great lesson in prayer

A true believer is concerned about God's name. Thus our text is really important for us to think about. From an eternity past, God always moves for the sake of His name. God has no beginning, meaning He always existed. God then created everything in this world. God even moved Satan out of Heaven for the sake of His name. God acts now, in the present and will act in the future, for the sake of His name. In our prayer life, we need to have an urgency concerning the holy name of God. We must think His thoughts after Him. We must plan each day for the sake of His name.

The third commandment says, *"You shall not take the name of the LORD your God in vain, for the LORD will not hold him guiltless who takes His name in vain,"* Deuteronomy 5:11. His Spirit gives us guilt and sadness when we are not concerned about the holy name of God. We must ask God to forgive our sin, primarily so that the holy name of God will not be dishonored.

"For the sake of Your name, O LORD, forgive my iniquity, though it is great." In praying this prayer, we understand that our iniquity is great in two ways. There are great sins of commission, those things we do wrong. We also have great sins of omission, those are the things we should have done but did not do. Even though we are great sinners, we will sin far less when we are concerned about the name of God.

When God forgave us in the salvation process, He took our sin and gave us the righteousness of Christ. So the prayer in our verse is asking God to see Christ's perfect life, not only for our salvation, but now also for our growing up in Christ, for our sanctification. The secret of joyful living is to stay near to the heart of God. His Spirit gives us much joy when we do.

Prayer: Holy and good Lord, give us the burden to pray this verse for the sake of Your name. Move us closer to Your heart. O God, make Your concerns, our concerns. Place us at the foot of the cross and keep us there for our salvation and sanctification. Grab us by Your Spirit for the sake of Your holy name. In Jesus' name we pray. Amen.

Psalm 25:16-18

"Turn to me and be gracious to me, for I am lonely and afflicted. The troubles of my heart have multiplied; free me from my anguish. Look upon my affliction and my distress and take away all my sins."

The lonely must turn to God

David is *"lonely and afflicted."* Many of us go through painful trials, like David is now experiencing. In our painful trials, we are tested by God, for His glory and for our good. Always remember, there is no testimony without a serious test. After our time of testing, we are now called to give a reason for the hope that is in us. For when there is an absence of hope in any life, loneliness can quickly fill the void.

Loneliness is very different than being alone. David said, *"the troubles of <u>my heart</u> have multiplied."* That shows something is wrong in the heart, meaning, divorce, disease, death, relationship problems or a lack of money are not the cause of loneliness. It is far more about a wrong response to events like these. Too often we put our hope in circumstances changing, instead of hoping in God.

Elizabeth Elliot said, "Loneliness can be a wilderness or it can be a pathway to God." We need to go to God. We have a personal responsibility to walk on God's path, not hide in a cave. God told the lonely Cain, *"If you do well will you not be accepted."* But Cain was not interested in doing well, and he remained lonely for life.

It is possible for us Christians to be unwilling to be fully submitted to God's plan for our life. If we have a bitter attitude, we blame God for what has happened or may happen. David admits there are troubles in his heart. Is he not fully trusting in God at this time? Is David doubting that God is good? That's Satan's goal in our trials.

Loneliness most often includes a relationship problem with others. A self-pity response of any kind is not godly living. We are to have fellowship with God and with others, in that order. God's prescription for loneliness is in Matthew 22:37-40. If we are stuck in the mud with what happened yesterday, it is rather difficult to enjoy the beauty of today. We would be wise to agree with what David said earlier in this psalm, *"forgive my iniquity, though it is great,"* Psalm 25:11b.

Prayer: Lord, our loneliness shouts to us that we need more of You and less of us. Lord, fill us with Your hope. In Jesus' name we pray. Amen.

Psalm 26:1-3

"Vindicate me, O LORD, for I have led a blameless life; I have trusted in the LORD without wavering. Test me, O LORD, and try me, examine my heart and my mind; for Your love is ever before me, and I walk continually in Your truth."

"Vindicate me, O LORD"

When we are accused of something that we did not do, we must see David's anguish here. David was being judged unfairly by Saul, who wanted to bring him down. Jezebel did this to Naboth. Judas did it to Jesus. Today, there are those who want us out of the way. If Jesus, the perfect Man, was falsely accused, then so will we be. What is our attitude when falsely accused? We have here, the excellent response of David to guide us.

"I have led a blameless life." David is speaking to God here, not to others. David does not claim to be without sin, but that he has lived for the will of God. David has God's interests in mind. From this platform, he is now going to make a solid prayer request to God. Notice that he does not whine to man, but appeals to God!

"Test me," meaning, "God, You test me. Don't allow anyone else to unjustly try me and come to wrong conclusions about what I have done for You. Lord, You see all and know all. Lord, You are all wisdom and all power. I appeal to You who are the highest judge in both Heaven and on Earth. Lord, hear my prayer."

Lord, *"examine my heart and my mind."* Look at my motives for doing what I do. I have acted out of compassion for others. I acted for their good and for Your glory. Lord, most people may not understand, much less care that I have spent myself zealously for Your kingdom. But Lord, I know that You care. Lord, please be zealous for my cause, for it is Your cause. O God, hear my prayer.

David was humble and prayerful in this great trial and so must we. If we humble ourselves before the Lord, He will lift us up in due time. Sooner or later, God will make it clear that we are innocent.

Prayer: Lord, give us the wisdom and patience to look to You. We want our great trials to be over. But we know that You want to teach us something about Your grace and mercy. In the end, Lord, we are grateful that You are in charge. In Jesus' name we pray. Amen.

Psalm 27:1

"The LORD is my light and my salvation — whom shall I fear? The LORD is the stronghold of my life — of whom shall I be afraid?"

"The LORD is my light"

If God is David's light, then God has to be light Himself. *"God is light; in Him there is no darkness at all,"* 1 John 1:4. God gives light, just as the sun gives light. The sun helps us to physically see everything. So too, God does that for us spiritually. How does God give us light?

God is omniscient, meaning that God knows all, sees all and He understands everything. No one can tell God one thing that He does not already know. Therefore, we should not spend time in prayer by telling God what is going on in our life. He already knows. Pray for His wisdom in how to respond to what is going on

God is light means that God is pure and holy. He remains holy regardless of what we ourselves do. Our dark sins do not in any way, take away from His light or holiness. A storm does not disturb the sun! The sun remains shining above it all and so does God. Our sin storm clouds block the Light, for what fellowship has Light with darkness?

Jesus, as the Light, came into our dark world to give us light. Israel was dark with sin. Calvary was dark. The grave was dark. But Jesus dispelled the darkness, giving us life and immortality. As Christians, we too can say with David, *"The LORD is my light and salvation."*

We do evangelism because the Lord is light. Jesus went into dark Gentile Galilee, teaching people to repent from darkness. Yesterday, I used a pail to wash the car. Today, the water looked clean but you could see the black dirt at the bottom. I took a stick and stirred the water to clean the pail. So too, the rod of affliction in the hands of the Light of the world, stirs our dark souls, exposing the dirt. We and others then confess our sin and repent. We walk in newness of life, all because *"The LORD is my light and salvation."*

Prayer: LORD, how precious it is that You light up our world in so many ways. Your divine light drives my fears away. My only comfort in life and in death is that I, in body and in soul, both in life and in death, am not my own, but belong to my faithful Savior Jesus Christ. What a beautiful light You are. We praise You for lighting up our lives. In Jesus' name we pray. Amen.

Psalm 27:4

"One thing I ask of the LORD, this is what I seek; that I may dwell in the house of the LORD all the days of my life, to gaze upon the beauty of the LORD and to seek Him in His temple."

"Gaze upon the beauty of the LORD"

David absolutely loved to go to the house of the Lord to worship God. Here in this psalm, we can see two important elements of worship. David's soul was fed, and God received the glory and honor due His name.

David gazed on the beauty of God. But what does that mean? God cannot be seen, since He is a Spirit. David's heart was one with God, enjoying His beautiful presence. David's day was not complete until he met with God in worship and prayer. David, by experience, knew God as a close, personal friend. But more importantly, God knew and enjoyed David's relationship.

"The beauty of the LORD," according to Stephen Charnock, is God's holiness. God's omnipotence is His almighty sovereign power. God's omniscience is His eye, seeing all things. His mercy is His bowels. Eternity is His duration. There is no blemish in God for He is perfect! Our God is totally beautiful in His character. It is God's holiness and beauty, that makes us beautiful! God cleans our hearts, now and for all eternity. The smiling heart He gives us, makes our faces also smile.

Just imagine that you were bankrupt and ready to be put into prison because you could not pay your debt. Then along comes a rich man and he totally pays your bill and you are totally free. You would think that man was beautiful. Well, God did more than that for us! He gave us life instead of death; beauty instead of ashes. God gave us what we needed instead of what we deserved, and for that alone, He is beautiful beyond description!

Prayer: O wondrous Lord, we worship You for Your beauty. Your amazing grace and boundless mercy are unlimited and eternal. We will forever gaze upon Your dazzling beauty. We worship You, Father, Son and Holy Spirit for who You are and for what You have done for us. In Jesus' name we pray. Amen.

Psalm 27:12-14

"Do not turn me over to the desire of my foes, for false witnesses rise up against me, breathing out violence. I am still confident of this: I will see the goodness of the LORD in the land of the living. Wait for the LORD; be strong and take heart and wait for the LORD."

"Wait for the LORD"

It is so hard for us impatient believers to wait for the LORD. That is why we have a command here to do so. David sees the desire and the effort of his foes to bring him down. People are saying things about him that simply are not true. They are even threatening to do him harm. But David says, "No" to the temptation to give up the fight for God's truth. In our own strength we cannot stand against evil. But God will strengthen us if our hearts remain steadfast, believing in His ability and desire to deliver us. After all, our enemy is God's enemy!

Think of Job in his severe trial. His friends tried to convince him that he did something wrong to deserve his fate. His own wife told him to curse God and die. By faith, Job said, "No," even though he had *"painful sores from the soles of his feet to the top of his head,"* Job 2:7b. It was then that *"his wife said to him, 'Do you still hold on to your integrity? Curse God and die!'"* Job 2:7b-9. But Job chose to *"wait for the LORD."* We need God's help to wait in faith and in obedience. There is a good song that pleads with God in prayer.

"Jesus Savior pilot me over life's tempestuous sea. Unknown waves before me roll, hiding rocks and treacherous shoal; chart and compass come from Thee. Jesus Savior pilot me."

There are four things we must do to wait for the Lord in Psalm 37:1-5. We must <u>put off envying</u> what others may have concerning money, looks, relationships, and the list goes on. After that, we can <u>trust in the Lord</u>. If we trust in the Lord, we will be able to <u>delight in the Lord</u>. After that, we can obediently <u>commit our ways to the Lord</u>. Then finally, we can *"wait for the LORD,"* for guiding us according to His perfect will.

Prayer: Dear Sovereign Lord, we thank You that You build our faith one trial at a time. You teach us to wait for You, even as You fill us with real hope. May You be glorified in us and through us, even as we glory in You. In Jesus' name we pray. Amen.

Psalm 28:7

"The LORD is my strength and my shield; my heart trusts in Him, and I am helped. My heart leaps for joy and I will give thanks to Him in song."

"Give thanks to Him in song"

Our text tells us to give thanks to the LORD in song. Martin Luther wrote a beautiful song that explains why and how the LORD *"is my strength and shield."*

1. Without God's strength and shield we can't stand against Satan.

A mighty fortress is our God, a bulwark never failing;
Our helper He amid the flood of mortal ills prevailing.
For still our ancient foe doth seek to work us woe. His craft and
Pow'r are great, and armed with cruel hate, on earth is not his equal.

2. The battle is the Lord's.

Did we in our own strength confide, our striving would be losing,
Were not the right man on our side, the man of God's own choosing.
Dost ask who that may be? Christ Jesus, it is He. Lord Sabbath
His name, from age to age the same. And He must win the battle.

3. God's truth will triumph through us.

And tho this world, with devils filled, should threaten to undo us;
We will not fear, for God has willed His truth to triumph through us.
The prince of darkness grim. We tremble not for him; His rage we
Can endure, for lo! His doom is sure. One little word shall fell him.

4. The Holy Spirit is with us!

That word above all earthly powers. No thanks to them abideth;
The Spirit and the gifts are ours, thru Him who with us sideth.
Let goods and kindred go, this mortal life also; The body
they may kill: God's truth abideth still. His kingdom is forever.

Prayer: Dear Lord and Friend, You are our strength and shield today and forever. Our hearts leap for joy, for You give us more of Your strength to serve You every day. In Jesus' name we pray. Amen.

Psalm 29:3-4

"The voice of the LORD is over the waters; the God of glory thunders, the LORD thunders over the mighty waters. The voice of the LORD is powerful; the voice of the LORD is majestic."

"The voice of the LORD"

The voice we listen to is the one that we worship! This psalm begins with one of the most beautiful calls in the Bible to worship God. *"Ascribe to the LORD, O mighty ones, ascribe to the LORD glory and strength. Ascribe to the LORD the glory due His name; worship the LORD in the splendor of His holiness,"* Psalm 29:1-2. Biblical worship is giving God the glory due His name. After all, God did create everything, and He still sustains all things, including us.

"Mighty ones," are especially directed to worship God. This call to worship, especially includes rulers and those in power. It is so easy for them to think that glory and honor is due them. The psalmist reminds those in power that there is a God, one who sits enthroned above all kings. There is a King of kings! So, *"mighty ones,"* kings and others, God is the one that deserves the praise and glory. Psalm two said to kings, *"kiss the Son, lest He be angry and you be destroyed in your way."*

God's voice thunders, "Worship Me." The very first time it ever "thundered," was after Noah entered the ark. The people yet living were surely terrified. They knew God was speaking. Except for Noah and his family, the people were being severely judged, for they did not worship God. Will we worship *"the voice of the Lord"*?

There are voices that bombard us from every side. Many voices compete for our attention. The ones we choose to listen to reveals the true condition of our hearts. The Lord's voice is never silent. To not hear God's voice, we would have to purposely block it out. For the voice of the Lord *"thunders,"* is *"powerful"* and is *"majestic."*

Prayer: Majestic Lord, we are so quick to listen to other voices, even ones that pull us away from You. The next time we hear the thunder in a storm, may we be reminded that it is a call to worship You! Help the leaders of our nation to understand this urgent need to worship You also. In Jesus' name we pray. Amen.

Psalm 30:4-5

"Sing to the LORD, you saints of His; praise His holy name. For His anger lasts only a moment, but His favor lasts a lifetime; weeping may remain for a night, but rejoicing comes in the morning."

Our attitude is everything

David pleads, *"you saints of His,"* have a right attitude toward God when His discipline is on you. David knew from his painful experience, God's frowning providence was upon him, *"for a night."* God did this out of love for David's soul and for the building of His own kingdom. David learned an important life lesson. Now he is concerned that all believers may see how God's loving hand of discipline *"lasts only a moment."* After being corrected, *"rejoicing"* soon follows! His weeping lasted until morning when a new attitude dawned.

The writer of Hebrews was also concerned about our attitude in suffering. *"Endure hardship as discipline, God is treating you as sons. For what son is not disciplined by his father?"* Hebrews 12:7.

James was concerned about our attitude. *"Consider it pure joy, my brothers, whenever you face trials of many kinds, because you know that the testing of your faith develops perseverance. Perseverance must finish its work so that you may be mature and complete, not lacking anything,"* James 1:2-4.

Peter was also concerned about our attitude in suffering. *"Dear friends, do not be surprised at the painful trial you are suffering, as though something strange were happening to you. But rejoice that you participate in the sufferings of Christ, so that you may be overjoyed when His glory is revealed,"* 1 Peter 4:12-13.

Satan will surely tempt us to doubt the goodness of God when we suffer. At this point, we need to trust God. Every believer has the love of God in them, today and for all eternity. We are joint heirs in Jesus Christ and nothing can separate us from the love of God. Therefore, we should not be fearful, worried or depressed. Let us then fully learn the importance of our text. May God move us out of our remaining unbelief, that we might praise Him more.

Prayer: O Lord, we spend so much time in worthless self-pity. Forgive us for doubting Your goodness. We know we must look up to You with a more trusting faith. Help us to do that. In Jesus' name we pray. Amen.

Psalm 30:11-12a

"You turned my wailing into dancing; you removed my sackcloth and clothed me with joy, that my heart may sing to You and not be silent."

"That my heart may sing"

Our wonderful Lord makes us sing. David and his son Solomon also, wrote many songs. The most famous song of all is called the Song of Solomon. That song is one of the 1005 songs that Solomon wrote, according to 1 Kings 4:32-33. Solomon's song is an allegory. The same words express the love of Christ and the church, and the close relationship of a husband and wife. Solomon's famous song is not in this study, yet he agrees with father David who wrote Psalm 30.

The Gospel of grace is the Father, Son and Spirit kissing believers. We, in turn, respond to that love in song. We see a picture of that throughout the psalms and in the Song of Solomon. Even in the parable of the prodigal son, the father kissed the son, even before the son makes his confession to the father. Truly the Christian life is an intimate relationship with God, driven by God, *"That my heart may sing."*

"Let Him kiss me with the kisses of his mouth – for your love is more delightful than wine," Song of Solomon 1:1-2. Jesus' electing grace "kissed" us, even before the world was made, says Ephesians 1:4-5. Before we were born, He already planned the *"kiss."* In the day of our salvation, God planted that personal kiss. Christ took our sin and gave us His perfect righteousness, kissing us eternally! The intimate love of God meets the deepest need we will ever have! Our love fails often, but God's love never fails. One result is, *"That my heart may sing."*

True believers desire to be intimate with God using intimate words. How wonderful that Christianity is not a religion, but a most wonderful, eternal relationship with our God and every believer. As believers, we must sing on Earth now and in Heaven forever!

Prayer: O Lord and Lover of our souls, when we don't desire You, humble us. For we can't live without Your divine love. Help us to learn and experience more about Your amazing love so that we may love You more for it. You so deserve our worship in song! In Jesus' name we pray. Amen.

Psalm 31:5

"Into Your hands I commit my spirit; redeem me, O LORD, the God of truth."

Do we trust our souls to God?

These words of the psalmist were the same as the last words Jesus spoke before He died. It would be most fitting if these were ours also. However, Jesus did not say the two words, "redeem me," for He had no sin of His own. He Himself, is our personal Redeemer! And that is exactly why we can trust God's Son. A redeemer buys. Jesus bought us with His blood, which is more precious than gold. Our redemption cost Him everything, and us nothing. Through faith in Him, we can say, *"Into Your hands I commit my spirit; redeem me, O LORD, the God of truth."* This is our prayer for today and our last words on earth.

The words *"I commit,"* show how no one took Jesus' Spirit from Him. They took His body away, but not His Spirit. No one could possibly take it because He is God. No one can take our spirit/soul from us either. If Christ, the Son of God has redeemed us, we belong to Him. Jesus clearly said about us, His chosen sheep, *"No one can snatch them out of My hand. My Father, who has given them to Me, is greater than all; no one can snatch them out of My Father's hand,"* John 10:28b-29. If we are His child, our soul is safe with God. Are we comfortable that God has complete control of our soul, now and for all eternity? Can we trust our soul to God for all eternity? If we say "Yes," that's good, but that brings another question. Can we also trust our soul to God for today's living? These are trust and faith questions that have everything to do with our attitude in life as well as in death.

The first question of the Heidelberg Catechism is a great one. "What is your only comfort in life and in death?" The answer is: "That I am not my own, but belong - body and soul, in life and in death - to my faithful Savior Jesus Christ. He has fully paid for all my sins with His precious blood, and has set me free from the tyranny of the devil." How comforting it is that the King of the universe not only bought us, but also holds on to us!

Prayer: O loving Lord, what a benefit, what a joy divine, leaning on Your everlasting arms! What a privilege, that in Christ, I can say, *"into Your hands I commit my spirit."* In Jesus' name we pray. Amen.

Psalm 31:9

"Be merciful to me O LORD, for I am in distress; my eyes grow weak with sorrow, my soul and my body with grief."

"Be merciful to me, O LORD"

David knew that part of God's character is that He is merciful. In the midst of incredible trials, David remembered that God could deliver him. David cries out to the only One who can help. God's grace to David and to us, is partiality our responsibility to cry out, *"LORD have mercy on me, a sinner."* Before the world was created, way before we were born, the Triune God had already put that desire to cry out to Him in our hearts! Christ knew us and loved us already then. In fact, that is exactly why Christ came to world. He came to have mercy on His elect sheep who were lost and hurting. How can we not love God and follow Him who is so merciful?

Blind Bartimaeus cried for mercy, saying, *"Jesus, Son of David, have mercy on me!"* Mark 10:47b. The point is, sinners cry for mercy. Jesus taught in Mark 10:45 that He came *"to give His life as a ransom for many."* Then immediately we read of this blind man. Perhaps the biggest shock of all is that this blind man is us, who would someday believe. Blind, we cannot see our way through life without Jesus. In fact, Bartimaeus' father was blind before him. Our fathers were spiritually blind, all the way back to Adam. Blind Bartimaeus was also physically blind. He cries for mercy to the Great Healer, desperate to see physically. But Jesus heals him spiritually also. Are we desperate to see spiritually?

Think of the various people in the Bible who cried for mercy and received it! David cried *"Be merciful to me, O LORD"* in Psalm 31 and 51. The Canaanite woman said, *"Have mercy on me, O Lord."* If we cry out to God like that, we will also receive His sure mercy. God's grace and mercy is our biggest need in life, and God is willing to give it to us when we cry out to Him for His powerful help.

Prayer: Dear Merciful Lord, we thank You for moving in us by Your Holy Spirit to cry out for Your much needed mercy. We praise You that You forgive sinners and then continue to be merciful to us throughout our life. We worship You. In Jesus' name we pray. Amen.

Psalm 31:15-16

"My times are in Your hands; deliver me from my enemies and from those who pursue me. Let Your face shine on Your servant; save me in Your unfailing love."

"My times are in Your hands"

What a comforting thought, our times are in God's almighty hands. If God and all of His amazing and perfect attributes are for us, then those who are against us matter little.

In Luke 11, Jesus taught "The Lord's Prayer." In commentating on this prayer, Jesus added some examples to teach us to have faith in God. Jesus taught that in a time of great need, a close friend may fail you, but God won't. Jesus asked, *"What earthly father would give his son a snake to eat instead of fish? What father would give a scorpion instead of an egg?"* Jesus then concludes that if we who are evil and imperfect can give good things, how much more can our perfect and powerful God give His Spirit to those who ask Him? And Jesus is the One who takes our prayers to His Father and ours!

Paul taught in 2 Corinthians 1:8b, *"We were under great pressure, far beyond our ability to endure, so that we despaired even of life."* Why did all of this hardship happen, Paul? *"This happened that we might not rely on ourselves but on God,"* 2 Corinthians 1:9b. Paul concludes, *"God has delivered us... and He will deliver us. On Him we have set our hope that He will continue to deliver us,"* 2 Corinthians 1:10. God delivers us in three ways. God *"has delivered"* us in the past. He *"delivers"* us in the present and *"will deliver"* us in the future!

All of God's adopted children belong to God, both body and soul! He planned our salvation. He purchased us with His Son's blood. He loves us like His own Son. Yet we do have a personal responsibility to ask for God's protection and direction. James, the brother of Jesus, said, *"You do not have, because you do not ask God. When you ask, you do not receive, because you ask with wrong motives,"* James 4:2b-3a.

Prayer: Almighty Lord, for Your kingdom's sake hear our cry for help. Our times are in Your hand. Like Paul, our enemies are too strong for us, but never too strong for You. Lord, You feed the birds and care for the animals. But Lord, Your image is in us. Save us *"with Your unfailing love."* In Jesus' name we pray. Amen.

Psalm 32:4-5

"For day and night Your hand was heavy upon me; my strength was sapped as in the heat of summer. Then I acknowledged my sin to You and did not cover up my iniquity. I said, 'I will confess my transgressions to the LORD' and You forgave the guilt of my sin."

Confession, the cleansing of the soul

Confession is perhaps the simplest of all doctrines and the easiest to understand. Yet it is here, that we fail and fall. Part of the reason is that sin is a topic most of us don't want to talk about. At first, David was unwilling to confess his sin, especially to God. That negligence, cost him his spiritual health, and then his physical health. A Biblical confession is, when I agree with God about the sins I have committed against Him and against others, with a commitment to forsake that sin.

David's stubbornness to confess his sin told God he did not agree or care about God's thoughts at this point in his life. David's failure to confess was a lack of commitment to forsake the sin. A believer who holds on to a pattern of sin is on dangerous ground. God will respond to such a challenge and will exercise His right to discipline every believer. When God's discipline does come, it is a fruit of His displeasure, yet it is also the very proof of His love. God's Spirit made David miserable, forcing him to confess his wrong doing. God's holy character, demands that His children are also holy!

I hear my grandchildren pray, "Lord, help me to be good." That is a good concern and a good prayer, but still lacking. Better to pray, "Lord, I just fought with my sister and hurt her and she cried. Lord, I never want to do this to her again. Please forgive me. Help me to always love my sister."

Why do we, our children and grandchildren so easily pray without confessing any specific sin? Because, that is the way we adults pray! As parents, we do not openly confess our sins to God. So whose fault is it that the children are not open with what they do wrong? More on this import point tomorrow.

Prayer: O holy Lord, You show us that confession is good for our souls. You even move us to the cross to cleanse us. Lord, we thank you for convicting us or we would never confess anything. What a loving concern You have for our holiness. In Jesus' name we pray. Amen.

Psalm 32:3-4

"When I kept silent, my bones wasted away through my groaning all the day long. For day and night Your hand was heavy upon me; my strength was sapped as in the heat of summer."

Confession, to overcome depression

When David kept "silent" he was not confessing any sin in his life. We do the same. Do we really think that we are more spiritually mature than Peter, Elijah, and David, who were depressed because of their sinful actions? The events or the schedules of these lives were *"written to teach us, so that through endurance and the encouragement of the Scriptures we might have hope,"* Romans 15:4b. Their Biblical examples, both good and bad, are for our benefit. God spoke to them about their personal depression. They listened to God and He healed them. They got over their depression and so can we. Are we willing to handle life's difficulties God's way?

David was experiencing the pain of depression. He said about God, *"Your hand was heavy upon me."* David had feelings of dejection and guilt. The result was hopelessness, and a ceasing of the activities in life. The Bible uses various words to describe depression: such as *"face downcast"* in Genesis 4:6, *"a burden too heavy to bear"* in Psalm 38:4, *"weary with sorrow"* in Psalm 119:28, a *"crushed spirit"* in Proverbs 17:22, 18:14 and *"grow weary and lose heart"* in Hebrews 12:3.

College students, business workers, housewives, even people in ministry are often depressed. Why? The Bible is ready to teach us; are we willing to listen? The problem is that so many of us have listened to the "world's ideas," that have tried hard to reinvent the real causes and solutions of depression. Psychology focuses almost entirely on fixing the feelings of depression. God deals more with thoughts, words, and actions that lead to depressed feelings. In Ecclesiastes 12:14, every thought, word, or action is a "religious" issue. David confessed his sin and was healed. Are we willing to listen to God also and be healed?

Prayer: O caring Lord, like David, we keep silent about certain sinful habits. In love, You convict us so we will change. Lord, we seek Your forgiveness and Your righteousness through the blood of Christ. In His name we pray. Amen.

Psalm 32:5

"I will confess my transgressions to the LORD."

I will confess my own sins

When we kneel to pray, it is very tempting to bring up what others did wrong, not what we did wrong! As we meet with friends, we confess what others have done wrong to us. Little children learn this at a very young age. We say to our young son or daughter, "Why is the little neighbor boy crying?" Our child will say, "He called me names, so I hit him with a stick." We instruct our child that even if someone calls you names, you don't have the right to hit them. "Now, go tell this little boy that you're sorry and ask for his forgiveness." The child goes and this is his confession, "Please forgive me for hitting you, <u>when you called me names</u>." The confession started good, but as soon as the neighbor boy's wrong was added in, your child was really saying, "I had a good reason to do what I did." That is not a confession. It is blame-shifting, just like Adam and Eve in the Garden of Eden.

Our motive for confessing sin must be that we are convicted that we are 100% guilty, and we cannot possibly ever make up for our wrong. With this in mind, we are now asking another person or God to forgive us from the guilt of what we have done wrong. True confession begins when we quit trying to justify our sin. We need to finally judge the log in our own eye and stop acting the part of the hypocrite. Biblical change begins with judging our own life.

What about saying to someone; "If I hurt you, I'm sorry." Is that a confession? No. Too often, such a question tempts the other person to lie, to make us feel better about what we have done wrong. We don't like to admit that we are wrong. If we have offended God and others also, it matters not what others think. Failing to confess is the worship of self. Biblical confessions worship the holiness of God. *"I will confess my transgressions to the LORD."*

Prayer: Forgiving Lord, we have so often confessed more of other people's sins than we have our own. Lord, forgive us and help us to stick to the basics and confess our own wrong living. May we copy David who said, *"I will confess my transgressions to the LORD."* May we praise Your holiness with our confessions. In Jesus' name we pray. Amen.

Psalm 32:5

"Then I acknowledged my sin to You and did not cover up my iniquity. I said, 'I will confess my transgressions to the LORD' and You forgave the guilt of my sin."

Our sin has physical consequences

Sin has consequences. God completely forgives, and forever removes the guilt of our sin, but there may still remain physical and material consequences. When David finally confessed his sin of adultery and murder, God forgave him from the *"guilt"* as our text shows. However, God made sure there were tragic consequences to King David's sin of adultery and murder. Why? So all Israel, along with us today, may know for certain, sin has consequences. Why? So we will stop sinning. It is called God's discipline of us, to make us more holy.

There were physical consequences of David's adultery. The baby died. Furthermore, the sword did not depart from David's house, (2 Samuel 12:10-11). As a physical consequence today, a person may get HIV and then AIDS. Sin has consequences, even *"to the third and fourth generations,"* Deuteronomy 5:9. Guilt is a different issue than consequences. The guilt of sin does not pass on from father to son. Ezekiel 18:1-20 is clear about that. See another practical example of physical consequences of sin.

A son gets into a fight at school. When daddy comes home from work the little boy says, "Daddy, I was wrong, please forgive me." Daddy must forgive, but discipline is still needed. Why? When the child feels some pain as a consequence of his actions, it serves as a reminder to not sin again. If Daddy does not discipline, the child would quickly learn to say, "I'm sorry" as a false confession, without changing his heart. Then, a father would be making a Pharisee out of his child. Outward actions do not change if the heart is not changed first. Of course, the father must discipline in love, not in anger, and then comfort the child afterwards, as God does to us. God gives us physical consequences, usually painful, always as a blessing, so we will stop sinning.

Prayer: O Lord, it is good for us to see that sin has consequences, so that we stop sinning. Help us to appreciate how important it is that You discipline us for our good. In Christ's name we pray. Amen.

Psalm 33:1-3

"Sing joyfully to the LORD, you righteous; it is fitting for the upright to praise Him. Praise the LORD with the harp; make music to Him on the ten-stringed lyre. Sing to Him a new song; play skillfully, and shout for joy."

"Sing joyfully to the LORD"

God loves music! Billions of birds sing endlessly to their Creator. If a bird with a little brain knows how to openly praise God, then how much more should Christians, who have been given a redeemed soul? Not every bird sings so sweetly. The crows are a bit raucous in their singing but still they sing. We are commanded to sing joyfully.

Paul sang while in prison. Anyone who is put into prison and can still sing, cannot really be imprisoned. Those who are in an abusive household and can still sing, have a sure hope in God. We must sing praises to God, believing that He is the One who is really in control. Singing is a way of responding in a right way to the evil that people do to us. Singing to God (not the self-pity blues) is a right response of gratitude for what God has done and will do. Singing expresses our love and commitment to God and to others in our daily living.

Those who can sing while enduring affliction have learned what James, Peter and Paul finally learned. Their personal joy was made complete, through their suffering. Our singing is a sweet prayer of dependence on God. Singing honors God and praises His powerful attributes. Singing moves God to act in mercy!

Back to Paul's example of singing in prison. He did not sing in the night because he was afraid. He sang because being thrown in jail for the sake of the Gospel didn't matter. Paul knew for certain that God was still in complete control. Paul sang praises to God knowing that God knows best how to advance His sovereign agenda in this broken world. Paul sang, then God responded!

Prayer: Dear Lord, "I will sing of my Redeemer and His heavenly love to me. He from death to life has brought me, Son of God with Him to be." We sing because You are on Your heavenly throne, Lord of the entire world. We sing because nothing can happen to us apart from Your holy will. Lord accept our songs of praise. In Jesus' name we pray. Amen.

Psalm 33:8

"Let all the earth fear the LORD, let all the people of the world revere Him."

God, the perfect designer

I recently read an article in a farming bulletin that points to our great Creator. It is amazing how our God is so orderly. His creative genius is seen even in the hatching of eggs. The eggs of a potato bug hatch in 7 days. A canary's eggs hatch in 14 days. A hen's eggs hatch in 21 days. A goose egg hatches in 28 days. A mallard egg hatches in 35 days. The baby parrot comes out of the shell in 42 days. All are divisible by 7. There are 7 days in a week. Seven is God's number of completeness and perfection.

God's incredible wisdom is seen in the making of an elephant., whose super strong legs all bend forward in the same direction. No other animal with 4 legs is made like this! The elephant's huge body was given four huge legs that act as fulcrums to raise it from the ground easily. How could an elephant evolve from something else?

See God's attention to the exact details in His arrangement of sections, segments and even the amount of seeds in fruit or in a head of grain. A watermelon has an even number of stripes. An ear of corn has an even number of rows. A head of wheat has an even number of grains. And God did all this by just speaking it into existence!

God causes the various flowers to blossom at certain specified times during the day. A botanist said that if he had controlled growing conditions for the flowers, he could tell the time of day or night just by the flowers that were open, and by those that were shut.

If God is so particular about eggs, elephants, seeds and flowers, will He not order our lives to carry out His divine purpose in us? God created us to recognize Him, to love Him, to worship Him and to live for Him. By recognizing who God is, by believing what He says about Himself, we will find our exact purpose in life.

Prayer: O Perfect Lord and Savior, what a majestic God of order and design You truly are. Your loving plans do stand firm forever. The purposes of Your heart are in every generation. All created things, and us too, are totally under Your sovereign control. We praise and worship You. In Jesus' name we pray. Amen.

Psalm 33:11

"The plans of the LORD stand firm forever, the purposes of His heart through all generations."

God doesn't change, what a blessing!

God's Word and work never changes because God's character never changes. The fact that God never changes is called the immutability of God. In fact, God cannot change. Our text shows us why: *"The plans of the LORD stand firm forever"* even *"through all generations."* God Himself said, *"I the LORD, do not change,"* Malachi 3:6a. God is the same yesterday, today and forever. He is eternally unchanging. He cannot change for the better as He is already perfect. His Word, the Bible, will never change or go out of date. It will always be relevant, meeting our deepest needs!

When we study the Bible to learn the will of God, we must see that how God related to our ancient fathers, He also relates to us. James 5:17 says, *"Elijah was a man just like us."* Their lives are meant to show us the unchanging will of God. It will forever be God's will, for us to be restored, conformed to the image of Christ. He created us to have a relationship with Him and that will never change.

Think of how the fact that God does not change is a blessing. If God could change, we would not know how to pray or even how to worship Him. Jesus said that no one can pluck us out of His or out of the Father's hand. If God could change, we could lose our salvation. If God could change, Heaven would be a dream and Hell would be nonexistent. But the truth is: Hell in the hands of an unchanging God is horrible beyond description.

The fact that God does not change is of great benefit for us as believers, already today! *"The eyes of the LORD are on those who fear Him, on those whose hope is in His unfailing love, to deliver them from death and keep them alive in famine,"* Psalm 33:18-19. There will never be a day or night when God will leave us or forsake us! What a loving and practical, unchanging God we serve.

Prayer: Beautiful, unchanging and holy Lord, David was so right in saying, *"We wait in hope for the LORD; He is our help and shield. In Him our hearts rejoice, for we trust in His holy name."* Lord, we worship You, thankful that You do not change. In Jesus' name we pray. Amen.

Psalm 33:20

"We wait in hope for the LORD; He is our help and our shield."

"He is our help and our shield"

Psalm 33 is a beautiful call to look to God, for He is *"our help and our shield."* This means, it's our Creator, not created things, that are our help and shield. The Psalm begins by calling us to worship God. Verses 4-5 praises God for His love, faithfulness, righteousness, and justice. Verses 6-7 praises the wisdom and the sovereign power of God. In verse 6 we are reminded that God spoke and the world was created. With all of these facts about the amazing attributes of God, the Psalm now states certain things will surely happen.

"The LORD foils the plans of nations; He thwarts the purposes of the peoples," Psalm 33:10. God does this because the world is moving according to His agenda. *"The plans of the LORD stand firm forever, the purposes of His heart through all generations,"* Psalm 33:11.

God *"blesses"* all who belong to Him. His omniscient eye *"sees all mankind,"* Psalm 33:13b. He *"watches all who live on earth,"* Psalm 33:14b. He *"considers everything they do,"* Psalm 33:15b. Then God specifically pours out His blessings on those who are His.

God *"helps"* His own. He gives them exactly what they need, exactly when they need it. His mercy is never early so that our faith is not exercised, nor is it ever so late so that we would lose hope! *"Let us then approach the throne of grace with confidence, so that we may receive mercy and find grace to help us in our time of need,"* Hebrews 4:16. God is our helper, so we need not fear what man can do to us.

God also *"shields"* His own. Satan cannot afflict us without God's permission. Job 1 teaches us that. That is why we pray in the Lord's prayer, *"Deliver us from the evil one."* God can and will do it. *"The eyes of the LORD are on those who fear Him, on those whose hope is in His unfailing love,"* Psalm 33:18. *"The Lord will rescue me from every evil attack and will bring me safely to His heavenly kingdom. To Him be the glory for ever and ever. Amen,"* 2 Timothy 4:18. God is our help and shield, now and forever!

Prayer: Dear Father in Heaven, Your Fatherly goodness in Psalm 33:22 is our need and our great comfort! *"May Your unfailing love rest upon us, O LORD."* In Jesus' name we pray. Amen.

Psalm 34:2-3

"My soul will boast in the LORD; let the afflicted hear and rejoice.
Glorify the LORD with me; let us exalt His name forever."

"Boast in the LORD" not in your ministry

Too often we openly or secretly boast in the ministry that God has given to us. David never boasted in his ministry. David never looked at the people and thought this is my ministry. David found greater satisfaction in following God than in leading people! O how we must learn that our lot in life is to, *"exalt His name forever."*

I saw a problem in others boasting in their ministry before I saw a problem in myself. One pastor in south India said to me, "these are my believers." After three days of teaching at that place, it became very apparent that the people did not know how to confess sin, nor did they understand forgiveness. I said to the pastor in private, "these are your believers, but they are not believers in God." This man was boasting in his ministry.

In reading many ministry letters, decisions for Jesus are counted like the ministry workers are the best salesmen and saleswomen in the world. They act like a gunfighter in the west who put notches on his gun when he killed someone. When did we ever get someone to decide for Jesus? Is that not the work of the Holy Spirit, the work of God? Why are we trying to take credit for what God does? What if we did some good thing and others took credit for it? Would we not be upset? God is not pleased with our soul counting and ministry boasting.

After salvation, sanctification is still the work of God's sovereign grace in a believer's life. It is our work to tell the good news and to disciple those God saves. *"My soul will boast in the LORD; let the afflicted hear and rejoice."* Paul had the right idea in 2 Corinthians 1:3-4. *"Praise be to the God and Father of our Lord Jesus Christ, the Father of compassion and the God of all comfort, who comforts us in all our troubles, so that we can comfort those in any trouble with the comfort we ourselves have received from God."*

Prayer: Dear Lord, forgive us for trying to steal the glory that belongs to You. Let us exalt Your name forever. In Jesus' name we pray. Amen

Psalm 34:11-14

"Come, my children, listen to me; I will teach you the fear of the LORD. Whoever of you loves life and desires to see many good days, keep your tongue from evil and your lips from speaking lies. Turn from evil and do good; seek peace and pursue it."

God's children need a Biblical world-view

God teaches His children to have a Biblical world-view. God wants children to view the world through His eyes, to respect His rules for living in the Bible. The opposite of God's way of living is man's way. Man's path in life says, we are the center of everything and whatever we want to do, that is best. There are two world-views.

God's children are to put off evil. The psalm here teaches us to have a *"fear of the LORD."* That means, to greatly respect God's will for our lives. God then gives us an example of what that looks like. *"Keep your tongue from evil and your lips from speaking lies."* We know from Luke 6:45, *"the mouth speaks that which comes from the heart."* So if we are prone to lie, it shows our heart is still *"evil,"* with very little fear or respect for who God is.

God's children *"turn from evil and do good."* The first thing God did in creation was to separate light from darkness. His children know the difference between light and dark living. They love what God loves, and they hate what God hates. God's children are not in love with sinning because they know it is not pleasing to Him.

God's children honor their parents and others because God tells them to love and respect them. They know God wants forgiveness to grace their relationships, whereas Satan wants them to be angry with others. God promises His children, *"good days,"* if they listen to Him!

God's children have hope. The secret to hope is not what you know, but Who you know! A child with hope has contentment. And again, that is not what you have in your hand, but what you have in your heart. There is no peace without a healthy *"fear of the LORD."* God's children can sing with a smile when their life is being rocked. For they know their God will never leave them or forsake them!

Prayer: Dear Sovereign Lord, we see that Your children need to trust in You and You will bless them. We praise You for being so faithful and loving. In Jesus' name we pray. Amen.

Psalm 35:22b-24a

"Do not be far from me, O LORD. Awake and rise to my defense! Contend for me, my God and my LORD. Vindicate me in Your righteousness, O LORD my God."

"Defend and contend for me, my God"

As a shepherd, David knew first-hand how it was his sole responsibility to contend for his defenseless sheep. He regularly killed snakes and other predators, along with at least one lion and bear. David with affection and dependence could say, *"The LORD is my Shepherd."*

Our God not only wants to defend us, He loves to defend His children! A mother or father may hesitate to protect or defend their child. God will never do that. God is more like a mother bear. If the little cubs are even threatened, whether it is real or not, there will be a most serious defense. God has much more care than a bear. Our cry for help will get a sure response from God. He will either change the circumstance or give us the grace to accept it.

Look at God's defending us from His perspective. His reputation is at stake. One of the names of God in the King James Version is *"Jehovah Nissi"* meaning our banner of defense. David wrote in Psalm 91:14-16, *"Because he has set his love upon Me, therefore I will deliver him; I will set him on high because he has known My name. He shall call upon Me and I will answer him; I will be with him in trouble; I will deliver him and honor him. With long life I will satisfy him, and show him My salvation."* Now that is a lot of *"I wills"* on God's part!

We must then pray seriously to God. "For Your name's sake defend us. For Your name's sake, contend for us so that we might contend for Your kingdom." Our *"Jehovah Nissi,"* was the God of Daniel in the lion's den. Our God defended Esther from the wicked Haman. Now it is our turn. We must praise and worship God when He defends us. *"My tongue will speak of your righteousness and of Your praises all day long,"* Psalm 35:28.

Prayer: O Powerful Lord, forgive us for our doubts about Your ability and desire to defend us. How vast the benefits divine that we in Christ possess! Your unlimited power is so amazing. Our privileged status is beyond our limited understanding. We praise and worship You for defending us and contending for us! In Jesus' name we pray. Amen.

Psalm 36:7a

"How priceless is Your unfailing love! Both high and low among men find refuge in the shadow of Your wings."

God's priceless unfailing love!

Gold and diamonds are cheap kid's toys when compared to God's *"priceless unfailing love."* As Christians, we desire more of God's *"priceless"* love, but not more than God's love! My favorite song is, "The Love of God." The words in the verses are so beautiful. The great words of the chorus are, "O love of God, how rich and pure! How measureless and strong! It shall forever more endure – the saints' and angels' song." As Christians, we are exactly like the prodigal son who was kissed by the Father, even before the son opened his mouth to confess any of his sin! God's unmeasurable love gives us a look into His heart that is beautiful beyond description.

How we act in response to God's love to us will echo throughout eternity. Do we personally value the priceless and unfailing love of God enough to tell others about it? Jesus cried in Luke 13:34, "*O Jerusalem, Jerusalem, you who kill the prophets and stone those sent to you, how often I have longed to gather your children together, as a hen gathers her chicks under her wings, but you were not willing.*"

Jesus cried over lost souls. Do we?

Many are rushing towards an eternity where they will face the wrath of God forever. If our neighbor was about to drown, would we rescue him? Do we care? Keith Green sings a great message!

"Do you see? Do you see? All the people sinking down? Don't you care? Don't you care? Are you going to let them drown?"

"How can you be so numb? Not to care if they come. You close your eyes, and pretend the job is done"

"Oh, can't you see such sin? Cause He brings people to your door, and you turn them away as you smile and say: God bless you!"

Prayer: Loving Lord, we say Your unfailing love is priceless, but we are so slow to show it in how we live. Forgive us and move our lips to tell others of Your unfailing love. We praise You for the cross, the proof of Your priceless love. In Jesus' precious name we pray. Amen.

Psalm 37:1-2

"Do not fret because of evil men or be envious of those who do wrong; for like the grass they will soon wither, like green plants they will soon die away."

The secret of contentment

We want contentment. We strive for it, but so few of us have it. Why? Part of the reason is, it is not what we do to get it, but what God does in giving it. Psalm 37 is instructive and has five key thoughts that show us that contentment is *"in the LORD,"* and *"to the LORD."*

1. Don't worry or envy as the world does! 2. *"Trust in the LORD."* 3. *"Delight yourself in the LORD."* 4. *"Commit your way to the LORD."* 5. *"Rest in the LORD."* All these are, *"in the LORD,"* because it is through His Spirit, that *"rest"* or contentment finally comes. But, we can't *"rest in the LORD,"* in number 5, until we *"commit our way to the LORD."* And we can't *"commit our way to the LORD"* until we *"delight in the LORD."* We can't *"delight in the LORD"* until we *"trust in the LORD."* And finally, we will never *"trust in the LORD"* until we put off worry and envy of all kinds. So then, let's first address the problem of worry and envy.

Worry is misplaced trust, because it's not trusting in God. Worry trusts in our ability to solve our greatest needs. The real problem is, that we are not self-sufficient. A Christian who thinks he or she is self-sufficient will be shown by God, that He is their sufficiency. Biblical trust is about the sufficiency of God. Worry ends where faith begins!

Jesus called worry, *"little faith"* in Matthew 6:30. God shows us envy is a deed of the flesh. Envy is not a spirit-filled life as seen in Galatians 5. In fact, envy indicates a depraved mind in Romans 1:29. If we really want to be content, we first need to be convicted that our worry and envy are wrong. In the process of change (repentance), we must put off sin and the love of things (idols), before the love of God can be put on. We then need to confess it and put it off. Only then we can begin to *"trust in the LORD."*

Prayer: Almighty Lord, we want to trust in You, to delight in You, to commit our ways to You, and finally to rest in You. Lord help us to put off our bad habits and put on trusting You. Lord, forgive our sin and help us to stop sinning! In Jesus' name we pray. Amen.

Psalm 37:3

*"Trust in the LORD and do good; dwell in the land and
enjoy safe pasture."*

Trusting, *"in the LORD"*

Trusting in God is all about having faith in God's ability to do what
He says He will do. We must know something about the character of
God to trust Him.. *"Faith is being sure of what we hope for and certain
of what we do not see,"* Hebrews 11:1. But our faith must be tested to
see if it is real! So God allows difficult situations to come along, just to
test us. Can God do what He says He will do in His Word? Or, will we
trust in our own ability to get through each trial?

Biblical contentment comes as God in Trinity provides for us in
every trial. *"I can do everything through Him who gives me strength,"*
Philippians 4:13. Paul was content with having little or much. Paul fully
trusted in God to give him what he needed, when he needed it. Trust is
an intimate and deep relationship with God. So God teaches us contentment when we trust Him for it. That is exactly why Paul could say,
"I have learned to be content whatever the circumstances," Philippians
4:11b. God taught him!

Like Paul, David learned contentment. God convicted him and
changed him also. He then confessed; *"My heart is not proud, O LORD,
my eyes are not haughty; I do not concern myself with great matters,"*
Psalm 131:1. He no longer went to God with great demands! Instead,
he humbled himself before God saying, *"I have stilled and quieted my
soul; like a weaned child with its mother,"* Psalm 131:2a. David finally
trusted in God's wise providence and timings for his life. Through his
trials, David learned that the battle is the Lord's. The big question for
us is: "Are we content to belong to the Lord, trusting that He will guide
us and use us as He so pleases?"

Prayer: Dear Faithful Lord, we want to know Christ, to abide in Him,
to live for Him! But Lord, we know that we need to trust You more. Our
selfish ambition gets in the way. Lord, Paul said in Philippians 2:13,
*"It is God who works in you to will and to act according to His good
purpose."* So fill us Lord with Your holy presence. In Jesus' name we
pray. Amen.

Psalm 37:4

"Delight yourself in the LORD and He will give you the desires of your heart."

"Delight yourself in the LORD"

We want to "*delight*" in God more, but our hearts, our wills, still have so many other "*delights*" that get in the way! We can only pray that God will do His work in us, convicting us, so that Christ is our ambition in life. No one can serve two masters. We can't delight in idols, (things or people) as if they are more important than God. How can we have contentment, if we are too preoccupied with the things of this world?

Another problem we have is that we are too controlling. We are "stressed out" wanting to know what God is doing in all parts of our life. We demand to know what God plans to do with our future. We are not yet ready to "*delight*" in whatever happens, or wherever God places us. When we question God, we act as if God reports to us. The truth is: we deserve nothing from God. We earn nothing. We need to get to the point where we can truly say to God, "*Nothing in my hand I bring, simply to Thy Cross I cling!*" That is the kind of "*delight*" in the providence of God that we need.

We are much like Adam and Eve in the Garden of Eden, when they sinned. They were not content with God. They wanted more. Our hearts need to be satisfied with God if we are going to "*delight*" in Him. Our Christian contentment comes as a fruit of having no higher ambition than belonging to God, totally at His disposal. That means, we have to give up our perceived rights.

As servants of God, we must do what is good and pleasing in His eyes. And even then, <u>we must leave the results totally up to God</u>. That point is so important. We insult God when we worry and fret about the results of our Christian service, after we give it to Him as worship. That is like giving someone a gift, then asking for it back. May we delight in God more and more as we grow in the faith.

Prayer: Beautiful Lord, too often we don't "*delight*" in You as our Shepherd. We do not yet fully trust in You. Our lack of contentment accuses You of doing something wrong in our lives. Lord, change us to "*delight*" in You more. Lord, work in us and through us, we pray. In Jesus' name we pray. Amen.

Psalm 37:5-6

"Commit your way to the LORD; trust in Him and He will do this: He will make your righteousness shine like the dawn, the justice of your cause like the noonday sun."

"Commit your way to the LORD"

We have a "*commit*" problem in the Christian camp. We do not yet fully "*trust in the LORD*" or "*delight in the LORD*." Therefore, we do not fully "*commit our way to the LORD*." As a result, we do not always do things for God's glory. We do too much for our own glory. We are still so sinfully in step with a lost world.

Years ago, a commitment to responsibilities was far more common. Now, we are more concerned with our "rights." We ask, "Why is there so much pain and suffering in the world?" By doing so, we imply God gives needless pain and suffering. We think that what God does for us is too little, and what we do for God is too much! By nature, (that is our sinful nature,) we have negative minds that are selfishly preoccupied with who we are. We do have serious commitment problems.

Our trusting and depending more fully on Christ must increase. Think of how we first received Christ. We were dependent on Him for forgiveness, for strength and for eternal life. We were in love with His grace and mercy. What happened? Do we now depend more on "our performance" for contentment, than in "His provision"? I think so. We sing, "His grace will lead us home!" But we live more like our great performance will get us there.

When we lose sight of who God is, we have a commitment and worship problem. It is good to keep coming back to the attributes of God and study them. We all need to review His character points and His promises to us as believers. God has not changed over the years. The way He dealt with the people in the Bible, He deals with us.

"Commit your way to the LORD; trust in Him and He will do this: He will make your righteousness shine like the dawn, the justice of your cause like the noonday sun." When we live for Him and experience Him, the result is that He gives us even more grace and makes us "*shine.*"

Prayer: O Wondrous Lord, help us "*commit*" all our ways to You, for Your glory and for Your praise. We want our relationship with You to grow. Fill us with Your presence. In Jesus' name we pray. Amen.

Psalm 37:7a NKJV

"Rest in the LORD, and wait patiently for Him; do not fret because of him who prospers in his way."

"Rest in the LORD"

Resting in the will of the Lord is the spiritual maturity we need. But the resting and waiting are hard lessons to learn. We would rather run like a chicken with its head off, than wait. It is not just children that have a hard time waiting. We all want answers, now! We want to know what to do now. We are filled with tension. We can even pray for a long time, not even waiting for God to speak to us. In the end, God must teach us to "rest in Him," for we never learn it on our own.

God teaches us concerning our selfishness. The order of His Ten Commandments point that out. When self is big and God is small, we are ready for a fall. The psychologist Maslow was very wrong. Self-actualization is not the apex of the triangle, God is. We may say we don't believe Maslow's insane theology, but we sure do live it. We are still too much like the drunk, the adulterer, gambler, glutton or the greedy who live to please self. How can we be content with God when the way we live is all about us? It is a relationship with Jesus that satisfies us. Contentment is a heart and soul issue. As Christians, our body and soul belong to God. He purchased us and now we need to live like we are His possession.

Contentment and resting in God will not be ours in abundance, until we realize God owes us nothing. Our faith needs to grow-up to be able to say with David, *"Whom have I in Heaven but You? And earth has nothing I desire besides You,"* Psalm 73:25. I believe that God will eventually teach every Christian to *"rest in the LORD."* God will make sure we learn contentment. He may even strip us of our health and possessions. God will somehow show us that He is "more" and "better" than anything or anyone! God has something far better for us than more of this world's possessions! He wants to give us Himself, to live in us and to live through us. When He does, we will *"rest in the LORD."*

Prayer: O Comforting Lord, we want to rest in You and we want to be content. Take my life and let it be consecrated, Lord to Thee. In Jesus' name we pray. Amen.

Psalm 37:16-17

"Better the little that the righteous have than the wealth of many wicked; for the power of the wicked will be broken; but the LORD upholds the righteous."

Contentment needed!

We continue on the lack of contentment subject, because it is a great problem. We strive for it with all kinds of misplaced human effort. We somehow think that if we have more material things we will find contentment. We look at what others have and want it. We want a better job. We want a bigger bank account. We want a great spouse and nice children. We think better health, a bigger car, and a nicer house would really satisfy us. We think a lengthy vacation and even retirement will bring a peace we do not currently have. And if only we would get a little more respect, then we would have contentment. And so on and on we think, while an aching void remains in our heart.

In review, David started Psalm 37 by saying, *"do not be envious"* of what others have. Envy is a form of bitterness that drives spiritual, mental and physical torture. We must replace all forms of such selfish thoughts, words and actions. But what do we replace it with?

"Trust in the LORD and do good." Why? Because envy is quite the opposite of trust, faith and hope in God. Check out Hebrews 11:1. Faith is all about hope. Where is our hope in envy and bitterness?

If we *"trust in the LORD,"* we can now *"Delight in the LORD."* For by delighting in other things, we held on to idols. If we can live life without prayer or opening the Bible, we do not delight in the Lord. When we *"delight in the LORD"* we can now, *"rest in the LORD."*

In our text, it says, God *"upholds the righteous,"* those who are committed to Him and resting in Him. I find it amazing that Paul said, *"I have learned to be content."* Equally amazing is how God, through the process of trials, teaches us contentment. Praise the Lord!

Prayer: Heavenly Father, contentment is so elusive because we think and act too much like pagan idol worshipers. Lord, fill our hearts with Yourself. Take our eyes off things of less value and place them on You. For we can see that Jesus had contentment even with only a stone for a pillow. Make us more like Him. In Jesus' name we pray. Amen.

Psalm 37:25 NKJV

"I have been young, and now am old; yet I have not seen the righteous forsaken, nor his descendants begging bread."

God's faithfulness to His children

What a beautiful testimony of David concerning the faithfulness of God! The truth about God's faithfulness must not only comfort us, but direct us to trust God in our daily living.

God's faithfulness is to His children. That is what our text is teaching. But more than that, God's faithfulness is also to His children's children. Our God is a covenant-keeping God. He blesses Christian families, up *"to a thousand generations"* as He promised He would in Deuteronomy 5:10.

God's faithfulness is part of His character. We can count on God to do what He says He will do. His promises are *"Yes, and Amen."* God is gracious to those who serve Him. He is full of compassion to those who need Him. He is slow to anger when we offend Him. He is most merciful when we seek Him. He is just as ready to give, as He is to forgive. Faithfulness is part of God's character.

God's faithfulness is given to the obedient. Elijah was a faithful servant of God. When there was a huge drought in the land, by the will of God, God did not forget obedient Elijah or a Christian widow and her son! *"For this is what the LORD, the God of Israel, says: 'The jar of flour will not be used up and the jug of oil will not run dry until the day the LORD gives rain on the land,'"* 1 Kings 17:14. We cannot out give God as we serve Him. God's response is, He faithfully gives back to us the best pension plan in the world.

God's faithfulness must be worshiped. We are called to praise God for His covenant faithfulness, which is to all generations. The Bible wants us to be sure that we understand. *"It was not with our fathers that the LORD God made this covenant, but with us, with all of us who are alive here today,"* Deuteronomy 5:3.

Prayer: Dear Faithful Lord, we do not deserve to be Your children. We receive Your beautiful blessings that come with Your/our covenant relationship. Lord, accept our worship and praise for Your eternal faithfulness! In Jesus' name we pray. Amen.

Psalm 38:1-2 NKJV

"O LORD, do not rebuke me in Your wrath, nor chasten me in Your hot displeasure! For Your arrows pierce me deeply, and Your hand presses me down."

God's counsel on depression

The subject of depression is not so difficult, if we look into the Bible. Today, many people want to hide their depression, embarrassed by it. God made David write about it for our benefit and also for God's glory. David's problem was that he sinned by committing adultery and murder, and then he did not confess it. He tried to ignore his wrong pattern of living for a time. God then got David's attention. The point is, God wanted David depressed! David admits, *"Your hand presses me down."* David took the pills of confession and repentance.

David knew the pain of depression. *"There is no soundness in my flesh because of Your anger, no health in my bones because of my sin."* David's "sin problem" was that his schedule stunk, and God corrected it. God's discipline does that. If we Christians do not honor God with our time, He will adjust our schedule. We can't correctly talk about depression without including schedule issues. At one point, David was living as a playboy instead of a war-boy. God raised up David to shine for Him, not to shame His name. David admits, God put him back on course.

Note, David's feelings of depression were not sinful. Actions that led up to his depression were. If we simply try to fix the feelings of our depression, and give excuses for it, our healing will be delayed. God wants us to get serious with any sin that is connected to our daily schedule. Then, He will quit pressing us down. Feelings of guilt, from the Holy Spirit, John 16:7-8, pain us for a good reason. They are supposed to. Why do we try numb it with drugs, alcohol, food, or buying things, etc.

Many people say a chemical imbalance caused their depression. True, they do have a chemical imbalance. But we will get chemical imbalances as a result of our anger, bitterness, worry or anxiety. It is foolish to say that these wrong responses to personal and difficult situations are caused by a chemical imbalance.

Prayer: O Lord, You are bluntly clear yet loving. Our devotion to You needs to change. Thank You for making David write to us on this important subject. In Jesus' name we pray. Amen.

Psalm 38:1-2 NKJV

"O LORD, do not rebuke me in Your wrath, nor chasten me in Your hot displeasure! For Your arrows pierce me deeply, and Your hand presses me down."

"Your arrows pierce me deeply!"

In Psalm 32 & 38, David records both his depression and his way to victory over it. He starts the discussion with our text, admitting God's rebuke for his recent self-centered living. God's corrective hand pressed him down. The Ten Commandments and the whole Bible teach us to love God first and others second. A depressed person has a self-first problem. Self-pity, self-exaltation and a controlling nature are serious pride issues. That is not how God wants us to live.

The way out of depressed and suicidal thoughts is not to crawl into a hole and hide in a self-preservation mode. Instead, meditate on how big God is, on His wondrous attributes. Forgive others and be gentle to them. We do not have a right to feel sorry for self, just because someone hurt us! A bitter response is not how Jesus lived. In Hebrews 12:15, James 1:20, and James 3:14-16 an angry or bitter response is not a *"righteous life."* It is *"of the devil,"* *"misses the grace of God,"* and it *"defiles many."* If we want to justify our self-pity, God does not agree. He demands better living habits for His children.

The very point at which we are tempted to have a pity party for self is right where we need to stop the downward spiral. We must quickly put our hope in Christ, not on our difficult trial. Meditate and think about what Christ went through. Then we won't think we have it so bad. Think of how Christ promises to never leave us or forsake us. Think of how no one can take us from Jesus' hands. Think of how Christ is bigger than our problem. He will give us the power to gain the victory. Our problem is always a common one to God who tells us: *"No temptation has seized you except what is common to man,"* 1 Corinthians 10:13a. God gives us trials so we will learn to trust Him. He understands our trials and has a promise for us. Let's pray.

Prayer: O Precious and Faithful Lord, You tell us that You will not let us be tempted beyond what we can bear. Your faithfulness, never fails us, even though we fail you. Our trials only strengthen us, if we respond by trusting You. We praise You. In Jesus' name we pray. Amen.

Psalm 39:4-5

"Show me, O LORD, my life's end and the number of my days; let me know how fleeting is my life. You have made my days a mere hand breadth; the span of my years is as nothing before You. Each man's life is but a breath."

"Each man's life is but a breath"

The older we get the more we realize that each and every human life is but a breath. It is over so quickly. We are here one day, gone the next, often without warning. Only God knows the date of our death! When we compare the few years we live to endless eternity, our life measures less than a drop of water in the ocean. Our life is like the blink of an eye compared to endless time.

The second point in our text is, every breath is valuable. Our time on earth is so important that the way we live, determines our eternity. Do not be deceived. There is just one life to live. Reincarnation is a dream of many, but not the truth. Satan lied to Eve when he said you will not die. But since we will someday die, we need to live the one life we have for the God who gave it to us.

Jesus has a divine urgency concerning two things. He knew that man's life was but a breath and that man's soul was precious. Jesus loving warning was: *"Verily, verily"* (meaning truly, truly, doubly true). *"I say unto you, 'He that heareth My Word; and believeth on Him that sent Me, hath everlasting life, and shall not come into condemnation; but has passed from death unto life,'"* John 5:24 KJV.

Jesus is concerned about our personal resurrection! He warned, *"The hour is coming, in which all that are in the graves shall hear His voice, and shall come forth; they that have done good, unto the resurrection of life; and they that have done evil, unto the resurrection of damnation,"* John 5:28b-29 KJV. Our loving God warns us, that life is precious and short, so live it with meaning. And real meaning in life is to seek Him, find Him and love Him. Will we give our all to Him who gave His all for us?

Prayer: *"Show me, O LORD, my life's end and the number of my days; let me know how fleeting is my life."* Lord, put an urgency in our hearts concerning eternal things! In Jesus' name we pray! Amen.

Psalm 39:10-11

"Remove Your scourge from me; I am overcome by the blow of Your hand. You rebuke and discipline men for their sin; You consume their wealth like a moth - each man is but a breath."

God may use a whip to turn us around

David is here speaking from personal experience. He knows all about the painful, yet loving, "blow of God's hand" in discipline. We might ask, "Why would God so severely discipline His beloved son David?" Why would God discipline us? What if we get "too comfortable" in going our own way? What if we foolishly live a bit selfish as a child of God, then what? *"A whip for the horse, a halter for the donkey, and a rod for the backs of fools,"* Proverbs 26:3. We are foolish when we say "No" to God's rightful authority. Foolish people need discipline. It is for this reason we discipline our children, not for mistakes, but for when they are foolish, when they want to be the boss of the home. Foolish believers want to do their own thing, their own way.

When I was young, my father drew a line across the end of the driveway. We were not allowed to cross it because of the dangerous traffic on the road. We would soon foolishly ride our bikes on the line, even over the line, to try set our own rules. Well, my dad had a stick that gave me pain to train my brain not to cross the line again! God has a whip to teach us to respect Him and then we cry and think God is not fair. We see others who are sinning more than us, which brings up a question. Did my earthly dad discipline other children that were not his? No, for they did not belong to him. God disciplines His children because He loves them. He bought His believers (not everyone) with the priceless blood of His Son.

God wrote: *"Do not withhold correction from a child, for if you beat him with a rod he will not die. You shall beat him with a rod, and deliver his soul from hell,"* Proverbs 23:13-14 NKJV. Some say that discipline is not good. God would rather have children cry now, than to cry for all eternity, in a place we do not want to go.

Prayer: Our great Teacher, what love You have for us. You lovingly correct us to bring honor and glory to You and to bless us. We worship You for Your loving wisdom. In Jesus' name we pray. Amen.

Psalm 40:1

"I waited patiently for the LORD; He turned to me and heard my cry."

Respectful waiting and listening

Children are impatient, but then so are mommy and daddy. We are told again and again to be patient, to wait, and to listen. We not only need to wait on others patiently by listening, but we also need to wait on the Lord. The words of our text are for all of us.

If we are unwilling to wait, we are unwilling to listen. If we do not listen, we will not understand each other, or God either. In the Bible there were many who did not want to wait. Kings fought battles and lost because they did not pray to God or wait on His advice. The impulsive Peter cut off a soldier's ear when he would not wait. Peter learned to wait on God. He later taught that we must also wait on each other, as well as on God.

Peter taught believing wives who had difficult husbands, to "*Be submissive to your own husbands, that even if some do not obey the Word, they, without a word, may be won over by the conduct of their wives,*" 1 Peter 3:1b NKJV. If a wife can win over a difficult husband with patient waiting, as she does her work, then so must we. Who have we been impatient with? Who have we been unwilling to listen to? Listening to others shows that we value them.

It is not only wives and children who need to be submissive and wait on each other. Peter clearly said to us husbands, "*Likewise you husbands, dwell with your wife with understanding, giving honor to the wife,*" 1 Peter 3:7a NKJV. If we are going to understand anyone, we will need to wait on them. Listening to others honors them. Listening to others is the loving option that replaces our evil anger or bitterness that is pushing them away from us.

Those who are important to us, we must respectfully listen to and wait on. How much more then, do we need to wait on God? Waiting includes seeking God's will in prayer, and not run ahead of His answer. May God help us to patiently wait on Him as we seek to do His will.

Prayer: Dear Lord, Your wisdom is precious. May we show that we value You, Your commands and others by obediently waiting on You. Thank You for guiding us to holy living. In Jesus' name we pray. Amen.

Psalm 41:1-3

"Blessed is he who has regard for the weak; the LORD delivers him in times of trouble. The LORD will protect him and preserve his life; He will bless him in the land and not surrender him to the desire of his foes. The LORD will sustain him on his sickbed and restore him from his bed of illness."

God is merciful to those who show mercy

What encouraging verses! We know that as Christians, we must show mercy to others. After all, God put mercy in our hearts. God drew us to Himself by His Spirit and put His love into us at the time of His salvation. Mercy is one of His attributes that now must flow out of our new heart, to others who need God's mercy. In fact, we must show mercy to honor God and to bless others. However, we still have a third reason to show mercy in our text. We show mercy to others for our own personal good, for our own protection.

God owes no man anything! He is a debtor to no one. Yet when we honor God, He returns the honor to us. When we are merciful to others in His name, He is merciful to us in our time of need. Far more than that, our text clearly says, *"The LORD delivers him in times (plural) of trouble."* How comforting, practical and timely God's mercy is, and how thankful we must be for God's sure mercy.

Jesus backs up what David says in the psalm. *"Blessed are the merciful, for they will be shown mercy,"* Matthew 5:7. Jesus taught His disciples this truth about His giving of mercy in "The Sermon on the Mount." Jesus was giving His disciples, and us, very practical reasons why we should love Him and follow Him. His truth has not changed over the years, so let us get practical.

Young child, are you kind and merciful to that boy or girl that gets picked on? Or, are you the one who likes to pick on others? Do not look for mercy from God, if you like to trouble others. God is never blind to your efforts to give mercy. He will repay!

Prayer: Dear Heavenly Father, You give us the gift of mercy. With mercy in our hearts, we show mercy to others and then, You in turn, gift us with more mercy. Since we sinners never deserve Your mercy, how grateful must we be for it. Forgive us for the times we complain in our hearts about Your care of us. In Jesus' name we pray. Amen.

Psalm 42:5,11

"Why are you downcast, O my soul? Why so disturbed within me? Put your hope in God, for I will yet praise Him, my Savior and my God."

"Why are you downcast?"

A vibrant faith has hope in a close communion with God, which David was missing here. The occasion likely happened when David was not able to go to the house of God, during Absalom's rebellion. Three times in Psalm 42 and 43, David cries out in agony. It is like David is arguing within himself. He sees his gloom and doom. He realizes that his hope in God is lacking. Even though David is down and somewhat depressed, he knows the only way up and out, is through a closeness with God. That is why David is preaching to himself, "Seek God!" Others had been asking him, *"Where is your God,"* in Psalm 42:3b. David was learning that when God is silent, something is about to happen.

David is being attacked spiritually, and then physically. God is allowing a serious trial to sharpen David's spiritual walk which will also sharpen his spiritual pen. We will do anything God asks of us, when God has been so silent. We can't live without God's smile and encouragement. God is not finished with David, but is recharging his spiritual battery for another strong run!

Like David, we are in a battle for truth. Soldiers are the ones who get shot at, especially those who are on the front lines. That is where arrows fly. Satan's demons intensify their attacks on those who are in the heat of the battle for God. Satan's main goal is to hurt the believer to try get back at Christ. We should not conclude from this that David has necessarily been sinning, kind of like Job. However, through pain and misery, God is moving David into an even greater holiness and usefulness for Him. Trials keep us humble so that God can safely bless us more. In the process, God brings more glory to His Own name.

Prayer: Gracious Lord, it is because of Your great compassion that we are not consumed! Your compassions never fail. They may seem late to us at times, but You always give us mercy, *"in our time of need,"* as the book of Hebrews teaches us. It is so amazing how You are able to quickly make us more like Christ. We praise You for Your concern about our holiness. In Jesus' name we pray. Amen.

Psalm 43:1 Amp.

"Judge and vindicate me, O God; plead and defend my cause against an ungodly nation. O deliver me from the deceitful and unjust man!"

"Judge and vindicate me, O God"

The King James version says, *"judge me."* The NIV says, *"vindicate me."* The Amplified Version says both. Now the question is: Why would David appeal to God to judge him here and now? The answer is all about God's justice in Heaven and in His courtroom on earth. Can any person be tried twice for the same crime in a court of law? No, that would not be fair or just. No one should pay twice for the same offense.

Here is the comfort for every believer: If you are a believer in Jesus Christ, then Jesus died on the cross for your sins, not His own. He was sinless. Let this truth sink in. He died for your sins. More than that, He gave you His perfect righteousness. Can you now be found guilty when God has said you are innocent? We are talking about salvation here.

David is appealing to God, not to man. David is asking God to defend his "right actions" that unrighteous people do not like. Peter also knew the pain of being judged unjustly. That is why he said, *"If you suffer for doing good and you endure it, this is commendable before God,"* 1 Peter 2:20b. Why then are we upset when we are unjustly examined? We should expect to be judged unfairly by the world. *"To this you were called, because Christ suffered for you, leaving you an example, that you should follow in His steps,"* 1 Peter 2:21.

Jesus is our perfect example in how to respond to unjust suffering. *"When they hurled their insults at Him (Jesus), He did not retaliate; when He suffered, He made no threats. Instead, He entrusted Himself to Him Who judges justly,"* 1 Peter 2:23. It is clearly God's right to judge.

Paul writes about how it is God's responsibility to pay back to those who cause the unjust suffering. In Romans 12:19, God himself says: *"Vengeance is Mine, I will repay."* So, David's crying out to God is really good theology for a Christian.

Prayer: O LORD, we see Jesus was judged for our sin, and now we have His righteousness. May we live like Jesus, waiting for You to judge and change others, while we love them. In Jesus' name we pray. Amen.

Psalm 43:3

"Send forth Your light and Your truth, let them guide me; let them bring me to Your holy mountain to the place where You dwell."

Lord, *"bring me to Your holy mountain"*

We desire a mountain top experience with our God. These times are moments of great inspiration. But we do not stay on the mountain top very long. In fact, God in His wisdom does not allow us to stay there. Mountain top experiences are specifically designed to charge our spiritual batteries for the difficult work in the valleys! God gives us some great and moving experiences, so that we will not doubt His leading, guiding, purpose and protection.

"Your light and Your truth, let them guide me." Yes, but guide us to what or to whom? Lead us to God Himself, for when His light and truth are placed in us, we need to give it to others. It is in the valleys that others are also hurting and are looking for direction. God's Word speaks truth to direct us. There are too many people who will say God is guiding them, but they seem to be lacking direction.

There is a children's book that shows caterpillars coming from all over the world to climb a mountain. They are crawling on top of each other, fighting their way to the top. Only a few make it to the top, only to find out, nothing is there! Their dream was the pursuit of nothing important! Then, they too get knocked off the "Caterpillar Mountain" and tumble down in great despair. Our God gives us a mountain top experience to fill us with hope and purpose.

God gives us a great time on the mountain, because He is there! He wants to convince us that He is real. He wants us to know that He is both the author and the finisher of our faith. Our God gives us His, *"light"* and His *"truth"* to "guide" us up His *"holy mountain."* We meet with Him, and He fills us. He prepares us, giving us purpose for living. Then our God helps us climb down the mountain and into the valley where we live and work. Our God is so good to us!

Prayer: Dear compassionate Lord, we thank You for Your light and truth that lead us to You. You are so good to us and we praise and adore You. In Jesus' name we pray. Amen.

Psalm 44:26

"Rise up and help us; redeem us because of Your unfailing love."

Dependent on God's *"unfailing love"*

The 44th psalm opens with David reminding us that our fathers have told us about what God had done for them. Our forefathers witnessed the hand of God on their behalf. They did not brag about what they personally had done, but what God had done for them.

In verse five, David comes to the present, to his difficult situation. He has his eyes on God's *"unfailing love."* *"Through You we push back our enemies."* *"Through Your name we trample our foes."* It is clear that David had a personal responsibility to stand up for God. The best human fighting weapons in David's day were a bow and a sword. With a bow, he could fight the enemy from a distance. With a sword, he could fight in hand to hand combat. It was David's responsibility to fight the enemy both near and far. But, God also has His sovereign responsibility to His beloved believers. This is our lesson to grasp. Our human will must work together with God's divine grace!

We have a responsibility to stand firm and observe the sure and real faithfulness of God. We have battles that seem way too big! So were David's battles. David was disgraced, covered with shame and beaten down. But what stands out is that David never took his eyes off from God. He cries out, *"Awake, O LORD! Why do You sleep? Rouse Yourself! Do not reject us forever."* Are we allowed to talk to God like that? Jesus invites us to come to Him when we are weary. It is a human habit to complain to others, yet David registers his complain to God alone. We would be wise to do the same!

David passionately appeals to God's *"unfailing love."* In faith, He stretches out his hand to God, not to others or to an idol. The strength of our faith is in God's powerful attributes. His perfect character is for all the ages, for all of His sheep, forever. God's love and faithfulness are to His church, to those who are bought with His Son's blood!

Prayer: Dear LORD, Your *"unfailing love"* is our need and prayer. Like David, we too are scorned and disgraced by the world. Our hope is in You. Deliver us for Your name's sake, so we can testify to what You have done for us also. In Jesus' name we pray. Amen.

Psalm 45:6

"Your throne, O God, will last for ever and ever; a scepter of justice will be the scepter of Your kingdom."

The Justice of God

A few days ago we looked at the justice of God as it relates to how people mistreat us in our daily lives. In this lesson, we will focus mostly on God's justice in The Judgment, at the end of the world.

The justice of God is far more strict than the justice of man. Man's justice is filled with imperfections in looking at things. The justice of God flows out of His perfect and holy character. It is not possible for God to ignore or overlook even one sin. In fact, the holy justice of God is proof of His flawless character! We read that *"Righteousness and justice are the foundation of Your throne,"* Psalm 89:14a. From that throne, God, who created everything and everyone, uses His sovereign authority to execute His laws with unlimited power.

God cannot possibly act contrary to His own perfect character. God cannot possibly sin and neither will He wink at evil of any kind. This means that God cannot possibly pardon any sin apart from the atoning blood of His perfect Son! Jesus prayed, *"Father, if You are willing, take this cup from Me."* God was not willing, because His justice demanded our sin must be paid for in order that we might walk in close fellowship with Him.

God created us for Himself, that we might enjoy Him forever. His justice against our sin was fully satisfied with His Son paying for our every sin. To that end, we must praise God for His justice. Forgiven, we are free to love Him with great joy for His undeserved grace and mercy to us whom He saved from His wrath. Covered by Christ's blood, we are in the sovereign will of God both now and forever. Nothing in life and death is greater. Nothing brings more glory to God. Nothing does us more good than to be in His holy will and loving it. True faith submits to the will of God!

Prayer: Loving Lord, how amazing is it that Christ shed His innocent blood to pay for our guilty blood. How beautifully You then reach out to us lost and dying sinners with Your scepter of justice. Your holy justice is now completely satisfied by Jesus, our Savior! We thank and worship You. In Jesus' name we pray. Amen.

Psalm 45:10-11

"Listen, O daughter, consider and give ear: Forget your people and your father's house. The King is enthralled by your beauty; honor Him, for He is your LORD."

"The King is enthralled by your beauty"

Our Father in Heaven is talking to us directly here with a message that is of utmost importance. The *"daughter"* here is each church member. Together, we are the body of Christ, God's adopted daughters and sons. Our Lord and Savior, *"the King"* wants us to *"give ear"* to what He has to say.

"Forget your people." What is the meaning? At one time Jesus said, *"Anyone who loves his father or mother more than Me is not worthy of Me; anyone who loves his son or daughter more than Me is not worthy of Me,"* Matthew 10:37. Of course, Jesus is not telling us to hate or neglect our family members. It's just that our love for Him must be so much more than it is for our family.

"Your father's house" also refers to Adam. As children of Adam, we are sinners with much to forget! *"Forget"* is a command to repent, meaning to change Biblically from being a child of Adam, to living like a child of King Jesus! This is Ephesians chapter four language, where the process of repentance is one of putting off the old and putting on the new. Living the Christian life, then, is not thinking or dwelling on our former way of living that we must forget or put off. Replace, repent, concentrate on how to live a godly is the secret to real Biblical change.

"The King is enthralled by your beauty." Why? Because God is pleased by how He has washed us sparkling clean through His Spirit. We shine for God, because He has shined us up. Mary Magdalene washed Jesus' feet with her tears,. But only after Jesus washed her with His precious blood. Jesus takes our guilty blood and gives us His innocent blood. He takes our hard heart of stone as Ezekiel 36 teaches, and gives us a soft heart of flesh. We are now Adam, recreated perfectly! And God sees that it is good!

Prayer: Beautiful Lord, we too are beautiful in Christ because of Your love. In Christ, You remade us in Your image. Just as You enjoyed the perfect Adam, You enjoy us. May we not forget to live for our Creator and our Recreator. We worship You. In Jesus' name we pray. Amen.

Psalm 46:1-2

"God is our refuge and strength, an ever-present help in trouble.
Therefore we will not fear, though the earth give way and the
mountains fall into the heart of the sea."

Singing, *"God is our refuge and strength"*

As parents, you have faithfully taken care of Shelly, your little girl. She is now a happy and content, six year old. While playing with the little neighbor girl next door, she learns that this little girl's father has left his wife and daughter, permanently. The neighbor girl is so sad and so afraid! What will happen to her mother and what will happen to her own life? Mother and daughter pray for the husband and father to return home.

Your little Shelly remembers to pray for the neighbor family. She thinks about how good she has it and that her father and mother love her so much. They protect her in every way as they care for her. One night Shelly breaks out in song about how her parents are her refuge and strength. They help me in all my troubles. Therefore, I will never be afraid. My parents will never leave me. Even if an earthquake were to come, my parents will hold me and comfort me! Little Shelly is secure in her firm faith in the dedication of her parents to the family.

More than praising a parent, the psalmist here sings praises to God. The song does not ask God to be our refuge and strength. It praises Him for it! Think of how often we unprofitably plead with God in prayer to be with us and other believers. Moses said to Joshua, *"The LORD Himself goes before you and will be with you; He will never leave you or forsake you,"'* Deuteronomy 31:8. Again in Hebrews, *"God has said, 'Never will I leave you; never will I forsake you.'"*

God is our refuge, because we are needy refugees. Like the psalmist, we must thank God for His excellent care of us in song and in prayer. May we sing about how God is our refuge and strength.

Prayer: Blessed Lord, our faith in You is well placed. Because of You, we are not shaken to despair. Because of Your refuge and strength, we do not lose hope. Nothing can ever separate us from Your love. We worship You. In Jesus' name we pray. Amen.

Psalm 46:10

"Be still and know that I am God; I will be exalted among the nations,
I will be exalted in the earth."

"Be still and know that I am God"

The psalm begins by telling us, *"God is our refuge and strength, an ever present help in trouble,"* Psalm 46:1. In the rest of the psalm, we get to see just how God is our *"refuge and strength."*

God reminds us that He Himself, is the *"river whose streams make glad the city of God."* Big cities had rivers of water to protect them in case of a long siege. God says, *"I am your river of protection."* Jesus said, *"Surely I am with you always, to the very end of the age,"* Matthew 28:20. A mature faith believes that and rests in that fact.

God's amazing protection is not true for the rest of the world. In fact, *"Nations are in uproar, kingdoms fall; He lifts His voice, the earth melts,"* Psalm 46:6. Our God is so in control of this world and of us.

Twice, we are comforted with this same truth, of God's Almighty *"strength."* *"The LORD Almighty is with us; the God of Jacob is our fortress,"* Psalm 46:7 & 11. Because God is with us and for us, we need to calm our hearts when He says, *"Be still and know that I am God."* We worship God for His forever, real presence.

"Be still," because we live in a noisy world. From cell phones, to T.V.'s blaring, to street noise, the world is in our face. Satan loves it when we go until we are so exhausted and have no time left for any close communion with God.

"Be still," involves a patient waiting on God. After all, faith is a respectful expectation in God! When we read Genesis 15, we find that Abraham waited on God all day in patient expectation. Then, *"as the sun was setting"* God answered Abraham, directed him and blessed him. We need a greater respect for God so we can *"be still."*

"And know that I am God." In the coming Psalm 48:9 devotion, we will see how *"being still"* helps us to *"know"* God. That is a primary reason to *"be still."*

Prayer: Majestic Lord, we are busy people, too busy. We run after many things that have so little value in eternity. Forgive us! Teach us so that we learn to be still. Lord, You are God and we want to love You more. In Jesus' name we pray. Amen.

Psalm 47:4

"He chose our inheritance for us, the pride of Jacob whom He loved."

God chose our lot in life to suit Him!

Have you ever wondered why your lot in life is what it is? Are we ever dissatisfied with where God has placed us? Do we think we should be in a better place, have a better position or family? If we could choose our parents and the places we would live and when we would live there, what would we do? Would we be content if we could change our *"inheritance"* in life? If we say "Yes," then God is not our hope and joy. Then, our circumstances changing are our hope. That's a problem.

The psalmist says, God loves *"Jacob,"* His church, His body, His believers. They are dear and precious to Him. God knows what is best for each of us. Our road may be difficult, but it is His road. He knows what will happen along the way, before we do. He knows how we will respond. Perhaps the many steep hills on our road of life are too difficult, because we are in too high a gear. God helps us to shift to a lower gear to make it up the mountain. His hand is on us, for our good!

God has put us where we are, to find Him. *"From one man He made every nation of men, that they should inhabit the whole earth; and He determined the times set for them and the exact places where they should live. God did this so that men would seek Him and perhaps reach out for Him and find Him,"* Acts 17:26-27a.

God put us where we are to be used by Him. God uses each of us in different ways to reach some for His kingdom. Think of the rough road Joseph was on. He was sold as a slave by his own brothers, a road took him to Egypt, a symbol for sin in the Bible. Joseph's road also included prison, even though he did nothing wrong! Why all the difficult twists and turns? Joseph was clear about his journey. He told his brothers, *"You intended to harm me, but God intended it for good to accomplish what is now being done, the saving of many lives,"* Genesis 50:20. What is our response? Will we be faithful in life's journey? May God give us His vision, for His glory and for our good!

Prayer: Lead on, O King eternal! You know the safest and most productive road for us to travel on. Help us to see it and be content in it, trusting Your plan. In Jesus' name we pray. Amen.

Psalm 48:9

"Within Your temple, O God, we meditate on Your unfailing love."

We can know God's *"unfailing love."*

People are knowable and we grow to love them for who they are. So too, our God is knowable! Other gods are unknowable. We can know God and love Him because we are not just a human body that exists. We also have a spirit. God gave us that spirit, or soul, to know Him, to be one with Him. God made us for Himself. The writer here wants us to meditate on who God is and on His *"unfailing love"* to us.

Like the psalmist, disciple John was also concerned that the people would know God's *"unfailing love."* John saw false prophets who did not teach about knowing the one, true God. John saw with a clearer view of Christ than the psalmist did. John saw people in the church, going through the motions of a spiritual life, without a close communion with God. They knew about God, but did not really "know God."

John simply, and so accurately, taught us in 1 John to confess our sins, to know God. How we need to learn the holiness of God, and the confession of sin helps us to do just that. We must fully experience God's *"unfailing love."* It needs to be said that those who really know God, confess their personal sin, not the sins of others! Dwight Moody said, "Sin will keep you out of the holy Word of God and the Word will keep you from sin."

Many people in John's day doubted their salvation. John pounded on the words, *"you may know."* *"I write these things to you who believe in the name of the Son of God so that you may know that you have eternal life,"* 1 John 5:13.

In fact, God's wants us to know Him, closely and personally. God says concerning mankind starting with Adam, *"From one man He made every nation of men, that they should inhabit the whole earth; and He determined the times set for them and the exact places where they should live. God did this so that men would seek Him and perhaps reach out for Him and find Him, though He is not far from each one of us. For in Him we live and move and have our being,"* Acts 17:26-28a. We can know God's *"unfailing love."*

Prayer: Personal Lord, we praise You that You are knowable, our very close friend. We worship You. In Jesus' name we pray. Amen.

Psalm 49:16-17

"Do not be overawed when a man grows rich, when the splendor of his house increases; for he will take nothing with him when he dies, his splendor will not descend with him."

No suitcases to Heaven!

When we fly to another place, we often take just one suitcase. We are limited on what we can take, so we take the essentials. What then are the basics we need to take in our suitcase to Heaven? The answer is, no luggage, no suitcase, no carry-on!

We only need a Passport to get into Heaven! God said to Israel, *"When I see the blood, I will pass over you,"* Exodus 12:13b. Our legal passport is the blood of the Lamb. In the Old Testament, the blood payment to get into Heaven was required by God. Why is the blood so important? God's profound answer is: *"For the life of a creature is in the blood, and I have given it to you to make atonement for yourselves on the altar; it is the blood that makes atonement for one's life."*

The passport to Heaven in the Old Testament was the blood of an innocent animal paying for the guilty man. The innocent blood, God accepted as full payment for a person's sin! That blood sacrifice pointed to Jesus, who shed His innocent blood in the New Testament. The gates of Heaven will never open without it. And our passport to Heaven can only be obtained on earth, only at Mount Calvary. No one can purchase it in Heaven. Don't leave home without it!

Jesus assures us that He alone shed His perfect blood for sinners to give them that new perfect life they need to enter Heaven. Jesus said, *"I tell you the truth, no one can see the kingdom of God unless he is born again,"* John 3:3b. As the Judge of all the world, Jesus said, *"So if the Son sets you free, you will be free indeed,"* John 8:36.

No one can take your passport from you! You can't lose it. There is a duplicate copy in Heaven, written on God's omnipotent hand. Your passport never expires. Jesus said, *"I give them eternal life, and they shall never perish; no one can snatch them out of My hand,"* John 10:28.

Prayer: Merciful Lord, You not only give us a passport to Heaven, You are that Passport! In Revelation 20:15, we read, *"If anyone's name was not found written in the book of life, he was thrown into the lake of fire."* What a great salvation in Jesus. In His name we pray. Amen.

Psalm 50:14b-15

"Fulfill your vows to the Most High, and call upon Me in the day of trouble; I will deliver you, and you will honor Me."

The keeping of vows

A vow is a voluntary pledge to fulfill an agreement. We make New Year's resolutions to live differently. We need to lose weight; to draw closer to God; to be a blessing to the family; to work more faithfully. And the list goes on. Vows are good, but they must be taken carefully and prayerfully. Once made, a vow is binding. *"When you make a vow to God, do not delay in fulfilling it. He has no pleasure in fools; fulfill your vow. It is better not to vow than to make a vow and not fulfill it."* Ecclesiastes 5:4-5.

A vow has curses if it is done foolishly. In 1 Samuel 14:24. *"The men of Israel were in distress that day, because Saul had bound the people under oath, saying, 'Cursed be any man who eats food before evening comes, before I have avenged myself on my enemies!' So none of the troops tasted food."*

Later, the army was out in the woods and came across some honey, *"but Jonathan had not heard that his father had bound the people with the oath"* and he ate some. Because the selfish King Saul made a rash oath, the soldiers were faint from hunger, and after that, some of the soldiers even ate raw meat because they were so starved! Saul would have killed his own son for breaking the vow, but the more righteous soldiers rescued him.

A vow has benefits if done wisely. *"Jacob made a vow, saying, 'If God will be with me and will watch over me on this journey I am taking and will give me food to eat and clothes to wear...then the LORD will be my God...and of all that You give me I will give You a tenth,'"* Genesis 28:20-22. Jacob kept his vow and God blessed him greatly.

Prayer: O Holy Lord, we are grateful for Your wisdom concerning vows. Lord, it is our desire to serve and love You more faithfully. We have so much to be thankful for. We praise You with words from King David. *"From You comes the theme of my praise in the great assembly; before those who fear You will I fulfill my vows,"* Psalm 22:25. In Christ's name we pray. Amen.

Psalm 50:15a

"Call on Me in the day of trouble; and I will deliver you."

Persistent in prayer

"Then Jesus told His disciples a parable to show them that they should always pray and not give up. He said: 'In a certain town there was a judge who neither feared God nor cared about men. And there was a widow in that town who kept coming to him with the plea, 'Grant me justice against my adversary,'" Luke 18:1-3. Jesus knows the power of our prayers, and He loves to respond to them. Satan hates it when we pray. That's why Jesus tells us about a widow woman who was being mistreated badly. He does not say exactly what the gross injustice was to this woman. Jesus wants us to know that He is a just and holy God. He cares much about every injustice we will ever face.

This widow who is suffering at the hands of others, is you and I. She has no one to help her out. Her only possibility for relief is to go to the local judge who is totally unjust in how he operates. This wicked judge's common practice is to make a decision based on how much it would benefit him personally.

The persistent widow has nothing. She has no money. She has no "rights." She has little of this world's goods. She can't even give a small bribe to move this judge to act on her behalf. All this widow can do is bombard the unjust judge day and night for his mercy! This is exactly our position as a poor sinner. We stand before the just judge Jesus, who is encouraging every sinner to be persistent in prayer. If an unjust judge is willing to give mercy to an undeserving sinner, how much more will Jesus, our just judge, give mercy to His own children!

Prayer: Dear Heavenly Father, we thank You for showing us the truth about persistently coming to You and pleading for Your mercy. Awe us with Your presence. Inspire us through Your Spirit. Save us through Your Son. It is not just Your saving mercy that we seek, but Your protecting and providing mercy also. Lord, we need You to move mountains for us. Do that so we can praise You more for Your amazing grace. Do this for Your name's sake. Then we will testify of Your goodness. In Jesus' name we pray. Amen.

Psalm 50:16-17

"But to the wicked, God says: "What right have you to recite My laws or take My covenant on your lips? You hate My instruction and cast My words behind you."

Can the unconverted preach/teach for God?

Before a great revival 300 years ago, Gilbert Tennent noticed many pastors and teachers were unconverted. What follows is a brief and timely meditation on where we are yet today. Our text spells out the problem. Spiritual food is necessary to have real spiritual health. Jesus and the disciples knew this.

What is a critical need in God's preacher/teacher? Is it precise doctrine, or is it having a personal, noticeable faith in Jesus Christ? Both are important, but what is most important? Sadly, we often see big degrees and precise "orthodoxy," to the neglect of humble service to God and to His children. This is not new. The Pharisees were bad examples of proper doctrine and life. Five P's describe them.

1. The Pharisees were very proud. They loved to be noticed and be heard for their long prayers. 2. The Pharisees were picky. They loved to argue. Jesus said they would strain a gnat and swallow a camel. 3. The Pharisees were perplexed about salvation. Nicodemus asked about being born again because it was not his experience. 4. The Pharisees had a pious pretense about living the Christian life. They talked a good line in public, but lived selfish and horribly in private. 5. The Pharisees had a party spirit. They made disciples like themselves, not like Christ. Today, putting a church's denomination policy before Jesus' truth, is the same spiritual disease.

An unconverted preacher/teacher has no call from God. Jesus said, *"Follow Me."* An unconverted preacher or teacher is concerned about their name and their salary. They love those who love them. Those who love Jesus are often enemies. If denomination or the love of our ministry come before our love for Christ, we are guilty. Paul said in 2 Tim. 2:2 , seek *"reliable men who will also be qualified to teach."* An unconverted preacher or teacher is unprofitable and unqualified.

Prayer: Lord, help us to see that blind men cannot lead blind sinners on the narrow path to You. Help us to see that a chained man cannot free others. In Jesus' name we pray. Amen.

Psalm 51:1

"Have mercy on me, O God, according to Your unfailing love;
according to Your great compassion blot out my transgressions."

Those who cried for *"mercy"*

Think of the people in the Scriptures who cried for mercy, and then received it! David here in Psalm 51 cries, *"Lord 'have mercy on me.'"* The Canaanite woman cried out, *"Have mercy on me, O Lord."* Blind Bartimaeus said, *"Jesus, Son of David, have mercy on me."* There was an anonymous beggar on the road to Jericho who said, *"Have mercy on me."* If we cry out like that to God, we too will receive mercy! We will receive a love relationship between us and God. And just think, even our crying out, *"Lord have mercy on me, a sinner,"* is only because in an eternity past, before the world was even created, before we were even born, the Triune God already established that relationship with us. It happened when the Father gave His sheep to His Son. Christ knew us and loved us already then. In fact, that is exactly why Christ came to this wicked and sinful world. He came to rescue His sheep who were not only lost, but needed His mercy to live.

If we have not cried out, *"Lord have mercy on me, a sinner,"* do it today. Then on the Judgment Day, we will not even think of bringing up anything that we have done to earn our salvation. It will only be because of His mercy that we loved Him. Christ Himself will bring up all the fruit and the works and deeds we have done because of our relationship with Him. All we need to say is, "Lord, here am I, a sinner, upon whom You had mercy and grace." "Lord, who am I that the Lord of the earth would care to know my name?" How great is our merciful God. Let us pray to Him, who is our Father in Heaven.

Prayer: O Father, how important it is to cry out to You, the One who is the way, the truth, and the life. How wonderful that You are eternally God and Lord, eternally holy and eternally all-knowing. For You will not only know us today, but on that great day You will still know us. How wonderful it is, we will be to be with You eternally, along with characters in the Bible. How wonderful it will be to see friends and loved ones. All who are Heaven will be there because You had mercy on them. For that, we praise You. In Jesus' name we pray. Amen.

Psalm 51:1-3

"Have mercy on me; O God, according to Your unfailing love; according to Your great compassion blot out my transgressions. Wash away all my iniquity and cleanse me from my sin. For I know my transgressions, and my sin is always before me."

David's healing confession

Satan will try to convict us not to confess our sin. We must be fully aware that he wants us to hide it. David listened to the devil for some time. As a result, David was suffering physically as well as spiritually. He was even greatly depressed from his failure to confess his sin, as we saw in the Psalm 38 devotion. David's healing started like this: God sends the prophet Nathan to convict him and help him to see the importance of confessing his sin. This confession of David here in Psalm 51, is one of the spiritual highlights of his life and ministry!

David's adultery with Bathsheba and the murder of her husband is now out in the open. Instead of being proud by ignoring his sin, he humbly acknowledges it. After confessing it, he quickly experiences the amazing forgiveness of God. O that we might confess our sin more often, more openly and more specifically!

David pleads with God, *"Restore to me the joy of Your salvation and grant me a willing spirit, to sustain me,"* Psalm 51:12. He did not say, "my salvation" but *"Your salvation."* Have you lost the joy of His salvation? A failure to confess sin may be one reason. Granted, you are still saved, but is your joy gone? If so, tell God about your sin in as much detail as you can. Confess it specifically, for that is how we change. Often we are way too vague in how we confess our sin. David said to God, *"a broken spirit; a broken and contrite heart, O God, You will not despise,"* Psalm 51:17b. A big part of being broken is to finally be fed up with our sin and to cry to God about it clearly. That is exactly what David did and encourages us to do also!

Prayer: O Triune God, we have a great stubbornness when it comes to confession. How much we need Your Spirit to convict us of our sin and for You to then forgive us through the blood of Jesus Christ. How gracious Your forgiveness of sin is. You give us what we need, not what we deserve. We praise You for your amazing forgiveness. In Jesus' name we pray. Amen.

Psalm 51:5

*"Surely I was sinful at birth, sinful from the time
my mother conceived me."*

Why do we sin?

We are not sinners because we sin. We sin, because we are born sinners. Every single person in this world was born with a nature that is completely 100% a slave to sin. This is exactly what it means to be born with "original sin." This is also what David is teaching in our text. David had that "sin gene" in him already at the time of conception. The very first cell in David's body had sin written all over it.

We have original sin, because our father Adam is the father of every human being. When Adam sinned, he was our representative, meaning, he sinned for all of us. A well-known verse explains this: *"Just as sin entered the world through one man, and death through sin, and in this way death came to all men, because all sinned,"* Romans 5:12. Later in verse 18, the same point is presented to help us understand God's salvation message: *"Just as the result of one trespass was condemnation for all men, so also the result of one act of righteousness was justification that brings life for all men."* The first Adam condemned us, whereas the Second Adam, Jesus, saves us. The first Adam made us like him, morally and spiritually, totally depraved. The Second Adam, Jesus, makes us like Him, totally righteous, just as if we never sinned.

Why do we need to know that we were born sinners? So we seek Christ and His righteousness. So we don't get the wrong idea that we might have been born Christian. So we understand what the root of our spiritual problem is. So we can see how lost we really are. So we can fully understand, *"There is none righteous, not even one;"* Romans 3:10b. How important the grace and mercy of God is. The grace and mercy of God makes no sense if we are not sinners through and through.

Prayer: Merciful Lord, we praise You for helping us see what complete sinners we really are. We needed to know how hopelessly separated we are from You with our in-born sinful nature. Lord, be merciful to us sinners. Cleanse us Lord, because as slaves to sin, we cannot cleanse ourselves. In Jesus' name we pray. Amen.

Psalm 51:10a

"Create in me a pure heart, O God, and renew a steadfast spirit within me."

"Create in me a pure heart, O God"

David is troubled. He knows that his heart has some "sin dirt" in it and he is spiritually uncomfortable. He is finally contrite, sorry for his sin. He is now humbling himself before God. David seriously wants his relationship with God to change. He is asking for God's forgiveness, realizing that it is God who must restore him and strengthen him. When we are also burdened with sin, may we follow David's beautiful example here of how to open up our heart to God.

By saying, "Create in me a pure heart, O God," David realizes that it is God who needs to make something out of nothing once again. For to create, is only something God can do! Who else in the world can make something out of nothing? In using the word "create," David's is showing us and God that his self-sufficiency has just ended. That is a major Biblical change, one that God quickly honors!

David wants his purity back. He wants his close walk with God to return. David has not lost his salvation, but he has lost the joy of God's salvation, which is his sweet communion with God. His sweet hour of prayer is no longer sweet. His problem is not only that he sinned, but that he did not confess it to God. Convicted, David speaks as a blind man, a beggar and a leper who needs God's healing. When we say: "Create in me a pure heart O God," we worship the holiness of God.

Praying, *"renew a steadfast spirit in me,"* is asking God's Spirit to fill our spirit once again. Notice how God works this out. In Ephesians 4:22, it is our responsibility to, *"put off, concerning your former conduct."* Then see what God does in verse 23. *"And be renewed in the spirit of your mind."* We don't *"be renewed"* our own minds. God does that when we repent. To complete the process of repentance, we *"put on the new man which was created according to God, in righteousness and true holiness,"* Ephesians 4:24. Through David's life, God is in the process of teaching us how to repent. May we listen.

Prayer: Lord, give us pure hearts that beat for You. Renew our spirits for Your name's sake, and for our eternal good. In Jesus' name we pray. Amen.

Psalm 51:11

"Do not cast me from Your presence or take Your Holy Spirit from me."

The work and evidence of the Holy Spirit

There are two spirits at work in the hearts of men. There is a *"familiar spirit,"* demonic in nature, described in Leviticus 20:6 NKJV. And then, there is the Holy Spirit, God Himself, the third person of the Trinity. God's Holy Spirit leads us to Christ, and then into a deeper relationship with Him. The Holy Spirit is active in salvation and sanctification, (our growing up in Christ). The *"familiar spirit"* imitates the real Holy Spirit for the purpose of leading us away from Christ, to Satan himself. A *"familiar spirit"* is a demonic helper of the devil. We need to know how demonic forces move to deceive us, to appreciate the beautiful work of the Holy Spirit, who alone makes us holy.

The evidence of the real Holy Spirit is a believer looking like Christ. With the Holy Spirit in us, we are willing to live for Jesus. Here David is praying for this. The truth is: A believer never gets more of the Holy Spirit on their own. Instead, the Spirit gets more of us, more of God's grace to us. David is praying for that in our text. The Spirit of God convicts us to lose our individuality, and replace it with love for God and for His kingdom! Love for God then, is not some emotional outburst of repeated words or phrases. It is practical living. Satan actually loves it when we go to church to tell God we love Him, and then live for the devil the rest of the week.

The Holy Spirit at Pentecost did not teach the disciples anything! It made them living messengers of the Word of God, just as Jesus said, *"You will be My witnesses."* The baptism of the Holy Spirit then, is never something apart from Christ. The baptism of the Holy Spirit changes no one. The ascended Christ does the changing. He directs His Spirit to come upon us. Baptism in the Holy Spirit is not a mystical experience, but a real work of Christ in us, changing our daily life.

Prayer: Dear Father, Son and Spirit, help us to see our unworthiness so that we can be filled with Your Holy presence. We see in the Bible that Jesus never went about shouting how great He was. Instead, He humbled Himself to death on a cross, giving Himself for us and for His Father's glory. Make us like Him. In Jesus' name we pray. Amen.

Psalm 51:12

"Restore to me the joy of Your salvation and grant me a willing spirit, to sustain me."

When we lose the joy of Your salvation

I wanted to title this "*When we lose the joy of our salvation.*" But that particular title is part of my problem! It is more accurate to say that our eternal place in Heaven is, "*Your salvation.*" David lost the joy of God's salvation. God did not take it from him! David sinned against God and was not interested in repenting. David damaged his relationship with God when he held Satan's hand, and then gave into temptation. David not only committed the sin of adultery and murder, he tried to hide it. Therefore, David's joy in God's presence suffered greatly. God's Spirit moved in David, giving him guilt instead of joy! A failure to confess sin does that to all of us. Nathan confronted and convicted David and now he is crying for forgiveness.

We also lose the joy of His salvation when we become too self-centered. As we lose our desire for God, our spiritual life becomes cold and our prayer life is not serious. Then God's Spirit in love, comes after us to convict us to seek God again! Like David, we plead with God to take the burden of sin away, for we can no longer bear it. God's Spirit makes us spiritually alive again. Like David, we plead with God to open our lips in praise. How true it is, after we admit our sin and confess it to God, He restores us to the joy of His salvation.

God did not create Adam to sin. Nor did God remake Adam and us to sin either. We simply are not able to carry the burden of sin! When we try, we stagger under the load. Then we lose the joy of His salvation. May the Spirit of God continually convict us when we stray from His presence. May we stay humble and not stumble. Through the Spirit's working, we will abide in Him, for we are His workmanship, created and recreated to enjoy God forever.

Prayer: O Majestic Lord, when our hearts don't desire You, create in us hearts that do. We want to be Your beautiful, joyful and productive Christians. Restore to us the joy of Your salvation and grant us a willing spirit, to sustain us. In Jesus' name we pray. Amen.

Psalm 51:13

"Then I will teach transgressors Your ways, and sinners will turn back to You."

Restored, to restore others

The context of Psalm 51 is just after Nathan the prophet confronted David for not confessing his sin. In the first twelve verses David pleads with God to forgive him of his sin of murder and adultery. David cries for mercy, asking God to make his impure heart, pure. David begged for a restored relationship with God. David needed the joy of God's salvation again. Now in our text, David makes a vow to God. If God will restore him, David promises to teach others what he has learned about God's restoration process.

What an excellent lesson for us about how to humbly approach God. David appeals to God to answer his prayer for the glory of God's name. David does not say "Restore me for my own good," but restore him for the good of God's kingdom advancing. Praying to be restored for God's glory is a very Biblical prayer. We can see this theme elsewhere in the Bible.

One of my favorite verses is Genesis 50:20. The context is Joseph's father is now dead. His brothers think Joseph will kill them for selling him into slavery for seven years, and then into prison for seven more. What a testimony of the grace of God that Joseph gives to his brothers and to us also. The brothers begged for their lives! This is a picture of us going to Jesus for forgiveness and restoration.

Joseph told his brothers, *"You intended to harm me, but God intended it for good to accomplish what is now being done, the saving of many lives."* Joseph knew that God allowed him to have some big trials in life so that God could use him for *"the saving of many lives."* We have the lives of many Bible characters who were restored by God, to be a testimony to us. We must testify to others about the grace of God.

Prayer: Dear Lord, we also see Your will for us in 2 Corinthians 1:3-4. *"Praise be to the God and Father of our Lord Jesus Christ, the Father of compassion and the God of all comfort, who comforts us in all our troubles, so that we can comfort those in any trouble with the comfort we ourselves have received from God."* In Jesus' name we pray. Amen.

Psalm 51:17

"The sacrifices of God are a broken spirit; a broken and contrite heart, O God, You will not despise."

God loves a *"broken and contrite heart"*

A Biblical sacrifice is something we give to the Lord that He desires, as an act of worship. On the human plain, a sacrifice is something we give to another person out of honor and respect. After a beautiful doxology, Paul begins Romans 12:1, *"Therefore, I urge you, brothers, in view of God's mercy, to offer your bodies as living sacrifices, holy and pleasing to God —this is your spiritual act of worship."*

It is only in view of God's mercy that we can put the words of our text into practice. A broken spirit and a contrite heart seeks the mercy and forgiveness of God. "*A broken spirit,*" puts to death selfishness and our living to sin. Think of what the prophet Samuel said to the proud and sinning King Saul in 1 Samuel 15:22-23.

"Does the LORD delight in burnt offerings and sacrifices as much as in obeying the voice of the LORD? To obey is better than sacrifice, and to heed is better than the fat of rams. For rebellion is like the sin of divination, and arrogance like the evil of idolatry. Because you have rejected the word of the LORD, He has rejected you as king."

We are not ready to live God's way until we humble ourselves before God. Humble people recognize that their former acts of pride do not please God. A proud spirit or pride, kicked Satan out of Heaven. God tells us why in Ezekiel 28:16-17:

"Through your widespread trade you were filled with violence, and you sinned. So I drove you in disgrace from the mount of God, and I expelled you, O guardian cherub, from among the fiery stones. Your heart became proud on account of your beauty, and you corrupted your wisdom because of your splendor. So I threw you to the earth; I made a spectacle of you before kings."

Prayer: Dear Lord, we see that Satan and King Saul were proud, not broken and contrite. May we humble ourselves and look to You for mercy and forgiveness. We are grateful that You have an abundance of mercy to give us, through Your Son. In His name we pray. Amen.

Psalm 52:1

"Why do you boast of evil, you mighty man? Why do you boast all day long, you who are a disgrace in the eyes of God?"

Who in "the church" is boasting of evil?

David writes here about Doeg, the evil Edomite, a descendant of Esau. Doeg observed David and Abimelech worshiping in the temple. The local priest Abimelech, prayed for the people. Doeg acted like one of Satan's demons to destroy God-centered worship. Who is doing this today? Who is trying to destroy the forgiveness of sin that only Christ can give? Who is trying to say that Christ's death on the cross is not the only way of salvation? It is evil people who deny that Jesus is both God and perfect Man!

Bible teacher Hank Hanegraaff in his book, "Christianity in Crisis - 21st century," warns us that an evil T.V. preacher said, "Jesus Christ knew that the only way He could stop Satan is by becoming one in nature with him." What blasphemy! Jesus' nature was perfect and remained perfect on the cross. Jesus took our sin but had no sin of His own. The Lamb of God had to be spotless, for God to accept the payment for our sin. Jesus was that Lamb, perfectly.

Another evil man said that Jesus was recreated spiritually in the Garden of Gethsemane. "Somewhere between the time He was nailed to the cross and when He was in the garden of Gethsemane, somewhere in there He died spiritually. Personally, I believe it was while he was in the garden." That too, is so evil. If Jesus Christ was recreated into the same nature as Satan, we have no forgiveness of sin. Salvation would have to come from another source.

Do we boast of evil? Do we like to tell stories of some of the evil that we did? Do we brag about how we were naughty or rebellious? God is not pleased with evil boasting from anyone. Paul said that if we want to boast, then boast in the cross of Christ. May God help us die to all selfish thoughts, words and actions.

Prayer: Dear Lord Jesus, we are so thankful that You save us sinners, because You are the perfect Lamb of God! We praise You that the gates of Hell cannot prevail against You, and us also, because we are saved by Your sinless life! In Your name we pray. Amen.

Psalm 53:5

"There they were, overwhelmed with dread, where there was nothing to dread. God scattered the bones of those who attacked you, you put them to shame, for God despised them."

God despises our foolish and evil enemies

Psalm 53 is the same as Psalm 14. Only verse five is different. Paul wrote Romans 3, quoting these two psalms. God wants us to know His promises. Psalm 53 begins, *"The fool says in his heart there is no God. They are corrupt, and their ways are vile; there is no one who does good."* Verse four is, *"Will the evildoers never learn — those who devour My people as men eat bread and do not call on God?"* Then in verse five, God is going to do something to our enemies, here and now, not just in eternity!

We have examples in the Bible of God rescuing Ruth, Gideon and others. Remember how Gideon had just 300 men against a huge army. In the height of the battle, *"While each man held his position, around the camp, the Midianites ran, crying out as they fled,"* Judges 7:21. God's enemies were, as our text says, *"overwhelmed with dread, where there was nothing to dread."*

God's real protection of His people is recorded in 2 Chronicles 20. God greatly encouraged me from this chapter. Three countries were invading Judah, surrounding them! King Jehoshaphat and the people seriously prayed! *"O our God, will you not judge them? For we have no power to face this vast army that is attacking us. We do not know what to do, but our eyes are upon You,"* 2 Chronicles 20:12. How true! The God who answered their prayer, is still our refuge and strength, and He delights to be so! *"This is what the LORD says to you: 'Do not be afraid or discouraged because of this vast army. <u>For the battle is not yours, but God's,</u>'"* 2 Chronicles 20:15b. God cares! Do not be afraid or discouraged. How we need to learn this truth.

"You will not have to fight in this battle. Take up your positions; stand firm and see the deliverance the LORD will give you, O Judah and Jerusalem. Do not be afraid; do not be discouraged. <u>Go out</u> and face them tomorrow, and the LORD will be with you,'" 2 Chronicles 20:17.

Prayer: O Lord, Your loving dedication to us, Your adopted children is awesome! May Your name be praised! In Jesus' name we pray. Amen.

Psalm 54:2

"Hear my prayer, O God; listen to the words of my mouth."

"Hear my prayer, O God"

David certainly knows that his enemy, and God's also, is after him. Satan is pressing with all the evil help he can get together, trying to eliminate David. Evil is trying to stop David, trying to stop the Lord's work. The powers of darkness want to be free to do their evil deeds. David's danger is so great and intense, that only the hand of Almighty God can protect him. So David cries out to God. Instantly, he comes to the point. There is no time for wordy prayers. David is 100% focused on the need of God's help. *"Hear my prayer,"* is his urgent plea! *"Listen to the words of my mouth."* David is pleading that God would give His immediate attention, for David was about to be swallowed up!

Have we been in prayer with such urgency? Have we yet had such a serious situation that we were convinced that only God could help us and rescue us? We were certain that there was no good way out of our pressing problem. It was only by faith and by past experience that we know that God will help us. We have already met the lion and the bear, and God helped us to survive those attacks! We are greatly comforted that God is our present refuge and is our present strength, just like He was in the past.

We are comforted in knowing that God is willing and able to deliver us completely. We know by experience that our strongest love language to God is fervent prayer! With our eyes fixed on God, day-dreaming is not possible. God wants to deliver us. After all, our Lord commanded us, *"Call on Me in the day of trouble; and I will deliver you,"* Psalm 50:15a. God allows our great trials so that He can show us His great deliverance. He knows how to build up our weak faith.

Prayer: O Lord, You are our refuge and strength. You graciously build our weak faith one trial at a time. Your power is so amazing. Your protection is beyond words. Your deliverance is always on time. You know exactly how to bring glory to Your Name that is far above all names. We love You so much, because You love us even more! Accept our praise and worship. In Jesus' name we pray. Amen.

Psalm 55:22

"Cast your cares on the LORD and He will sustain you; He will never let the righteous fall."

"Cast your cares on the LORD"

Christian brother and sister, God owns you as His Child. You bear His name. You are His relative. You are adopted with the full rights of God's born child. Jesus is your Brother. The Holy Spirit is your Friend. If your God in Trinity is for you, who can possibly be against you? For the sake of God's most holy and righteous Name alone, He will always care for you!

God is a perfect, loving Father who owns all, sees all, controls all, and has all wisdom and power. On top of that, your Father has an infinite storehouse of provision. He has angels at His dispatch and Satan under His foot! God will not let any difficulty or trial be greater than you, His believer, can ever bear. In fact, any trial you have will only serve to strengthen you and in the end, bless you. With these facts in mind, you have in this text a command, a promise, and a complete protection package!

"Cast your cares on the LORD" is a command. Faith demands that you act. God will test your faith to see if you do the casting. When the characters in the Bible cast their cares on God, He delivered them. When the people trusted in any other god or gods to care for them, it became a snare, not a care!

"He will sustain you," is a promise! It does not say He may or might sustain you, but that *"He will sustain you."* Has God ever broken a promise? Does He not always keep His Word? It is impossible for God who is holy and righteous to lie. He who is faithful, *"will sustain you."* How? That's His concern, not yours. You don't need to know. His ways are always higher than your ways. *"He will sustain you."*

"He will never let the righteous fall" is your complete protection package! *"Never,"* will He let a believer fall. Trouble may come, but there will be no danger in the trouble. So, *"Cast all your anxiety on Him for He cares for you,"* 1 Peter 5:7.

Prayer: O Lord, we commit our many cares to You, our Creator and Friend! Our *"cares"* are in the Best Hands. We are grateful that You are so able and willing to care for us. In Jesus' name we pray. Amen.

Psalm 56:8

"Record my lament; list my tears on Your scroll - are they not in Your record?"

"List my tears on Your scroll"

David wrote this psalm when the Philistines had seized him in Gath. He records what his enemy was doing to him and then pleads and prays for God to act on his behalf. We must do the same!

"All day long they twist my words; they are always plotting to harm me," Psalm 56:5. We are not the first to be persecuted for righteousness' sake. David here, and many others before us, have been abused by those who hate God and us. We must cry to God. There is some value in crying to others who will pray, but God's Word says that we are to cry to Him who is able to do something about our situation.

"They conspire, they lurk, they watch my steps, eager to take my life," Psalm 56:6. Man plans and schemes, but it is God who prevails! *"Many are the plans of a man's heart, but it is the LORD'S purpose that prevails,"* Proverbs 19:21. It was Thomas Kempis who wisely said, *"Man proposes but God disposes."* The eye of our God misses nothing. And then there is the fact that our God is all wise and all powerful. Who can harm us if God is for us? No one.

This is very personal. *"Record your lament"* because then it is no longer our personal concern, but God's. Our tears and our pain is on God's scroll. If our lament and tears are in God's hand, why do we doubt God's willing heart to act for us?

God allows our difficult trials to test us to see if we will trust His wisdom and power to deliver us from our enemy. God is looking for us to be faithful in our trials, and to respond well when He does act for us! God delivered David again and again to show him, and us, that He is the Great Deliverer. *"For You have delivered me from death and my feet from stumbling, that I may walk before God in the light of life,"* Psalm 56:13.

Prayer: Compassionate Lord, forgive our small faith in doubting Your ability to act for our good and for Your glory. May we walk humbly before You, fully trusting in Your promised ability to care about our daily living concerns. In Jesus' name we pray. Amen.

Psalm 57:2-3

"I cry out to God Most High, to God who fulfills His purpose for me. He sends from Heaven and saves me, rebuking those who hotly pursue me; God sends His love and His faithfulness."

"To God who fulfills His purpose for me"

David and others cried out to God, and He answered them. Now, it is our turn. We also have those against us, without a just cause. We cry out to God with the same thoughts as David. We cry because our God who was our help in ages past, is our hope for years to come. He is able to *"fulfill His purpose for me."*

David wrote this beautiful psalm, full of praise and worship to God. David was so aware of how he was appointed and anointed by God for a specific purpose, as all believers are. God creates us for Himself. We do not see this so much when we remain very selfish. God then conforms us to Christ some more. Paul wrote in Ephesians 2:10, *"We are God's workmanship, created in Christ Jesus to do good works, which God prepared in advance for us to do."* Doing good works for Him is all about purpose. In Jeremiah 29:11, God tells us, *"'For I know the plans I have for you,' Plans to give you a hope and a future.'"*

We must be careful to know the <u>order</u> of God's will for our lives. We can get so wound up in doing many "good works" for Christ, that we lose sight of the need to become more like Christ. <u>God is way more concerned about what we are "becoming," than in what we are "doing."</u> We can do so much more for Him, if we are becoming more like Him.

David admits his difficult situation. *"I am in the midst of lions; I lie among ravenous beasts - men whose teeth are spears and arrows, whose tongues are sharp swords."* What does David then do? He composes a song of faith about God's sure protection. Awesome!

Prayer: Most Holy Lord, what a blessing it is, to have beautiful psalms that speak hope and truth to our needy hearts. You were there for David. You are there for us. We depend on You! "Be exalted, O God, above the heavens; let Your glory be over all the earth." In Jesus' name we pray. Amen.

"The righteous will be glad when they are avenged, when they bathe their feet in the blood of the wicked. Then men will say, 'surely the righteous still are rewarded; surely there is a God who judges the earth.'"

"Surely the righteous still are rewarded"

In a few days, we will be in Psalm 62. There we see that God rewards believers eternally in Heaven. But what about here and now on this Earth? Does God reward believers in this life also?

David is believed to have penned this psalm after Saul passed a law that gave David the status of an outlawed wolf. Whoever would kill David, would be found innocent in the courts of the land. So the question is not only for David 3000 years ago, but for us today. Can God protect David and us with a horde of vigilantes after us? Can God keep us safe from governments and those who are working to eliminate us? David's sure answer is that God will not only protect us, but will reward us for standing for the truth.

"The righteous will be glad when they are avenged." It does not say if they are avenged. God said, *"It is Mine to avenge; I will repay."* The only condition for us as believers in Romans 12:19, is *"Do not take revenge, my friends, but leave room for God's wrath."* We are to daily trust and obey God, and then <u>leave the results to Him</u>. How will God repay? That is God's business, not ours.

Often in counseling sessions, I draw a line down the middle of a sheet of paper. On the one side I put "Our human responsibility to be faithful." On the other side is, "God's responsibility or results." How often we have fear and worry issues when we are more concerned about "God's results," than in our personal faithfulness.

"Surely the righteous still are rewarded." God is still God. Like King David, we too must look back in history and see that God rewards His faithful believers. His Word and His promises, which are based on His character, give us our needed hope. We are so thankful that our God is on a big throne and all kings and queens are on little ones.

Prayer: O Lord, we are so grateful for Your amazing grace to us! You not only give us salvation but deeply love us, Your children. May Your name be praised. In Jesus' name we pray. Amen.

Psalm 59:16

*"But I will sing of Your strength, in the morning I will sing of Your love;
for You are my fortress, my refuge in time of trouble."*

I will sing of Your strength and love

David begins his day, singing to God. In time of trouble, sing to God a song of faith. Sing a song that trusts in His awesome strength and abundant love. David is believed to have written this psalm soon after King Saul sent men to kill him. David knew that Saul wanted him dead and responds by singing of God's sure protection.

David began the psalm saying, *"Deliver me from my enemies, O God; protect me from those who rise up against me."* David then goes on to say how his enemies are on the move against him when he is not hurting them. Later on in Psalm 59:9-10, David sings, *"O my Strength, I watch for You; You, O God, are my fortress, my loving God. God will go before me and will let me gloat over those who slander me."*

The Apostle Paul sang in prison. His singing was a sweet prayer of dependence on God to act for his good and for God's glory. Our singing is a sweet prayer to God's ears of how we are dependent on Him! Our singing honors God and His powerful attributes. Our singing moves God to act in mercy towards us.

My favorite Bible chapter is 2 Chronicles 20. God greatly encouraged and strengthened me to move forward in faith, fully depending on Him. In this chapter, Jerusalem and Judah were surrounded by three enemies. King Jehoshaphat addressed the people: *"Have faith in the LORD your God and you will be upheld; have faith in His prophets and you will be successful."* After consulting the people, Jehoshaphat appointed men to sing to the LORD and to praise Him for the glory and splendor of His holiness. The people sang even while they were still surrounded by their enemies! They sang, *"Give thanks to the LORD, for His love endures forever."* <u>Then</u>, as *"they began to sing and praise, the LORD set ambushes against the men of Ammon and Moab and Mount Seir who were invading Judah, and they were defeated."*

Prayer: Dear Lord, our help in ages past, our hope for years to come. The last verse of Psalm 59 is a great summary of our heart song. *"O my Strength, I sing praises to You; You, O God, are my fortress, my loving God."* We praise You. In Jesus' name we pray. Amen.

Psalm 60:12

"With God we will gain the victory, and He will trample down our enemies."

The battle is the Lord's

Jesus came to save His people and He does so completely. *"With God we will gain the victory."* We will gain the victory over sin and Satan. *"We are more than conquerors through Him who loves us,"* Romans 8:37b. So then, if God is for us, who can be against us? God has a binding covenant agreement to bless His children in this world.

An earthly king has a covenant with his people, to both love and protect them, if they will faithfully serve him. God is our King, of all kings! His divine attributes are perfect, powerful and constantly at work for us. Our God is totally willing and able to save us completely. He is faithful and proud of His name. David was completely confident when he said, *"With God we will gain the victory, and He will trample down our enemies,"* Psalm 60:12

If God is so completely for us, then what must we do? We must do exactly what God told Joshua to do! *"Have I not commanded you? Be strong and courageous. Do not be terrified; do not be discouraged, for the LORD your God will be with you wherever you go,"* Joshua 1:9. We must be bold for God, who is so bold for us. "Let courage rise with danger," the song says. A soldier may have his hands full of weapons, but without courage he is already defeated. A coward is useless in both a physical and in a spiritual battle.

There are two big questions we need to answer with our head and with our heart. *"The LORD is my light and my salvation whom shall I fear? The LORD is the stronghold of my life - of whom shall I be afraid?"* Psalm 27:1. David fully believed in the size of His God. The giant, Goliath, was very small to him next to the mighty power of his God. David won the victory because he relied on God! May we too fully believe that God *"will trample down our enemies,"* for He will!

Prayer: Victorious Lord, so often our faith is weak. We often lack the spiritual strength that we need. Help us to _fully_ believe, like David here and like Paul who said, *"I can do everything through Him who gives me strength."* Lord, we look to You. In Jesus' name we pray. Amen.

Psalm 61:1-2

"Hear my cry, O God; listen to my prayer. From the ends of the earth I cry to You, I call as my heart grows faint; lead me to the Rock that is higher than I."

"Lead me to the Rock that is higher than I"

In the last psalm, we saw that the battle is the Lord's. However, we do have a responsibility to pray and cry out to Him. David also wrote, *"The righteous cry out and the LORD hears them; He delivers them from all their troubles,"* Psalm 34:17. Our great God allows trials, in part, just so He can deliver us and build our faith and trust in Him. God encourages us, *"So do not fear, for I am with you; do not be dismayed, for I am your God. I will strengthen you and help you; I will uphold you with My righteous right hand,"* Isaiah 41:10.

Who else cried out in prayer to God? Moses and the people of Israel did. They were fresh out of Egypt, rescued by God from a life of slavery. Egypt is a symbol of sin, and slavery to sin. In salvation, we too are also rescued by God. But Satan and his demons want us back, just as Pharaoh wanted the children of Israel back. Pharaoh and his many chariots and horses chased after the people of Israel. *"As Pharaoh approached, the Israelites looked up, and there were the Egyptians, marching after them. They were terrified and cried out to the LORD,"* Exodus 14:10. What happened next is for us to see the greatness of our God! *"Moses answered the people, 'Do not be afraid. Stand firm and you will see the deliverance the LORD will bring you today… The LORD will fight for you; you need only to be still,"* Exodus 14:13-14.

The people did as our text commands us to do in faith yet today, that is to pray. *"Hear my cry, O God; listen to my prayer. From the ends of the earth I cry to You, I call as my heart grows faint; lead me to the Rock that is higher than I."* That Rock is Jesus. Let us then, cry out to Jesus and God Himself will hear our cry.

Prayer: Almighty Lord, David's testimony is our need also. Help us to believe by faith and then to depend on You. David gave the reason to cry out. *"You have been my refuge, a strong tower against the foe."* Lord, we thank You for not only saving us from our sin but now also from our enemies. We worship You. In Jesus' name we pray. Amen.

Psalm 62:1-2

"My soul finds rest in God alone; my salvation comes from Him. He alone is my rock and my salvation; He is my fortress, I will never be shaken."

Resting in God *"alone"*

What a beautiful psalm to show us that God's salvation *"alone"* brings us a restful confidence. God's complete salvation gives us a trusting satisfaction in His present and future promises. Our resting in *"God alone"* is our willingness to remain prayerful and patient in the midst of uncertainty. We will still have temptations to rest in other *"things"* like money and other relationships, even more than in God. But then, our *"walk with God"* must teach us that past occasions of God's divine help should cause us to expect His kind assistance when new difficulty's come. Resting in God *"alone"* is a living faith that has learned to accept *"No"* or *"Not yet,"* as a permanent or temporary answer to our prayers. Spurgeon said, "Faith can hear the footsteps of coming salvation, because she has learned to be silent."

In verses five to eight, David talks to his soul to find rest in God alone. Even David had the temptation to think that all would not turn out well for him in his present trial. David teaches, *"My salvation and my honor depend on God, He is my rock and refuge,"* Psalm 62:7. Like us, David had fears, yet he appears here, calm and trusting! In other places, David cries out with a loud voice about his present burden. Both responses are faith responses. God is both a refuge for the calm soul and for the crying soul.

Two ways of living are contrasted as the psalm ends. David looks out at how others are handling their present troubles. He warns us all, *"Do not trust in extortion or take pride in stolen goods; though your riches increase, do not set your heart on them,"* Psalm 62:10. All other *"assets,"* besides God, are temporary possessions. There is no long term gain in them! God is working out our salvation for today and for eternity. *"He alone is my rock and my salvation."*

Prayer: Lord, we say with David, You are *"my fortress, I will never be shaken."* Lord forgive us for our lingering doubts about Your ability to totally save us today and for eternity. In Jesus' name we pray. Amen.

Psalm 62:11-12

"One thing God has spoken, two things I have heard; That You, O God, are strong, and that You, O LORD, are loving. Surely You will reward each person according to what he has done."

"You will reward each person"

The fact that God is *"strong'* and *"loving"* has been demonstrated again and again on the pages of the Bible and throughout history. God is strong and loving to us also, for which we are most grateful. Thus, David rightly reasons, because of these two perfect and powerful character traits, God has the desire and ability to fulfill this promise: *"Surely You will reward each person according to what he has done."* David was convinced of this fact, even without a full Bible. David only had the first five books of Moses.

We have a full Bible and still many Christians do not believe that God rewards *"each person according to what he has done."* Paul wrote, *"Do not be deceived: God cannot be mocked. A man reaps what he sows." "The one who sows to please his sinful nature, from that nature will reap destruction; the one who sows to please the Spirit, from the Spirit will reap eternal life,"* Galatians 6:7-8.

John had a clear vision of what was to come in The Judgment. *"I saw the dead, great and small, standing before the throne, and books were opened. Another book was opened, which is the book of life. The dead <u>were judged according to what they had done</u> as recorded in the books. The sea gave up the dead that were in it, and death and Hades gave up the dead that were in them, and <u>each person was judged according to what he had done</u>,"* Revelation 20:12-13.

Will God reward people in this life for what they do or don't do? In the Beatitudes, Jesus spoke of both earthly blessings and Heavenly ones, based on if we would love Him. The most complete list of God's blessings are listed in Deuteronomy 28:1-14. We do not deserve blessings, but God is merciful to those who show mercy to others.

Prayer: Gracious Lord, You are such a loving God. The wages of sin is death. That is what we deserve. But You give us this life in abundance and eternal life on top of that. We worship You. In Jesus' name we pray. Amen.

Psalm 63:3-4

"Because Your love is better than life, my lips will glorify You. I will praise You as long as I live, and in Your name I will lift up my hands."

"I will praise You as long as I live"

God's love is, *"better than life."* What a beautiful Christian truth. Why do you think David is so filled with joy and satisfaction concerning God's love? One reason stands out that is true for every believer, but is not true for those who do not believe. If a guilty man is on death row in prison, and then the highest judge of the land pardons him, extreme gratitude would describe him. Our God did just that for each of us who are Christian. Our pardon is for all eternity, not for just a few years on this earth. In Romans nine, God's love in pardoning Jacob, was far different than His love to Esau. What is true for Jacob is true for every believer.

David also says, *"My soul clings to You."* Then he gives the reason, because *"Your right hand upholds me,"* Psalm 63:8. David is sure of God's preserving love. Every believer will always stay saved, because God will not let go of him. Jesus said about believers, *"I give them eternal life, and they shall never perish; no one can snatch them out of My hand,"* John 10:28. In the next verse, Jesus says, *"no one can snatch them out of My Father's hand."*

The love that God gives to us is ours to offer back to Him as our reasonable service and worship. That is why Paul said, *"Therefore I urge you, brothers, <u>in view of God's mercy</u>, to offer your bodies as living sacrifices, holy and pleasing to God-this is your spiritual act of worship,"* Romans 12:1. Are we available to serve God wherever we are? <u>Our God is just as interested in our availability, as He is in our ability</u>! May we lift our hands in worship and in service for God as long as we live.

Prayer: Merciful and gracious Lord, You fill us with Your love. We will praise You as long as we live. We lift our hands to You in worship for restoring our souls. How comforting it is that in body and in soul, both in life and in death, we belong to You. In Jesus' name we pray give our thanks. Amen.

Psalm 64:6-8

"They (evildoers) plot injustice and say, 'We have devised a perfect plan!' Surely the mind and heart of a man are cunning. But God will shoot them with arrows; suddenly they will be struck down. He will turn their own tongues against them and bring them to ruin: all who see them will shake their heads in scorn."

God strikes down those who mock Him

In this psalm David respectfully voices a complaint to God. Once again, David does not complain to others, but to God. David noticed that evil people, *"sharpen their tongues like swords and aim their words like deadly arrows."* He saw how they ambushed the innocent. More than that, *"They encourage each other in evil plans."* If this is us who are using our words to take others down, we need to realize David is praying against us here also.

Paul warns us in Romans 12:19, *"Do not take revenge, my friends, but leave room for God's wrath, for it is written: 'It is mine to avenge; I will repay,' says the Lord."* Paul also wrote in Galatians 6:7, *"Do not be deceived; God cannot be mocked. A man reaps what he sows."* The saying, "what goes around, comes around," is true. If a man takes from others, God will take from him. On the other hand, if a man is merciful to others, God will be merciful to him. May we then be patient in adversity, knowing that we have a just God in Heaven who is always looking out for us.

God struck down the wicked Haman, who was a powerful man in a pagan land. Haman threatened the righteous Mordecai. Haman thought he had *"devised a perfect plan"* to defeat Mordecai. He built a high platform to hang Mordecai on. But God eliminated the wicked Haman on his own platform. God had all of this completely under His control. But notice, Mordecai was fasting and praying along with many others. Let us pray also.

Prayer: O Righteous Lord, it is so good of You to show us again and again, how much You care for us, Your adopted children. We cry out to You for help. You who are good, defeat evil. As You do, You are glorified, while we are blessed. We love You so much. Accept our praise and gratitude. In Jesus' name we pray. Amen.

Psalm 65:4 NKJV

"Blessed is the man whom You choose, and cause to approach You, that he may dwell in Your courts. We shall be satisfied with the goodness of Your house, of Your holy temple."

"You choose, and cause to approach You"

We may wonder, how did David understand about who would believe in God and who would not? David did not have the words of Jesus, like, *"No one can come to Me unless it has been granted to him by My Father,"* John 6:65b NKJV. David did not hear Jesus say, *"You did not choose Me, but I chose you and appointed you that you should go and bear fruit,"* John 15:16a NKJV. Yet still, David knew that the gift of salvation is limited to those whom God chooses.

David had the five books of Moses. He knew about Noah and the flood. David knew that God chose exactly which animals were to come two by two into the ark. David knew God called Abram to follow Him. David was also aware of how God called Moses to rescue His people.

David never forgot how the prophet Samuel came to his father Jesse's house. He saw Samuel pass by his seven older brothers, without choosing them. David was clearly aware that he did not deserve to be selected. And this is exactly where we have a bit of a problem. We think that everyone deserves salvation. The opposite is what is true. *"For the wages of sin is death,"* Romans 6:23a. Because of Adam's sin, we are all born sinners, separated from God, deserving death.

We do see that we, who are Christian, made a move towards God in the salvation process. Yes, but it was the Holy Spirit who convicted us and moved us to make that decision! God, by His Spirit, moved us to Himself. That is why David could say, *"Blessed is the man whom You choose, and cause to approach You."* God is to be praised, not us, for our relationship with Him. May we never cease to be grateful for what God has done in causing us to approach Him!

Prayer: Most blessed Lord, we are reminded again that You are to be praised for Your abundant grace in *"causing"* us to approach You. How great is Your salvation to us personally! May we love You with an undying love for adopting us to be Your children for all eternity. In Jesus' name we pray. Amen.

Psalm 65:9

"You care for the land and water it; You enrich it abundantly. The streams of God are filled with water to provide the people with grain, for so You have ordained it."

God's gift, NOT "mother nature's"

The famous radio announcer, Ernie Harwell, started every baseball season with a quote from God's Word. *"See! The winter is past; the rains are over and gone. Flowers appear on the earth; the season of singing has come, the cooing of doves is heard in our land,"* Song of Solomon 2:11-12. That sovereign blessing is from our personal and real God, not from a nonexistent, impersonal "mother nature."

God will continue to fulfill a covenant promise He personally gave to all mankind. Right after Noah and every creature came off the ark, God sealed His promise by putting His (not mother nature's) rainbow in the sky. God's beautiful rainbows are a covenant reminder to Himself and to us. God's specific words of promise were, *"As long as the earth endures, seedtime and harvest, cold and heat, summer and winter, day and night will never cease,"* Genesis 8:22. "Mother nature" does not bring us any of these promises or blessings!

David continues by praising God, *"You drench its furrows and level its ridges; You soften it with showers and bless its crops,"* Psalm 65:10. It is blasphemy to credit "mother nature" with giving us anything. Giving glory to anyone or anything that rightly belongs to God is a direct insult to God, an idol, and total unbelief.

Imagine, you sent the seasons, the sunshine and the rain in the right amounts, to feed your creation all over the world. And then foolish people all over the globe gave the credit for your wise planning, and continual provisions, to a person that does not exist.

Mother nature is a deliberate lie, another religion, meant to steal the genius of God's perfect work! Our holy and perfect God takes an insult every time mother nature is mentioned. We have a long-suffering God that patiently puts up with such foolishness, for now!

Prayer: O Lord, You are our great provider. We praise You for Your creation. We also praise You for caring for Your creation every day. The glory and the praise belongs to You alone. May Your name be lifted up and praised! In Jesus' name we pray. Amen.

Psalm 66:18

"If I had cherished sin in my heart, the LORD would not have listened."

When God doesn't hear our prayers

This verse explains why God sometimes does not answer our prayers. The word *"cherished"* is not a word we use anymore. It means to think highly of, or to admire. A still older version of the Bible uses the words, *"if I harbored sin in my heart."* If a ship is in a harbor, it is in safe water. God is telling us that if certain sins are safe in our hearts, if we will not confess them, then He will not listen to our other prayers.

Those who are close to God dread sinning and cannot wait to get to their prayer room. The Holy Spirit makes us pour out our hearts to God when we sin. Loving sons or daughters do not want to offend their caring father. Loving adopted sons or daughters of God cannot rest knowing that their sins hurts the relationship with their Heavenly Father. The reason is: Sin always separates.

Another verse that carries the same message as our text is: *"And when you stand praying, if you hold anything against anyone, forgive him, so that your Father in Heaven may forgive you your sins,"* Mark 11:25. Here we see that if we keep bitterness in our hearts, we should not be surprised that God seems silent to our prayers and petitions. The problem is not that God moved away from us, but that we moved away from Him with an uncaring attitude. By confessing our sin and asking for forgiveness, we worship the holiness of God. Then, our holy God forgives and blesses us.

There are times when God just says "No" in answer to certain prayer request. We then often think that God is not answering our prayer. Do we yet realize, that when God says "No," or "Not yet," that is an answer to prayer! When we pray that things should happen according to God's will, then we need to listen to God's will. God's "No" always serves to protect His kingdom, His honor, and our good.

Prayer: Holy Lord, we have offended You by holding tightly to some sins. In our pride, we have often loved sin more than You! Lord, forgive us! We pray that sin may never be safe in our hearts. Lord search our hearts and expose our sin so that we might confess it fully. We need You every hour and want to be in Your will and grace. We pray this in the holy name of Jesus Christ. Amen.

Psalm 66:19-20

"God has surely listened and heard my voice in prayer. Praise be to God, who has not rejected my prayer or withheld His love from me!"

God is worthy of our praise

As believers, it is a fact that our many prayers to God are not a burden to Him. God's children will never wear out their welcome to their Heavenly Father. Jesus Himself gave us an open invitation when He said, *"Come to Me, all you who are weary and burdened, and I will give you rest,"* Matthew 11:28. In John 16, Jesus said He was going to Heaven to send us the Holy Spirit, to walk with us. The Spirit of God moves us to prayers which are a delight to God.

How grateful we are then, that God hears our prayers. Are we guilty of being something like a selfish son or daughter who asks a parent for money and then moments later thinks or speaks bad things about their parents? The psalm before us reminds us to be grateful to God as part of our daily worship! After all, we have quite something amazing in God, that the pagans do not have. They pray to a god who cannot hear, who has no eyes to see, no hands to help and no storehouse of blessings. We however, pray to our loving Father in Heaven for His sure mercy in our time of need.

Once again, we know well how to ask God for His mercy. But do we praise God in prayer for His willingness to hear our prayers? In fact, the prayer of a repentant sinner is music to God's ears. *"The prayer of the upright pleases Him,"* Proverbs 15:8b.

David once asked God, *"Who praises You from the grave?"* Psalm 6:5b. Perhaps David's view of Heaven before the final judgment was that of a believer who could not praise God anymore. Yet, the point David is making is pointing out how necessary it is for us to praise God now. God is worthy of our praise!

Prayer: O Precious Lord, it is our beautiful experience that You answer our prayers graciously. Paul was right in His praise of You in Ephesians 3:20; *"Now to Him who is able to do immeasurably more than all we ask or imagine, according to His power that is at work within us, to Him be glory in the church and in Christ Jesus throughout all generations, for ever and ever! Amen."*

Psalm 67:5-7

"May the peoples praise You, O God; may all the peoples praise You. Then the land will yield its harvest, and God, our God, will bless us."

Praising God brings us His blessings

A few days ago we talked about the foolishness of praising "mother nature" for favorable weather we receive from the hand of God. We now see blessings flowing two ways, from God to man and from man to God. The psalm starts out with a benediction (blessing) to God's people. *"May God be gracious to us and bless us and make His face to shine upon us."* WHY? *"That Your ways may be known on earth, Your salvation among the nations,"* Psalm 67:1-2.

I love that blessing from God! God blesses us so we can bless Him in our evangelism efforts. He strengthens us to serve Him. God is an evangelistic God. He desires for people to know Him and to worship Him. He created us for Himself. Already in Genesis 3:15, a Savior was promised. A few verses later, *"The LORD God made garments of skin for Adam and his wife and clothed them,"* Genesis 3:21. God covered their sin, blessing Adam and Eve with salvation, so that, they would worship Him and have close fellowship with Him again.

"May all the people praise You, O God" is repeated three times in the seven verses of this psalm. God clearly wants us to know that it is important to praise Him. However, God does not just have the praise of Himself in mind. God also wants to bless us! When we praise God, He blesses us in return! We should never doubt God's blessings for that is a weak faith in His ability and willingness to care for us.

Is it possible to doubt God's blessings, even as we pray? Yes. How often do we pray and plead with God to please be with this or that believer? A better prayer would be, "We praise and worship You, O God, for Your loving promise of <u>never to leave or forsake a believer</u>. You promise to be with us always, even to the end of the age. How great is Your love for us, Your adopted children."

Prayer: Dear Lord, we worship You for Your sure faithfulness. You even make the land *"yield its harvest"* when we praise and adore You. We praise You that for being such a good and gracious God! In Jesus' name we pray. Amen..

Psalm 68:35

"You are awesome, O God, in Your sanctuary; the God of Israel gives power and strength to His people. Praise be to God!"

God, "gives power and strength to His people"

One of the main things that happens in a new believer's life is that God gives a new *"power and strength to His people."* There are two P's that are involved as a result of our salvation. The Penalty of sin is removed. The Power to overcome the strongholds of Satan is given. How does God give His power and strength?

God is a Spirit, with a capital S. Satan is a spirit with a small s. God was not created, He always existed. The Bible in Hebrew begins, *"God in the beginning."* The devil or Satan is a spirit, created by God. But then, Satan became proud and turned evil. As a spirit (no body) Satan still reports to his Creator, who is God. In Job 1:6-7, it says, *"One day the angels came to present themselves before the LORD, and Satan also came with them. The LORD said to Satan, 'Where have you come from?' Satan answered the LORD."* Satan still answers to God! Jesus told us to pray to God, *"deliver us from the evil one."* God, in trinity, has power over Satan. Without God, we don't.

Jesus already had power over Satan when He was born a baby in Bethlehem. Herod could not kill Him. In Matthew 4, Jesus had power over Satan again when He was tempted in the wilderness. Jesus had power over Satan in the Garden of Gethsemane when Satan tried to prevent Him from going to the cross. Jesus had power over Satan on the cross. Jesus had power over Satan when He came out of that grave. Jesus had power over Satan when He ascended into Heaven. Jesus now sits in Heaven as our Mediator, with power over Satan.

The Holy Spirit has power over Satan and his spirit demon helpers. Jesus called the Holy Spirit, *"our Counselor"* in John 16. *"But when He, the Spirit of Truth, comes, He will guide You into all truth,"* John 16:13. The Holy Spirit wrote the Bible, which is truth. When we walk in truth, we too stop Satan.

Prayer: O Lord of lords, what power we have when You, Father, Son and Spirit are in us. Without You, we are doomed. You alone preserve us for Your heavenly kingdom, for You have complete authority over Satan and his demons. We thank You. In Jesus' name we pray. Amen.

Psalm 69:30

"I will praise God's name in song and glorify Him with thanksgiving."

How well do I communicate praise to God?

The birds start singing praises to God, even before it is light outside. God created them to sing praises to Him and they faithfully sing. How much does a bird have to sing about compared to we who are redeemed Christian's? We read that in Heaven we will sing praises to God forever for His mercy to us who were lost sinners. Are we yet praising God in song here and now?

Our words communicate. Most of us have good communication skills because we learn that early in life. But are we communicating in song to God? How well do we communicate praise and worship to God that is due His name? God did create us to worship Him and in this psalm God directs us to that in song.

Are we quite foolish in our praise? Does our selfishness and pride still limit our ability to communicate praise to God? We may go to church for an hour or two on Sunday to glorify God and praise Him. But what do we do with the other 166 hours in the week? Who do we praise and glorify then? Are we singing praises to others about who we are and what we have done? Or, are we more impressed with who God is and what He has done and is doing? The words of our songs show the condition of our hearts. Our thoughts and words tell the truth about who we are.

We need to be into God's Word to have a song in our hearts! God must increase and we must decrease, in order to sing His praises. True spiritual maturity is learning to value God and what He has done. Christ esteem is the need of the day, not self esteem. Self-importance is our undoing, beginning with Adam and Eve. A real change of heart is needed to *"glorify Him."* May our lives lead a parade to the honor and glory of God. *"I will praise God's name in song and glorify Him with thanksgiving,"* now and forever.

Prayer: O Lord, You are worthy of praise. Forgive us for so often still singing our own praises. Forgive us for wanting our name to be glorified. Move our eyes from ourselves to You. Change us and make us more like Your Son. To You belongs all glory and praise. In Jesus' name we pray. Amen.

Psalm 70:5

"I am poor and needy, come quickly to me, O God! You are my help and my deliverer. O LORD, do not delay."

Prayer, a gift to *"poor and needy"* sinners

A problem we have in prayer is that we do not know how small we are. God knows we are made from dust, totally <u>dependent</u> on Him. We, on the other hand, tend to be rather proud and <u>independent</u>. God will bless His people, if it is safe for Him to do so. God is not in the habit of blessing proud people. It is humble people who are *"poor and needy."* Prayer is three things for the *"poor and needy."*

Prayer reminds us that we are unworthy. (God never needs a reminder). We are much like an empty cupboard. If God filled our cupboard without our asking, we would never in a million years, know how unworthy and needy we are. As Spurgeon said, "A true prayer is an inventory of our needs, a catalog of our necessities, a revelation of our hidden poverty." Prayer depends on God for His limitless supply. We who are *"poor and needy"* need just that.

Prayer is a confession of our physical and spiritual bankruptcy. The song says, *"Prayer is the contrite sinner's voice, returning from his ways, while angels in their songs rejoice and cry, 'Behold, he prays!'"* Prayer is the Christian's vital breath! It is the nature of prayer itself, to humble us, while at the same time esteem God as Almighty! We who are *"poor and needy"* have no one else to help us.

Prayer is a great privilege of the Christian! Without prayer we are dead to God and dead to the needs of this world. May we not forget the prayerful Moses. When he prayed' the enemy moved away. When Esther prayed, evil was stopped and God's mercy triumphed. When Daniel prayed, the hungry lions became like harmless kittens. Prayer gives us weak humans God's divine strength. Prayer trades in our foolish ideas for God's heavenly wisdom. Prayer gives our troubled minds the amazing peace of God. How we *"poor and needy"* sinners need privileges from God's hand!

Prayer: Merciful Lord, we praise You for giving us prayer. Without Your love and mercy we are lost in this world, damned in the next. Help us to see our dependence on You and thank You for it. In Jesus' name we pray. Amen.

Psalm 71:18

"Even when I am old and gray, do not forsake me, O God, till I declare Your power to the next generation, Your might to all who are to come."

Strengthen us to teach the next generation

This verse is our plea in prayer. Like David, we know the aches and pains of aging. We know that we will not always be on this earth. By God's grace, we now know what is important in life and what is foolish. We are aware of our many shortcomings as a parent and leader. But we must not dwell on these, by thinking "If only I had done it differently." Long ago God forgave us from all these sins and we are grateful. Like David, we know that we did not deserve God's abundant mercy! How we love God for His patience in teaching us over the years. We have learned that our Lord and Savior is fully trustworthy. With David we cry out, to our great God, *"I will always have hope; I will praise You more and more,"* Psalm 71:14.

David looks out into the church and world. He sees the multitudes and realizes that so many do not have the hope and faith that we need. He knows that so many of us just do not "get it." Many do not yet realize how strong and mighty God really is! If only the next generation would turn to God. That is our main focus now. Our desire is, *"My mouth will tell of Your righteousness, of Your salvation all day long,"* Psalm 71:15a. We long for others to have God's righteousness today and eternally. That is what spiritual leaders do.

David here cries out to God to give him the personal strength to carry on for God's glory! He pleads, *"Do not cast me away when I am old; do not forsake me when my strength is gone,"* Psalm 71:9. David pleads, *"Do not forsake me, O God, till I declare Your power to the next generation, Your might to all who are to come,"* Psalm 71:18. And that is our prayer today and every day.

A song says, *"Years I spent in vanity and pride, caring not my Lord was crucified."* We admit that, as we now press on.

Prayer. Dear covenant-keeping Lord, use us as Your mouthpiece to communicate the beauty of who You are! Lord give us the strength to do that as we age. By Your grace we now know that You are fully our everything, our all. Strengthen us in every way to communicate who You are and that Jesus saves. In His name we pray. Amen

Psalm 72:12-14

"For He will deliver the needy who cry out, the afflicted who have no one to help. He will take pity on the weak and the needy and save the needy from death. He will rescue them from oppression and violence, for precious is their blood in His sight."

How much does injustice bother you?

Christians are "commissioned" by God to care about injustice. We are commanded to be the arms and legs of God's mercy. God *"will take pity on the weak."* There are orphans without parents, and then, there are orphans with parents who have left them for selfish goals. There are women and children who are abused. Workers are being cheated. Does injustice really bother us, or is injustice less than a hungry mosquito buzzing by our head?

Israel was located on the crossroads of civilization, as are we! They went to the temple thinking they were religious. We go to church. They prayed, but then God lets Israel and us know something really important. God says that we are not to miss a key element in our worship and service. Do not ignore the oppressed. God speaks to all uncaring "churchgoers." *"Is this not the kind of fasting I have chosen: to loose the chains of injustice and untie the cords of the yoke, to set the oppressed free and break every yoke?"* Isaiah 58:6.

If we want God's blessing, then we need to think His thoughts. We need to see a hurting world as God sees it. His eye sees every single act of injustice everywhere. *"He will deliver the needy who cry out." "He will take pity." "He will rescue them from oppression and violence."* The only question is: Will we get involved as God's "mercy workers," or will we live in our own "little world"?

The love in God's heart motivates Him into action. *"For precious is their blood in His sight."* That really does beg a question to us. How precious is the blood of the oppressed who are suffering injustice? Will we help needy people? Be sure of this, if we are unwilling, God will send someone else! *"For He will deliver the needy."*

Prayer: Just and holy Lord, open our eyes to see what You see! Open our hearts to respond for You. May we not be so busy in things that have so little eternal value. Take my life and let it be consecrated Lord to Thee. In Jesus' name we pray. Amen.

Psalm 72:19

"Praise be to His glorious name forever; may the whole earth be filled with His glory. Amen and Amen."

"Amen and Amen."

Right after this double Amen, it says, *"This concludes the prayers of David son of Jesse."* What does the use of the word, *"Amen"* mean? *"Amen"* expresses our trust in God to answer our prayers. *"Amen"* is a faith response to the character of God. *"Amen"* says, I accept God as my God. *"Amen"* says Jesus is my Savior. *"Amen"* says the Holy Spirit is my friend and comforter. *"Amen"* says I believe God's Word is true and will always be so. The word *"Amen"* is very personal as we worship God. So then, when we say *"Amen,"* we acknowledge that God is the Lord and guide of our life in a very personal way. Bring my *"Amen"* to pass, dear Lord.

Wicked and unrepentant people cannot honestly say "Amen" and mean it. They do not yet agree with God or worship God in Spirit or in truth. However, that is not true of the wicked who have already died and are in the torments of Hell. There, in Hell, they fully believe that God exist as they experience His wrath. Paul tells us in Philippians 2:10, *"That at the name of Jesus every knee should bow, in Heaven and on Earth and under the Earth."* The words *"under the Earth"* describe Hell, and they will be saying "Amen" to who God was and still is: Lord for all eternity!

Jesus even used the words *"Amen and Amen"* at the beginning of a sentence. What has been translated, *"Verily, Verily"* is really *"Amen and Amen."* For example, *"Verily, verily, I say to you, He that heareth My Word, and believeth on Him who sent Me, hath everlasting life, and shall not come into condemnation; but is passed from death unto life,"* John 5:24. The word *"Amen"* is a word of emphasis whether in the beginning or at the end of a verse.

Prayer: Glorious Lord, the prayer in our text is our personal prayer, one we can say "Amen and Amen" to. *"Praise be to His glorious name forever; may the whole earth be filled with His glory. Amen and Amen."* Bring it to pass Lord! In Jesus' name we pray. Amen.

Psalm 73:2

"But as for me, my feet had almost slipped; I had nearly lost my foothold."

"My feet had almost slipped"

I am just about ready to lose it! The pressure is too much! I don't know how much more I can stand. I'm close to going crazy. These are exactly the psalmist's thoughts. We must admit they are ours at times too. The ones in the mental hospital are not the only ones who have mental stress. It's a good thing that God writes to us about our struggles, so then, we can see the way out of them.

The Psalm starts by saying "*God is good,*" meaning, "My poor mental outlook is not God's fault." God is not the problem. After all, "*my feet had almost slipped.*" The psalmist admits his problem exists because of how he has been thinking. He envied those who he thought had it better than he did. The psalmist thought, "It's not fair what I am going through." He saw the arrogant and "*prosperity of the wicked.*" He saw that, "*their bodies are healthy and strong.*" He saw others that were "*violent,*" "*wicked,*" and "*carefree.*" He selfishly says, "*Surely in vain have I kept my heart pure,*" Psalm 73:13a. In other words, God You are not fair, and following You is perhaps not worth it. Clearly, the psalmist is feeling sorry for himself, and that is a problem!

Then, hope arises. He now says, "*I entered the sanctuary of God; then I understood their final destiny,*" Psalm 73:17. He now makes a huge spiritual adjustment. He is reminded that the far greater comfort and glory is in Heaven, not always here and now. Instead of focusing on the very temporary blessings of God to the many, he now sees the eternal blessings of God's grace to a few, including him. As the truth of this fact sinks into his soul, something happens! Now he says to God, "*You place them on slippery ground,*" Psalm 73:18a. He has moved from self-pity and the worship of self, to worshiping God who is so worthy of our adoration. May God help us to do the same.

Prayer: Majestic Lord, we too are so "*senseless and ignorant*" at times. We lose sight of Your amazing grace. May we say with the psalmist in Psalm 73:26, "*My flesh and my heart may fail, but God is the strength of my heart and my portion forever.*" In Jesus' name we pray. Amen.

Psalm 73:2b-5

"My feet had almost slipped; I had nearly lost my foothold. For I envied the arrogant when I saw the prosperity of the wicked. They have no struggles; their bodies are healthy and strong. They are free from the burdens common to man; they are not plagued by human ills."

When self-pity almost buried Asaph

Because of its importance, we look further at Psalm 73. Asaph works through a serious down period in his life. He was very close to being depressed, and he openly admits it for our benefit. He recalls his self-pity thoughts and actions. He lost sight of the Ten Commandments that teach us to love God first and then others second. His "pity party words" of "I," "me" and "my" in the first half of the psalm shows his self-focus. How we must learn from him.

Asaph's envy and worry accused God of doing something wrong. Its amazing, how often we think we know better than God on how He should do things. Asaph's self-pity did not trust his life to God's wise caring. Thinking God is not fair, not good, and not able to care for us is idolatry and rebellion, much like King Saul in 1 Samuel 15.

Feeling sorry for self or having self-pity, kills us mentally, spiritually, even financially. We need to put it off and replace it just as Asaph does. See his repentance. *"I entered the sanctuary of God; then I understood their final destiny,"* Psalm 73:17. The self-pity Asaph had now turns to pity for those who are spiritually lost! That a big turning point as God helps Asaph regain his spiritual senses. Asaph's confession continuing in verse 22, puts his mind on God, the Author and Perfecter of his faith. Asaph now worships God, instead of self!

When we too fall into self-pity, that is the very point where we need to quickly repent also. If we continue down the self-pity road, we will soon experience, anger, bitterness, fear, worry and even depression. God's process of change outlined in Ephesians 4:22-24 explains how we need to put off the self-pity and replace it with trusting in God to care for us. A song correctly says, "The joy of the Lord is my strength." May God help us to see His all sufficiency.

Prayer: Sovereign Lord, through the pen of Asaph, You minister to our greatest need, Yourself. We need more of You in our hearts. Lord, be merciful to us sinners. In Jesus' name we pray. Amen.

Psalm 73:1-2, 23-25a

"Surely God is good to Israel, to those who are pure in heart. But as for me <u>my feet had almost slipped</u>; I nearly lost my foothold... Yet <u>I am always with You; You hold me by my right hand</u>. You guide me with Your counsel, and <u>afterward You will take me into glory</u>. Whom have I in Heaven but You?"

True faith believes in three tenses

Forgiven sinners were blessed in the past; are blessed in the present; will be blessed in the future, as underlined above. Asaph had a trial that he thought would finish him off. God again, amazingly, delivered him! With a smile, Asaph looks back at the past, remembering God's past deliverances. He has gratitude in the present. He now applies his faith to trusting in God, in the future. Faith, to be a living faith, must understand that God's faithfulness in the past is real in the present and will be there in the future. As we remember God's past faithfulness, we must not stay there. Our unchangeable God is the same today and forever, just as He was in the past. Our help in the past, is still our strength in the present, and our hope for the future. Never think that God will not bless and protect us, His children.

When David explained why he wanted to fight the giant. He looked to the past saying, *"God delivered me from the lion and the bear."* He applied it to the present when he said *"this Philistine."* And to the future by saying, *"will be like one of them."* Already, young David had a solid faith because he exercised it in three tenses!

"Now faith is being sure of what we hope for and certain of what we do not see. This is what the ancients were commended for," Hebrews 11:1-2. Faith brings the past to the present with eyes to the future. Job said, *"I know that my Redeemer lives, (present tense) and that in the end He will stand (future) upon the earth. And after my skin has been destroyed, yet in my flesh I will see God,"* Job 19:25-26. *"I am the Alpha and the Omega,"* says the Lord God, *"<u>who is,</u> and <u>who was,</u> and <u>who is to come,</u> the Almighty,"* Revelation 1:8.

Prayer: O Eternal Lord, like Asaph, may we be grateful for the past, restful in the present, trustful for the future. The truth is, *"My flesh and my heart may fail, but God is the strength of my heart and my portion forever,"* Psalm 73:26. In Jesus' name we pray. Amen.

Psalm 74:19

"Do not hand over the life of Your dove to wild beasts; do not forget the lives of Your afflicted people forever."

Lord see our affliction

Asaph is concerned and so are we. He feels rejected by God, but deep down he knows better. God seems silent, but Asaph also knows that God sees everything and hears all things. Asaph's affliction and doubts are real. Our hearts are also in turmoil at times. We need the grace of God in a big way. So, Asaph does the only thing by faith we can do. Look to God, who is also our only help.

Asaph is first of all concerned about God's name and about how He is being mocked. Asaph respectfully reasons with God about how in creation, He has firmly set "boundaries" for the summer and winter. He reminds God that He has a supernatural control of all created things. And now in our text Asaph likens himself to a dove that the wild beasts have their eyes on. Asaph lists three reasons God should have mercy on us and deliver us all.

"Have regard for Your covenant," Psalm 74:20a. Lord, we have a holy and solemn agreement to serve You and love You. Your part of the covenant agreement is to love and protect us. We know You are a holy God, committed to Your adopted children.

"Do not let the oppressed retreat in disgrace," Psalm 74:21a. Lord, we who are *"poor and needy"* want to *"praise Your name."* We want to do this more and more. We *"poor and needy"* sinners who were saved by You, now depend on You. Save Your sheep from the wolf. His teeth are showing and he has a hungry look in his eye.

"Rise up, O God, and defend Your cause," Psalm 74:22a. Lord, we are Your cause. Your mission is our mission. Together, we have a co-mission. Do not allow the enemy to mock You or us. We are in this together! Lord, come quickly to our aid!

Prayer: Great Lord and Savior, we look to You. Jesus taught us to pray, *"deliver us from the evil one."* We do that now, eagerly looking for Your protecting grace, eagerly waiting to praise You again and again for it. In Jesus' name hear us. Amen.

Psalm 75:4-5

"To the arrogant I say, 'Boast no more,' and to the wicked, 'Do not lift up your horns. Do not lift up your horns against Heaven; do not speak with outstretched neck.'"

'I Did it My Way'

Our title is a song by Frank Sinatra. The words describe how a person did exactly what he or she wanted to do in life's journey. Recently, this song by Sinatra was played at a funeral to describe and give tribute to a man who lived life his own way. As Frank crooned the words, "I did it my way," many of the people smiled at the careless life of the one who was deceased. God was not smiling!

Think about the saying, 'You need to be true to yourself.' Is this not a selfish belief system that refuses to be swayed by others, not even by God? In our text, we are warned by God not to live life our own way, but according to His way. Why? *"Know that the LORD is God. It is He who made us, and we are His; we are His people, the sheep of His pasture,"* Psalm 100:3. Worship God then, not self. The worship of self is called *"arrogant"* in our text. God says, *"Boast no more." "Do not lift up your horns."* Quit fighting God's design for your life.

"Do not speak with an outstretched neck." The God who made us has told us clearly how to live to honor Him. To arrogantly stick out our neck in protest to God is eternally foolish. When I think of an outstretched neck, I think of a snapping turtle. A neighbor man caught snapping turtles for food. When he butchered them, he would put a stick in front of the turtle. The turtle would snap at the stick and refuse to let go of it. You could pick up the turtle by the stick, and still it would not let go. With his neck completely stretched out, it would be cut off. And still, the severed head would not let go of the stick! When our necks remain out against God, our doom is certain.

Prayer: Lord, that snapping turtle was true to himself. He snapped at a stick in front of him. Even though his outstretched neck came out to stop many an enemy, his natural reaction was also his doom. May we see that if we live life our way, You will remove our outstretched neck. You ended Psalm 75 by saying , *"I will cut off the horns of all the wicked."* Make us live life Your way, for it is also true, *"The horns of the righteous will be lifted up."* In Jesus' name we pray. Amen

Psalm 76:10

"Surely Your wrath against men brings You praise, and the survivors of Your wrath are restrained."

God's wrath against men brings Him praise

The psalmist makes a statement about the wrath of God that goes against what so many believe. Some try to do evangelism by telling the unsaved that God loves them. Is that true? We ask this question because our text here teaches that God's wrath against men brings Him praise. God's love is ours through Christ alone.

In John 3:16, Jesus said, *"For God so loved the world that He gave His one and only Son that whoever believes in Him shall not perish but have eternal life."* The *"world"* spoken of here are the Christians that God is saving from every tribe and nation. In John 3:18, Jesus then said, *"Whoever believes in Him is not condemned, but <u>whoever does not believe stands condemned already</u> because he has not believed in the name of God's one and only Son."*

John 3 ends, *"Whoever believes in the Son has eternal life, but whoever rejects the Son will not see life, <u>for God's wrath remains on Him</u>."* *"Remains"* shows how God's wrath is ongoing against those who hate Him and His Son. In fact, when Jesus saves us, He saves us from the present and future wrath of God!

Was God glorified when He saved Noah but destroyed the rest of the known world? Was God's holiness and justice lifted up when He destroyed Pharaoh and all his host in the sea? *"For the Scripture says to Pharaoh: 'I raised you up for this very purpose, that I might display My power in you and that My name might be proclaimed in all the earth,'"* Romans 9:17.

When Daniel's three friends were thrown into the fiery furnace, an angel came and protected them. God was glorified when they did not even smell like smoke. But what about the soldiers who threw them into the fire? Was God glorified when these soldiers perished by those same flames? God's holiness and His ability to protect His children was clearly shown, bringing Him praise.

Prayer: Gracious Lord, we thank You that we can be saved from Your holy and just wrath by the blood of Your precious Son. We praise You now and for all eternity. In Jesus' name we pray. Amen.

Psalm 77:2

"When I was in distress, I sought the LORD; at night I stretched out untiring hands and my soul refused to be comforted."

Suffering, our souls alarm clock

We are "usually" wise enough to set an alarm clock to get us up in the morning. We know there is a great chance that we could be late. God knows that our precious soul also needs an alarm clock! And since our souls belong to Him, He sets the clock for when we need to get up from our spiritual slumber! God's suffering alarm clock comes with a very special design. It does not have a "snooze" button that we can so easily reach to get more spiritual sleep! For this reason, David cries to God, with hands lifted to Heaven. But the Author and Perfecter of our faith, will not so quickly turn off our "suffering alarm." After He awakens us spiritually, we still need to get moving in His direction.

God uses suffering two ways. First, He awakens us to the fact that we need a closer relationship with Him. A sharp brain with a sleeping soul, is a waste! We should not be surprised when God in His wisdom allows us to suffer, to wake us up. Peter wrote, *"Dear friends, do not be surprised at the painful trial you are suffering, as though something strange were happening to you. But rejoice that you may participate in the sufferings of Christ, so that you may be overjoyed when His glory is revealed,"* 1 Peter 4:12-13a. From various sufferings, God makes us experience spiritual blessings. As Ps. 23:3 says, *"He restores my soul."*

God also uses suffering to awaken us to get involved in the work of evangelism and discipleship of others. We normally care little that others suffer, until we ourselves know the pain of suffering! David said in his suffering, *"Restore to me the joy of Your salvation, and grant me a willing spirit to sustain me. Then I will teach transgressors Your ways and sinners will turn back to You,"* Psalm 51:12-13. Others who are suffering need God's answers. Our suffering prepares us to step forward to be a blessing to them, all for God's kingdom. How awake are we?

Prayer: Dear Lord, we praise You for using suffering to rouse a deaf world. Forgive us for complaining when we should be thanking You for Your wisdom. We do so now. In Jesus' name we pray. Amen.

Psalm 77:3b-4

"I mused, and my spirit grew faint. You kept my eyes from closing; I was too troubled to speak."

Bible characters were depressed

The godly Asaph was depressed in his life. In the same way, Christians are depressed yet today. In Psalm 77, we can see Asaph's depressed thinking process. He was overwhelmed and very self-focused. In the first 10 verses, the personal pronouns of *"I"* or *"my,"* are used 20 times. In the last 10 verses, Asaph begins to come out of his selfish thoughts as the *"I"* and *"my"* are used just three times. When he switched from being intent on his problem to being intent on the solution — that is God, Asaph's problem of depression was solved. As we read Psalm 77, we must notice how our hope returns when we meditate on the size of our God!

Peter, a man like us, was also a man of faith. Yet still, in Matthew 26:69-75, he fell in a time of weakness. He denied that he even knew the Lord, lying three times. Peter failed a major test in his life. After this, Peter wept bitterly. The depressed feelings were a direct result of Peter's denying Christ. Peter was a sinner, made of flesh and bone just like us. His depression was a result of his sinful self-focus. What do we do in our self-pity?

God said Job was *"blameless and upright,"* Job 1:1b. Yet still, he was depressed after a great trial in his life. Job struggled with the question, *"Why do the righteous suffer if God is loving and all powerful?"* It is recorded that Job was wrong when he was, *"righteous in his own eyes,"* Job 32:1b. God finally questioned him, *"Would you discredit My justice? Would you condemn Me to justify yourself?"* Job 40:8. This is a powerful question! The depression of Job shouts to us, about how incredibly self-centered we are. If one of the most godly men in the Bible needed to change, how much more do we need to change and become more focused on living God's way!

Prayer: Dear Lord, we praise You for giving us examples about those who were depressed at times in their lives. Help us to understand the principles You teach us through Bible characters. Forgive us for not clearly professing our love for You like Peter did. May we learn to trust in You fully, in every trial. In Jesus' name we pray. Amen.

Psalm 78:40

"How often they rebelled against Him in the desert and grieved Him in the wasteland."

Our rebellious sins grieve the heart of God

Beginning with the first sin of Adam and Eve, our sins grieve the heart of God. When Adam and Eve sinned against God in the Garden of Eden, God missed their fellowship. The first words God spoke to the hiding Adam and Eve were, "*Where are you.*" He was grieved over that broken relationship. God was filled with a divine sorrow. Our sins also grieve God, because they separate us from Him.

In our text, we can see that when the people of Israel "*rebelled*" against God in the desert, He was grieved. Israel was being tested by God in the wilderness, to see if they loved God. Their complaining did not pass the test! They were telling God He was not being fair to them and was not doing what He should for their welfare. The people charged God with not being good enough. Is it possible that we love God's blessings, more than we do God Himself? God grieves over such selfish living.

The prophet Samuel told King Saul that his rebellion was like the sin of witchcraft. Truly, the advice that the demonic world gives us is to rebel against God's wisdom for our lives. Saul's problem was that he claimed that he knew better than God about what was good for the people of Israel. God was grieved over Saul's sin.

Jesus was grieved at the end of His life, when looking out over Jerusalem. He knew the destruction that was coming. With compassion Jesus said, "*If you, even you, had only known on this day what would bring you peace,*" Luke 19:42b. The cold, unbelieving hearts of the people grieved God for not truly worshiping Him.

We bring joy to God when we listen to Him! God said, "*If My people would but listen to Me, if Israel would follow My ways, how quickly I would subdue their enemies and turn My hand against their foes!*" Psalm 81:13-14.

Prayer: O Lord forgive us for grieving You with our stubborn sins. May we love You more than sinning, for our sin grieves You. Strengthen us and bless us Lord. In Jesus' name we pray. Amen.

Psalm 78:52-53a AMP

"But (God) led His own people forth like sheep, and guided them (with a shepherd's care) like a flock in the wilderness. And He led them on safely and in confident trust, so that they feared not."

"But God"

The Bible shows us people who are in very serious situations. Then we often read two words, *"But God."* What follows next is a miraculous way God mercifully rescued them. Joseph was 14 years a slave and in prison. In Genesis 50:20, Joseph said to his brothers, the ones who put him there, *"You intended to harm me, but God intended it for good to accomplish what is now being done the saving of many lives."*

Four days ago, my older brother Ron passed away. The funeral was yesterday. There were many, *"but God"* events in his life. He was wounded so bad in Vietnam that he would have died within 5 minutes. *"But God,"* arranged for a medivac helicopter to be on the scene, one hour from the nearest base. Six months later my parents were on vacation and the state police found them and said that Ron was critical and that they should come to Fort Knox immediately. They drove all night. *"But God,"* again spared his life. Before being released from the hospital the doctor told Ron he would surely not be able to have children because of his extensive injuries. *"But God"* gave him and his wife three children and now many grandchildren. And there were other *"but God"* events.

How about us? How many *"but God"* events are there in our own lives? Do we recognize them? Do we praise God for them when we experience them? Are these *"but God"* events shaping us to become more humble, more faithful and more devoted to God? Our text verse is written for us today! *"But (God) led His own people forth like sheep, and guided them (with a shepherd's care) like a flock in the wilderness. And He led them on safely and in confident trust, so that they feared not."* Our God gives us grace upon grace until He brings us to Heaven with more eternal grace.

Prayer: Caring Lord, it is so wonderful that You as our Shepherd lead us *"safely and in confident trust,"* so that we need not fear. Lord, it is You alone that makes us lie down in green pastures. We praise You! In Jesus' name we pray. Amen.

Psalm 79:11

"May the groans of the prisoners come before You; by the strength of Your arm preserve those condemned to die."

"The groans of the prisoners come before You"

When I teach in jail I often remind them that It is not how you begin in life that matters most, it is how you end. Many prisoners are coming to Christ. God hears the groans of the prisoners and He loves to hear them. *"The LORD looked down from His sanctuary on high, from Heaven He viewed the Earth, to hear the groans of the prisoners and release those condemned to death,"* Psalm 102:19-20. God not only loves those in prison, he wants us to love them too. In Hebrews 13:3, God tells us to, *"Remember those in prison, as if you were their fellow prisoners, and those who are mistreated as if you yourselves were suffering."*

Many prisoners are very lonely. There are also prisoners in their own homes, so very lonely and rejected. One such prisoner wrote: "All my life I wanted to belong. Belong to my parents. Belong to my husband. Belong to my children. In the middle of my pain and depression God came to me. I heard a still small voice that said, 'You belong to Me.' The voice was gentle and sweet. God was telling me that I didn't belong to anyone on earth. I belonged to Him." The groans of that prisoner came to God, and He released that prisoner!

God is glorified when He pardons prisoners of all kinds and then restores them. Only God can forgive and restore. God saves weak people, the blind, the lepers and the crippled, us. That is our spiritual condition as prisoners to sin. We were all refugees at one time, lost, struggling, hopeless. Then God became our refuge and strength.

In Isaiah 58:6, some were fasting and praying but God was not listening. Why? They were fighting each other. God told them and us today, *"Is not this the kind of fasting I have chosen: to loose the chains of injustice and untie the cords of the yoke, to set the oppressed free?"* God wants His people to reach out to others who are not yet set free. That is the work of evangelism and discipleship that we do with God and for God. Praise God for His compassion and commission.

Prayer: Merciful Lord, forgive our lack of compassion for prisoners. You hear their groans and send us to comfort them and direct them to You. Lord strengthen the prisoner. In Jesus' name we pray. Amen.

Psalm 80:19

"Restore us, O LORD God Almighty; make Your face shine upon us, that we may be saved."

"Restore us, O LORD God Almighty"

Our greatest need in life is to be restored! But, restored to what? We have to go back to our first father Adam, to figure it out. Adam was created perfectly. *"God created man in His own image, in the image of God He created him; male and female He created them,"* Genesis 1:27. God the Father is a Spirit only, with no body. Adam was given God's perfect spirit or soul that was without sin. God in all of His holiness could walk with Adam in the garden because Adam was also perfectly holy.

Something happened in the Garden of Eden that changed the course of history all the way down to us. Adam was created with a free will, then chose to do something evil. In Genesis 2:17, Adam was told not to eat from a certain tree. If he did, he would lose his holiness and die. We know that he ate. Adam now needed to be restored. God did that in Genesis 3:21. God shed the blood of an innocent animal to cover Adam's sin, restoring him into full fellowship with God. Why blood? Why would God shed the blood of an innocent animal?

God clearly said, *"For the life of a creature is in the blood, and I have given it to you to make atonement for yourselves on the altar; it is the blood that makes atonement for one's life,"* Leviticus 17:11. In the whole Old Testament period, God accepted the innocent blood of an animal, to pay for our guilty polluted blood. After 4000 years, God sent His Son to do what Adam did not do, live a perfect life. Now His blood purifies us, restoring us to God.

We are yet today, all born children of Adam, all not righteous, all not restored. Our stubborn will pushes God away as we try to live life on our own, without Him. When we fight God, we are unwilling to be surrendered to Him and His restoring love. So God allows us to sink in our sin until His Spirit makes us realize that we can't live without Him! It is then that the prayer in our text pleads with God to restore us.

Prayer: Loving Lord, we can see already in Genesis that it is not Your purpose to punish sin, but instead it is to cure it, restoring us to Yourself. So, *"Restore us, O LORD God Almighty; make Your face shine upon us, that we may be saved."* In Christ's perfect name we pray. Amen.

Psalm 81:13-14

"'If My people would but listen to Me, if Israel would follow My ways, how quickly would I subdue their enemies and turn My hand against their foes!"

If only we would listen to God

What do I really want in this life? Is it to love God and listen to what He commands? Is it to listen to God no matter what the cost? Or, is it still my main desire to be selfish? The thoughts of martyred missionary Jim Elliot comes to mind. He spoke of a life changing truth concerning the giving of himself completely to the service and worship of God. He said, "<u>He is no fool who gives what he cannot keep, to gain what he cannot lose.</u>" Like Christ, he was willing to give up the things of this world for the eternal things of the world which is to come.

Why do we not really *"listen"* to God? Our ears are more tuned to what the world wants. We want more of this world than we do of God. How foolish to think that this world has the answers to life and will bless us for listening to them.

In Psalm 81, God recounts how and when He blessed His people Israel. Christians are still God's *"people."* God is our Father and He is still the King of kings and the Lord of lords. If we will but listen to God and follow His perfect advice, notice what God will do for us! He will quickly subdue our enemies and turn His hand against our foes.

Our lives are filled with struggles. God says to Israel and to us, *"In your distress you called and I rescued you,"* Psalm 81:7a. *"Open wide your mouth and I will fill it,"* 10b. Then, in our text verse, we have a responsibility that is ours. We need to *"listen"* to God, not to a world that is calling us away from God. Our obedience to God guarantees His blessings and protection! And God always keeps His promises!

God has not changed over the years. *"Jesus Christ is the same yesterday and today and forever,"* Hebrews 13:8. If this were not true, our faith in Him would be in vain. May we then, *"listen"* to our forever, unchanging, holy God.

Prayer: O most holy God, we have been so distracted by the world. We have not listened to Your Word or to Your Spirit. Lord, how true it is, we need more of You, not more of this world. Strengthen us to serve you completely. In Jesus' name we pray. Amen.

Psalm 82:3-4

"Defend the cause of the weak and fatherless; maintain the rights of the poor and oppressed. Rescue the weak and needy; deliver them from the hand of the wicked."

"Rescue the weak and needy"

God loves justice and therefore He hates injustice. His anger is shown against evil and it rests on evildoers now, and for all eternity. Our God is by nature, gracious and compassionate. He sees the cause of the weak and fatherless. He is concerned about their needs, telling us to *"rescue the weak and needy."* "Defend," *"rescue"* and *"deliver"* are His sincere commands! Our God sees and cares about social injustice. What are we doing to obey God in this?

Conviction and the courage to act is all about faith. David had courage when he fought the giant. Caleb had courage when at 80 years old, he still fought. Paul had courage to speak the truth about the gospel. Jesus courageously obeyed God to the point of death on a cross. Is our courage noticeable? Are we willing to speak up and do something when it is risky? We have injustice in our world. We know the character of God. Will we seize the opportunity to be faithful and make a difference? It was Edmond Burke who wisely said, "All that is necessary for the triumph of evil is for good men to do nothing."

The question is not what can this or that organization do but what can you and I do personally? For the past four years now, I have been going into the prisons to teach. Honestly, there are thousands there who want to change how they have been an abuser in various ways. They are sinfully sick and need a changed heart to live a different lifestyle. They are convicted of that. It is no longer surprising to me that in prison, names like Moses, David, Joel, Matthew and Mark are common. These are the wayward children and grandchildren of many believers. They are now convicted and ready to change. The harvest is plentiful but the laborers are few. Who will go and be the mouthpiece of God? Who will help *"rescue the weak and needy"*? There are many ways to get involved.

Prayer: Compassionate Lord, move us where You want us to confront wickedness. Give us the wisdom, strength, courage and desire to act. In Jesus' name we pray. Amen.

Psalm 83:1- 4

"O God, do not keep silent; be not quiet, O God, be not still. See how Your enemies are astir, how Your foes rear their heads. With cunning they conspire against Your people; they plot against those You cherish. 'Come,' they say, 'let us destroy them as a nation, let the name of Israel be remembered no more.'"

Israel's enemies are God's enemies

All of Psalm 83 is a song and a powerful prayer to God for His protection of Israel as a nation. Both history and the Bible testify to the fact that God loves Israel and has sworn to protect it. God very specifically promised Abram His divine protection and favor. Note the strong determination of God when He repeats "I will" seven times, His number of perfection, His perfect will. *"I will make you into a great nation and I will bless you; I will make your name great, and you will be a blessing. I will bless those who bless you, and whoever curses you I will curse; and all the peoples of the earth will be blessed through you,"* Genesis 12:2-3.

Soon after Abraham, Egypt was the greatest nation on earth. They opposed Israel, Abraham's children, and the Egyptian empire collapsed. In modern times, Britain became the main shelter for the Jewish people. Britain flourished all over the world. Yet when they turned their back on Abraham's children, they quickly weakened. Around 1900 America became a place where the Jewish people were safe. America became a most blessed nation. Will they too turn their backs on Abraham's children? If they do, their fall will be great, never to return to prominence on the world stage.

History is indeed His story. The Bible is clear. It is the sovereign will of God to protect his chosen people. It is wise to bless Abraham's children, for God notices and blesses accordingly. If God will move empires for Abraham's children, we must take notice. Israel's enemies are God's enemies. The psalm prays, *"See how Your enemies are astir, how Your foes rear their heads."* Be assured, God sees.

Prayer: O Lord, You are sovereign. Your will is done in Heaven and on Earth. In Psalm 2, You warn kings and rulers to be wise and not to stand against You. Lord, You alone are God and we are not. We can only accept Your will and worship You. In Jesus' name we pray. Amen.

Psalm 84:11

"For the LORD God is a sun and shield; the LORD bestows favor and honor; no good thing does He withhold from those whose walk is blameless."

Thinking and doing God's thoughts brings *"honor"*

To *"walk blameless"* we need to think God's thoughts after Him. Our mind matters! What we think in our mind, we become in life. It is the attitude of our minds, not our DNA or biological heritage, that will determine much about our quality of life. Marcus Aurelius said, "Our life is what our thoughts make it."

God made us in His image to love what He loves. God made our brains with the ability to make us healthy and happy. When Moses was about to leave the earth, God had him tell the Israelites, there are blessings for obedience and curses for disobedience. Our text again testifies about God's promised blessings for obedience. We must compare our text to what Moses said on his deathbed.

"What I am commanding you today is not too difficult for you or beyond your reach. It is not up in Heaven, so that you have to ask, "who will ascend into Heaven to get it and proclaim it to us that we may obey it?" No, the word is very near you; it is in your mouth and in your heart so that you may obey it. See, I set before you today life and prosperity, death and destruction. For I command you today to love the LORD your God, to walk in His ways, and to keep His commands, decrees and laws; then you will live and increase, and the LORD your God will bless you in the land you are entering to possesses," Deuteronomy 30:11-16.

God gave us the Bible to think Biblically, which comes before acting Biblically. God also gives us the power to choose wisely! Moses was clear in his farewell address: *"This day I call Heaven and Earth as witnesses against you that I have set before you life and death, blessings and curses. Now <u>choose life,</u> so that you and your children may live and that you may love the LORD your God, <u>listen to His voice</u>, and <u>hold fast to Him</u>. For the LORD is your life, and He will give you many years in the land,"* Deuteronomy 30:19-20. The mouth of God has spoken and His Word endures forever.

Prayer: Dear Lord, we praise You for giving us Your wise thoughts, so we may think Your thoughts after You. In Jesus' name we pray. Amen.

Psalm 85:10 NASV

"Lovingkindness and truth have met together; righteousness and peace have kissed each other."

Grace and truth, the balance we need

Our God in Trinity has such wonderful attributes, which are His character points. We need many of them to remake our personalities. God's character can be summarized in two great attributes, grace and truth. God reaches out to us in "grace," giving us what we need, not what we deserve. God also gives us *"truth,"* His Ten Commandments, which is His perfect law to guides us.

If God gave us His law without grace, everyone would go to Hell. If God gave grace without law, all would go to Heaven. John said of Jesus' perfect personality: *"The Word became flesh and made His dwelling among us. We have seen His glory, the glory of the One and Only, who came from the Father, full of grace and truth,"* John 1:14.

Our churches and homes need grace and truth! We commonly error one way or the other. There are those who are all truth. They love to study the Word but are unbending in their strict ways. There is no grace in them. No one is good enough. They find fault with many. If their kids make a mistake, they lower the boom and growl like a dog! They know little about crying with a sinner, looking for tears of repentance. They are so quick to judge and slow to forgive!

Then we have Mr. and Mrs. Friendly in the church. Anything that you want to do is no problem! Any moral issue to them is too legalistic. Bible Study is not that important. Just get along with everyone and any lifestyle is just fine. Why repent of anything, God loves you just the way you are. They are weak on truth but accepting of others.

There are so many problems in marriage, in parenting and even in the church, that have their roots in a poor balance between grace and truth. We need to be more like Jesus. He was *"lovingkindness and truth"* in one person. Sinners were comfortable with Him, even when He told them to sin no more.

Prayer: O perfect Lord, the song is so correct: "More like the Master we would ever be, more of His meekness, deep humility. More zeal to labor, more courage to be true." That is our prayer, Lord. In Jesus' name we pray. Amen.

Psalm 86:1-2

"Hear, O LORD, and answer me; for I am poor and needy. Guard my life, for I am devoted to You. You are my God; save your servant who trusts in You."

A needy believer petitions a merciful God

When we are in great turmoil, this psalm shines as a Spirit-inspired lesson in prayer. In this psalm, we can see David's humble <u>position</u> in prayer. We also see David's <u>pressing petition</u>, God's <u>practical provision</u> and God's <u>positive protection</u>, four P's.

A humble position in prayer. *"I am poor and needy."* We weak sinners need serious trials to highlight the poverty of our own resources to survive. We need God. A poor and needy child extends an empty hand to God in prayer. How God loves to fill our hand and lift up our person. After all, a main purpose of our trials, is for us to see how dependent we are on God.

Praying a pressing petition. David pleads, *"Guard my life."* He passionately presses God to answer him speedily. When we are being pursued by God's enemies and ours, we need His divine defense. By defending us, God's mercy is clearly being shown, just as God defended David from his "giant problem."

Praying for God's practical provision. Before this, David prayed for his physical protection. Now, David prays for his spiritual protection. He prays, *"restore to me the joy of Your salvation."* God through His Spirit gives joy, peace and contentment.

Praying for God's positive protection. Appeal to the justice of God. When God's sure mercy meets the injustice of *"ruthless men,"* God's mercy wins! David prays, *"the arrogant are attacking me, O God; a band of ruthless men seeks my life — men without regard for You."*

Truly, those who are against us have no fear of God in them. Right and wrong matter little to them. The evil they want to do drives them, which is why they are so "ruthless." Our great God protects us!

Prayer: Merciful Lord, how this prayer psalm fits us perfectly. We are weak in ourselves. Without Your divine mercy, we are in great trouble. Lord provide for us to shine for You. Protect us, O Lord, for we are Your dependent children. In Jesus' name we pray. Amen.

Psalm 86:16-17

"Turn to me and have mercy on me; grant Your strength to Your servant and save the son of Your maidservant. Give me a sign of Your goodness, that my enemies may see it and be put to shame, for You, O LORD, have helped me and comforted me."

When God's mercy and goodness meet

Great things happen in a believer's life when God's mercy and goodness meet. In fact, miracles may even happen! David here prays for God's strength again, remembering how he was strengthened to fight the bear, the lion and Goliath. David concentrates on the size of his God, not on the size of his problem. David prays for God's mercy and goodness.

Here is an important question! Did David earn God's mercy and deserve it? No! *"Who has ever given to God, that God should repay him?"* Romans 11:35. Yet in Psalm 18:20 David said, *"The LORD has dealt with me according to my righteousness, according to the cleanness of my hands He has rewarded me."* Are these verses teaching opposite doctrine? No. God's mercy ties them together. Jesus said in Matthew 5:7, *"Blessed are the merciful for they will be shown mercy."* We do not earn God's favor but He is more merciful to those who show mercy to others. Mercy is always <u>unmerited favor,</u> so David prays for mercy.

Look back at God's past mercies, to be confident of His future promises for more. God did promise that His mercy always will come, *"in our time of need,"* Hebrews 4:16. Charles Spurgeon said, "I should find it difficult to discover a season in which I have cried unto God and not received deliverance during the whole run and tenor of my life. In hundreds of instances I have had as distinct answers to prayer as if God had thrust His right hand through the blue sky and given right into my lap the bounty which I had sought from Him."

Prayer: O Lord, for the sake of Your holy name, give us Your mercy and goodness! Rescue us for the benefit of Your kingdom. You deserve that honor and praise. *"Give me a sign of Your goodness, that my enemies may see it and be put to shame."* May my enemies see that You are God and turn to You, that they too may believe. In Jesus' name we pray. Amen.

Psalm 87:1 & 6

"He has set His foundation on the holy mountain." "The LORD will write in the register of the peoples: 'This one was born in Zion.'"

Is our spiritual house Rock solid?

The meaning and importance of Mt. Zion in the Bible is important. Mount Zion itself, is mount Moriah. There, Abraham put his son on the altar. There, God provided a ram for the sacrifice. That ram in the Old Testament is looking forward to Christ in the new.

The church of God has a foundation built on rock and that Rock is Christ. The church has one foundation. Mountains are made of rock that cannot be moved. God's covenant promises in Christ are that rock solid. It cannot be moved or removed, so sure is our salvation. Compare our salvation that is built on a Rock to Psalm 24:2. The earth or earthly things in general are founded upon the sand, which has a moving and unstable foundation.

God's mountain is *"holy."* God's holiness is the stability and strength of the church. When God makes us holy through Jesus Christ, we will not sink. As the song says, a house built on a rock will stand firm.

The Jews are not the only ones who are God's people. God's promise to Abraham on Mount Zion was to all nations. Verse four of this psalm reads, *"I will record Rahab and Babylon among those who acknowledge Me; Philistia too, and Tyre, along with Cush and will say, 'This one was born in Zion.'"*

Gentiles and Jews make up God's holy family. Paul said to the new Gentile Ephesian church, *"You are no longer foreigners and aliens, but fellow citizens with God's people and members of God's household, built on the foundation of the apostles and prophets, with Christ Jesus Himself as the chief cornerstone,"* Ephesians 2:19-20.

"The LORD will write in the register of the peoples: 'This one was born in Zion,'" Psalm 87:6. If our name is in God's *"register,"* which is permanent, we are most blessed. Only those who have Christ in their heart and live for Him, are members of the Zion community.

Prayer: O Sovereign Lord, how privileged we are that our salvation is rock solid built on the Rock, Jesus Christ. Your Son is our Savior. You are our Father. The Holy Spirit is our Guide and Friend. We are blessed. Accept our praise. In Jesus' name we pray. Amen.

Psalm 88:10-12

"Do You show Your wonders to the dead? Do those who are dead rise up and praise You? Is Your love declared from the grave, Your faithfulness in destruction? Are Your wonders known in the place of darkness or Your righteous deeds in the land of oblivion?

The misery of a severe trial

The writer is in despair. Loved ones have been taken away from him. The psalm begins and ends with crying out to God for relief. Nowhere in the psalm is there any indication that his grief is yet over. Have we felt this kind of sadness and pain? Do we yet know the loneliness of separation from loved ones? There are those in our life who are now feeling the pain the psalmist is in. Will we reach out to them and give them even a ray of hope? What verse could we comfort them with?

We know that it is a blessing for us to go through these hard times, but it is so painful when we are in them. Here the psalmist cried out to God who is his help and shield. Often, God sends formerly broken people to reach out to those who are in tough times. Redeemed Christians with renewed hope, are also God's arms of comfort. "We can *comfort those in any trouble with the comfort we ourselves have received from God*," 2 Corinthians 1:4b. In recounting our trials, we must point to Jesus the Prince of Peace, not to ourselves.

Most often we must walk through the fire before we believe that God is good and can be trusted. Our divine given experiences have a way of moving head knowledge into our heart.

Peter was without hope often. He could later say, *"In this you greatly rejoice, though <u>now for a little while</u> you may have had to suffer grief in all kinds of trials. These have come so that your faith, of greater worth than gold, which perishes even though refined by fire-may be proved genuine and may result in praise, glory and honor when Jesus Christ is revealed,"* 1 Peter 1:6-7.

Our growing up as Christian's is sped up, *"in all kinds of trials."* It is through pain that God gives us a loving burden to help others in similar circumstances.

Prayer: Dear merciful Lord, we thank you for what You teach us in our trials. You are a merciful God. In Jesus' name we pray. Amen.

Psalm 89:1-2

"I will sing of the LORD's great love <u>forever;</u> with my mouth I will make Your faithfulness known <u>through all generations</u>. I will declare that Your love stands firm forever, that You established Your faithfulness in Heaven itself."

A life-long commitment to evangelism

The commitment to the work of evangelism in this psalm must be our passion. Sad to say, too often we are not very passionate in the work of evangelism. There are at least four reasons we are so indifferent to the Word of God going out to others.

We are lukewarm in our relationship to God! If passion for God is missing, why would we care if others know Him? In Acts 17:26-28 we are told to *"seek Him," "reach out for Him"* and to *"find Him."*

We do not love the lost! When Zacchaeus was saved by Jesus he immediately wanted other sinners to know what he now knew: that his sins were forgiven! He cared that his friends knew how they could be pardoned from their present and eternal death sentence. Why would we go to the lost if we do not love them?

We do not weep over the lost! When Jesus was approaching the city of Jerusalem, *"He wept over it and said, 'If you, even you, had only known on this day what would bring you peace,'"* Luke 19:41-42. Jesus had a passion for lost souls who were in the church and in the world. Do we weep over those in the church who just don't get it? These are our covenant brothers and sisters! There are lost people inside the church, sitting in pews who need evangelism. Also, we have a world that is spiritually dead. Do we have godly pity for them?

We do not seek the lost! *"The Son of Man came to seek and to save what was lost,"* Luke 19:10. If we do not love sinners nor weep over them, why would we reach out to them? Lost sinners are lost! They will not just suddenly go to church. The church has to go to them and seek them out. A hunter must go to the woods. A fisherman must go out on the lake. An evangelist must go into all the world! Are we too comfortable to do the difficult work of evangelism?

Prayer: Dear Lord, You left beautiful Heaven for wicked earth. It was Your love for Your Father's will and Your love for lost sinners that compelled You to come. We worship You. In Your name we pray. Amen.

Psalm 89:14

"Righteousness and justice are the foundation of Your throne;
love and faithfulness go before You."

The justice of God is our salvation

God's justice is His perfect and holy wrath against sin and sinners. We are naturally afraid of the justice of God. We know that God hates sin and punishes it both in this life and in the next. But did we ever consider that the justice of God can also be our friend?

If we lived in the Old Testament, the innocent blood of animals was shed to cover our sin. This sacrificial process satisfied the justice of God. In the same way, God told the Israelites to put blood on the door post and He would pass over that house. God's justice against sin was satisfied, because the sin was paid for by that innocent blood.

All the sacrifices of the Old Testament pointed to Jesus' coming. His sinless life totally replaced the animal sacrifices. Now, Jesus Himself satisfies the justice of God for us. It was when Jesus cried out on that cross, *"it is finished,"* that His perfect life fully satisfied the holy justice of God against our sin. In fact, when we become a Christian our Holy God forgives all our sin, past, present and future.

"Righteousness and justice are the foundation of Your throne." Yes, we are fully righteous as Christians, all because God's justice is fully satisfied for us personally. With God's justice satisfied, we are now just as righteous as Christ Himself. We are just and holy, as forgiven Abraham, David, Esther, Elijah, and the former prostitutes Rahab and Mary Magdalene.

"Love and faithfulness go before You." It is God's love for us that justifies us now. It is God's faithfulness that guarantees we are justified forever! We thank God for His beautiful justification, for covering our sin by the blood of Christ.

Prayer: Beautiful and loving Lord, how privileged we are in Christ! *"We are more than conquerors through Him who loved us. For I am convinced that neither death nor life, neither angels nor demons, neither the present nor the future, nor any powers, neither height nor depth, nor anything else in all creation, will be able to separate us from the love of God that is in Christ Jesus our Lord."* Lord, accept our praise and prayer of thanks in Jesus' name. Amen.

Psalm 90:10-12

"The length of our days is seventy years — or eighty, if we have the strength; yet their span is but trouble and sorrow, for they quickly pass, and we fly away. Who knows the power of Your anger? For Your wrath is as great as the fear that is due You. Teach us to number our days aright, that we may gain a heart of wisdom."

"Teach us to number our days"

The 90th Psalm is perhaps the only one written by Moses and is the oldest psalm of all. David wrote 75 psalms, Asaph 12, The sons of Korah 10, Solomon 1, Heman 1, Ethan 1, with 50 being anonymous.

This Moses' psalm is likely the last thing Moses wrote. It is his hope and prayer for the children of Israel. <u>Moses knew that his life is ending and he sees many who do not yet understand the journey they are on</u>! The people think they are on the way to Canaan, without seeing clearly in the present. They are complaining instead of praising God.

To better understand Moses' dying concern, think of how Jesus taught His disciples. He had them go out on the sea to a distant place. Then, in the middle of the sea, in the middle of the night, they were struggling as *"the wind was against them,"* Mark 6:48b. Then, when the disciples gave in to despair, Jesus comes walking on the water! At first they thought it was a ghost and were very afraid. But then Jesus said, *"Take courage! It is I. Don't be afraid."*

What was the purpose of the disciples' journey? Surely, it was the destination that was the goal of the disciples! Yet to Jesus, it was the learning process in getting to the destination that was His goal. And this is exactly what we, too, must learn. This is what Moses is speaking of here. His prayer to God is, *"Teach us to number our days."* Our days are so few, thus may we use them for the honor and glory of God.

May we not get so wrapped up in some big event four years from now, like a college degree, or getting married next year, or even a new car in six months. It is not what we will get or do in the future that matters, but how we prepare for it. Today may we number our days, and be faithful.

Prayer: Dear Lord help us to learn from Moses' excellent words! May we not miss the journey, life itself. Lord, teach us to number our days. In Jesus' name we pray. Amen.

Psalm 91:2-4a

"I will say of the LORD, 'He is my refuge and my fortress, my God in whom I trust.' Surely He will save you from the fowler's snare and from the deadly pestilence. He will cover you with His feathers, and under His wings you will find refuge."

My God, *"is my refuge and my fortress"*

It is possible that either Moses or David wrote this psalm. This Psalm is a personal testimony of how the Lord was the psalmist's personal *"refuge."* The psalmist saw first-hand how the Lord was his *"fortress,"* his hiding place, his defense against all his enemies. Here he praises God's almighty attributes that fully protect him. In James 5:17a we read that *"Elijah was a man just like us,"* as are all Bible characters. We too are sinners, <u>saved by grace</u>, then <u>protected by God</u>.

Now this gets very personal for us as the psalmist directly applies this to our own faith and life! *"Surely He will save you from the fowler's snare and from the deadly pestilence."* He is saying: God did this for me and He will also do this for *"you."*

"Surely he who dwells in the shelter of the Most High will rest in the shadow of the Almighty," Psalm 91:1. The very first verse of the Psalm identifies those who have God's extra protection. It is for those who are close to God, those who are intimate believers! The word *"feathers,"* compares God's protection to a mother hen. A hen can only protect the chicks that are close to her. The wandering chick can be quickly snatched by a hawk. Her wings of protection were spread but the chick that wanted to do "life" on its own, was not safe!

The question for us then is, what kind of faith do we have? How serious are we in our relationship with God? Is God really the love and passion of our life or do we basically give God lip service, not heart service? We run to God for protection in difficult times. But where are we in the "good times," when there are few trials and little persecution? If we are content to be away from God, then we are that wandering chick! May God move us to Himself, to His protection.

Prayer: O gracious Lord, what an encouragement and blessing You are. But we also see a warning to stay close to You. Lord, we need and desire that! Fill us with Your Spirit. In Jesus' name we pray. Amen.

Psalm 91:4b

"His faithfulness will be your shield and rampart."

God's faithfulness, our *"shield"*

The faithfulness of God is beyond amazing. His divine loyalty protects a believer. Our God is so totally committed to those He loves. *"Those He called He also justified; those He justified He also glorified,"* Romans 8:30b. God takes every believer to Heaven! How can He do it? By being faithfully committed to them! His faithfulness is far greater than we can see or ever understand. God faithfully keeps His covenant promises. Can God fail? No! Can His Word fail? No! The faithfulness of God is solemnly promised here in our text. The Scriptures give many examples of God's faithfulness.

God's *"faithfulness"* is our *"shield."* These are military terms. A shield blocks the thrust attempt of a sword or the flight an arrow. The forces of evil are against us as believers. But God so protects us that He even holds the shield!

God's *"faithfulness"* is our *"rampart."* A rampart is that stone wall of protection on the top of a fort or castle. God puts a strong wall of protection around every believer. On top of that, God even assigns His protecting angels to guard us. What a great God we have! It is not so much that our faith protects us, but that God's guaranteed faithfulness to us does!

A favorite verse on God's faithfulness that builds our hope in the trials of life is: *"God is faithful; He will not let you be tempted beyond what you can bear. But when you are tempted, He will also provide a way out so that you can stand up under it,"* 1 Corinthians 10:13b. This is so personal. Because of God's faithful protection, every temptation of Satan is limited to what we can bear. The trials/temptations will only serve to strengthen our faith as we see first-hand, the faithfulness of God's guaranteed protection package. We can only conclude then with Paul, *"If God is for us, who can be against us?"*

Prayer: Faithful Lord, it is a crying shame that we as believers lose hope and doubt Your complete faithfulness in the trials of life. Forgive our weak faith! We praise You for Your eternal faithfulness! In Jesus' name we pray. Amen.

Psalm 91:5 & 11 NKJV

"You shall not be afraid of the terror by night, nor of the arrow that flies by day." "For He shall give His angels charge over you, to keep you in all your ways."

We have God's guardian angels!

The disciple John wrote, *"Perfect love casts out fear."* That precious truth summarizes these beautiful verses. The amazing love of God was already very real as the Old Testament began. Adam and Eve were afraid for the first time, right after they sinned in the Garden. Their fear was removed by the love of God, when He covered their sin in Genesis 3:21. God's perfect love restored them to fellowship. Our closeness to God removes our fears.

Through many trials, God will teach us that it is not an enemy, a lack of money, poor health or the death of a loved one that <u>causes</u> us to fear. These are merely <u>temptations</u> to fear. The <u>cause</u> is in us, even in our hearts. God's perfect love removes our fear. Most often, we need to walk through the fire before we believe that God can be trusted.

We will *"not be afraid of the terror by night."* The night is like daylight to God. If He is for us, who can possibly be against us? God promised that He will not allow any trial to be more than we can bear. So great is His concern for us as His children.

Again, God promises us extreme protection. We are given a clear example of how God lovingly shields us when we are afraid. *"He shall give His angels charge over you, to keep you in all your ways."* God has protecting angels, ordained and charged by Him to protect us! We do not have a guardian angel, but we have, by the Word of God, guardian *"angels."* God's angels watch over us, *"charged"* to keep us <u>in *"all"*</u> of our ways. They have a great ability to protect us, along with a great affection in their devotion to us. Beyond that, we know that the Holy Spirit also walks beside us as our helper and shield. But there is even more! Jesus is our advocate in Heaven. He is the best lawyer ever, who never sleeps and is always on the job, for His Own.

Prayer: O Lord, we can only say, "You are an awesome God." Forgive us for our fear and worry, which is a lack of trust in You! May we stay close to You who cares so much for us! In Jesus' name we pray. Amen.

Psalm 91:14-16 NKJV

"Because he has set his love upon Me, therefore I will deliver him; I will set him on high because he has known My name. He shall call upon Me and I will answer him; I will be with him in trouble; I will deliver him and honor him. With long life I will satisfy him, and show him My salvation."

Seven "I will" promises of God!

The he and the him in this psalm is a believer who loves God. In this psalm we have already seen man's responsibility to love God. We have also seen the sovereignty of God's care for His elect children. Both of these points of doctrine are 100% true at the same time. We have seen that those who trust in God have His guaranteed protection and comfort. In these last three verses, we now have seven "I will" promises that God will surely bless us.

"He (that's us) shall call upon Me and I will answer him." We have a responsibility to pour our heart out in prayer to God! There is little or no value in complaining to others, yet there is great value in praying to God. We must plead our case before Him.

"I will be with him in trouble." God does not say I might help you. Our God says, *"I will be with him in trouble."* This does not mean that trouble never will come, but there will be no evil in the trouble, as God works it for our good.

"I will deliver him and honor him." Here again is an absolute truth. God will deliver us. And not just deliver us, but honor us as He did Mordecai when the evil Haman tried to kill him! Our God delivered Daniel in the lion's den; his friends from the furnace; Peter and Paul from prison. He will deliver and honor us also.

"With long life I will satisfy him." God's gives us, His children, a joyful life as He fills, refills and fulfills us. Our spiritual life in Him gives us new power to sustain positive relationships. And the best is yet to come, Heaven itself! *"I will show him My salvation."* Like Job we can say, *"In my flesh I will see God,"* Job 19:26b.

Prayer: Dear Lord, Your love is amazing. Your grace is so sure. Your mercy is always on time. Your power protects us. You preserve our souls through all eternity. We worship You. In Jesus' name we pray. Amen.

Psalm 92:12-15

"The righteous will flourish like a palm tree, they will grow like a cedar of Lebanon; planted in the house of the LORD, they will flourish in the courts of our God. They will still bear fruit in old age, they will stay fresh and green."

Flourishing and bearing fruit in old age

Growing old has "challenges." What will be our response when "old" comes? In this psalm we have a senior Christian flourishing like an old palm tree does in the desert. What is our God teaching us about how to stay healthy and productive, even in our elderly years?

We first read of palm trees after Israel crossed the Red Sea and went into the desert. *"Then they came to Elim, where there were twelve springs and <u>seventy palm trees</u>, and they camped there near the water,"* Exodus 15:27. In Revelation, *"a great multitude that no one could count, from every nation, tribe, people and language, standing before the throne and in front of the Lamb. They were wearing white robes and were holding palm branches in their hands,"* Revelation 7:9b.

Since *"The righteous will flourish like a palm tree."* What do the *"righteous,"* elderly and 70 palm trees have in common? Palm trees grow well in the desert, but it is not the richness of the soil that makes them grow! They are tapped into the living water far below the surface. A vibrant Christian lives in a world that is not rich spiritually. But, they are tapped into the living water, Jesus. He makes them flourish!

A *"flourishing"* Christian is *"planted in the house of the LORD."* Not even one person grows naturally in God's house. All have been transplanted there by the love of God, our Master Gardener. That is where the living water feeds the palm tree believer. But notice where they *"flourish"*? It is, *"in the courts of our God."* That is, the outer courtyard, not in the inner sanctuary. This is he or she who is greatly used by God for evangelism and discipleship *"in the courtyard."* They flourish right where the people of the world gather. Bearing fruit in old age is only possible if we are first *"planted in the house of the LORD,"* willing to be used by God outside the church walls for His kingdom.

Prayer: O Sovereign Lord, make us like a palm tree, filled with Your living water. Make us tall and straight, offering palm branches, Your peace through the Prince of Peace, Jesus Christ. In Him we pray. Amen.

Psalm 93:1-2

"The LORD reigns, He is robed in majesty; the LORD is robed in majesty and is armed with strength. The world is firmly established; it cannot be moved. Your throne was established long ago; You are from all eternity."

"You are from all eternity"

"The LORD reigns" is present tense, meaning today. The world is not out of control. It is in His control. *"He is robed in majesty."* Our God is dressed in King's clothing. He *"is armed."* Our God is not helpless. He has more strength than anyone. The world is 100% *"firmly established,"* going nowhere today or in the future without the will of its Creator! Our God established His throne *"long ago"* in an eternity past. We who live just a few years, can hardly wrap our minds around what it means that God is eternal, but we must try.

It is impossible to go back in history to the very beginning of God's existence. He always existed. That is what eternal means. God is outside of time. He was not created or made like we and the world are. God existed by Himself, independent from anything else. There was no earth, no sun, no moon, no stars and no angels. God eternally existed alone. The Father, Son and Holy Spirit alone existed.

One of God's amazing attributes is that He is self-existent. He is in need of nothing and no one. He does not need us! He surely does not need us to run His world. He does not need us to save His world either. That does not mean that we can abuse God's creation, but that He is in full control of it and always will be.

Because God is *"from all eternity,"* He will continue to be for an eternity in the future. That is such a great comfort to believers and a horrible curse to unbelievers. All of us, everyone, will exist in spirit form forever. After the resurrection, both believers and unbelievers will exist eternally in body and in soul. That means we will be *"for an eternity,"* either in Heaven or in Hell. Jesus said so in John 5:28-29.

Prayer: O Majestic Lord, what a solemn thought, You existed *"from all eternity"* and will exist *"for all eternity."* Every person and every angel will exist for eternity, in one of two places. What urgency we have to seek salvation in Christ today! In His name we pray. Amen.

Psalm 94:3, 5, & 7

"How long will the wicked, O LORD, how long will the wicked be jubilant?" "They crush Your people, O LORD; they oppress Your inheritance." "They say, the LORD does not see; the God of Jacob pays no heed."

The wicked say, *"The LORD does not see"*

David cries out to God, *"How long will the wicked be jubilant?"* These are wicked people in the church, who oppress God's servants and are proud of their oppressive spirit. They try to "crush" God's servants. Yes, there are jealous people in places of power, who try to move out those who humbly serve God and His people. Perhaps they do not realize that they are enemies of the Gospel.

David teaches us here how to respond in a right way to those who hate us. By faith, David knew what Paul later wrote in Romans 12:19, *"Do not take revenge, my friends, but leave room for God's wrath, for it is written: 'It is mine to avenge; I will repay,' says the Lord."* It is our responsibility to overcome evil with good. We need God's help to do that. Pity instead of anger is needed, because God wants to protect our minds from being poisoned. Pity, because God calls us to love our enemies, even as we hate what they are doing. If we do not pity those who do evil, we will be bitterly unproductive, with a spoiled mind.

The wicked act much like an ostrich who puts its head in the sand, concluding nothing can see them. The wicked who say, *"the LORD does not see,"* are blind. Unlike the ostrich, we humans are created in the image of God. We have a soul that was given to us by God. After death, Ecclesiastes 12:7b says that *"the spirit will return to the God who gave it."* We will all be accountable to God for how we lived and God knows exactly how we live each day.

Along with David then, we plead with God to act on our behalf to protect us. Since we belong to God, our Good Shepherd delights to care for us. When we pray and put our hope in God, our faith is exercised. God's attributes are then lifted up, and He is worshiped.

Prayer: O Lord and Father, like David, we are not strong enough to stand up to our enemies. Lord act for us, for Your name's sake. Defend Your name and Your possessions. In Jesus' name we pray. Amen.

Psalm 95:1-2

"Come, let us sing for joy to the LORD; let us shout aloud to the Rock of our salvation. Let us come before Him with thanksgiving and extol Him with music and song."

Called to worship God

Our text is a command and a call to worship God. At the beginning of a worship service, it is good to hear these words calling us to worship God. In the past, the church bell sounded out a call to come and worship God. It is God who is calling us into His presence! In worship, we acknowledge our need of God's help and He assures us of His blessing. In worship, we must see that we are sinners and that God pardons sin when we come to Him. It is our great privilege to worship God as we are literally transported into the throne room of Heaven to be with God. In worship, we realize how small we are and how big God is. In true worship, we are an adoring assembly who understands why we are here on Earth. We must be joyful in worship as well as reverent, as we offer our praises to God!

"Sing for joy to the LORD." Yes, we must sing! The Psalms were written to be sung back to God. When our hearts are full of Christ, we will sing. If God has put a song in our hearts, He wants to hear it! Think of how beautifully the birds sing to God! What do they have to sing about compared to us? We must sing in worship, with all our hearts, for the glory of God!

"Come before Him with thanksgiving." Grumbling is not thankful living or acceptable worship either. God wants us to have an attitude of gratitude. When our outlook on life is one of thanksgiving we will be praying without ceasing! God greatly delights in grateful people! Thanksgiving glorifies and worships God!

"Let us not give up meeting together, as some are in the habit of doing, but let us encourage one another - and all the more as you see the Day approaching," Hebrews 10:25.

Prayer: O great Lord, thank You for inviting us to worship You. May we come with a grateful song in our hearts, and with an attitude of thankfulness to You. For You have done so much for us and promise to do far more! May our worship be acceptable and pleasing to You. In Jesus' name we pray. Amen.

Psalm 95:7b-8a

"Do not harden your hearts."

Called to worship God, not to make excuses

In our text, we have a serious warning. Many in Israel did not see that something was wrong. So many in our churches do not see a problem either. How often we all return to God after a serious trial, only to lose our fervency in our walk with God once again. It is right here that God's warning comes, *"Do not harden your hearts."*

A hard heart in the Bible is an uncaring, selfish heart that wants to do its own thing. A hard heart will not listen to what God wants and to what "others" in our life need. A hard heart seeks its own agenda and its own praise. A hard heart does not really worship God, but instead, self. We know what we should not do, but do not put it off. We concentrate on what we must not do instead of what we must do. We are no longer interested in repentance. Our lack of real worship on the Sabbath, especially shows our hard hearts.

In Isaiah 58, God gives us a strong warning about how the true worship of God was slipping fast. The people of Israel were fasting and praying and yet God told them their hearts were hard, not right with Him. What were they doing wrong?

God tells us all: *"On the day of your fasting, you do as you please,"* Isaiah 58:3b. They would *"exploit"* their workers. Their life was full of *"quarreling and strife."* They were *"striking each other with wicked fists,"* even while they were fasting. They were not sharing food and other blessings with others. Instead they took things from others, even as they fasted. They provided for themselves without providing for others. The worship of God in church was replaced with doing what they wanted. With hard hearts, their love for God grew cold.

This is personal. How is our love for God doing? In Acts 17, we are told that we are all put into this world to seek God, to find God, and to know Him personally. A soft and caring heart seeks after God, and then loves what He loves.

Prayer: Beautiful Savior, King of creation, create in us pure hearts that are in awe of Your greatness. Create in us hearts that want to know You more. In Jesus' name we pray. Amen.

Psalm 96:9

"Worship the LORD in the splendor of His holiness; tremble before Him all the earth."

Worship the holiness of God

We are called here to worship the holiness of God, but what is the best way to do that? Surely, the answer for each of us is to pursue holiness ourselves! Peter emphasized personal holiness. *"As obedient children, do not conform to the evil desires you had when you lived in ignorance. But just as He who called you is holy, so be holy in all you do; for it is written: 'Be holy, because I am holy,'"* 1 Peter 1:14-16. We must be holy and worship the holiness of God because that's the purpose of every human life.

Happiness is not the purpose of life. Good health or material blessings is not our purpose. God's one purpose for every life is holiness! God created man to be holy. *"Without holiness no one will see the Lord."* In fact, all the people God saves, He does so that they might be holy!

Holiness is to be separated unto God, immersed in God and passionate about God. Jerry Bridges wrote in "The Pursuit of Holiness," "to live a holy life, then, is to live a life in conformity to the moral precepts of the Bible and in contrast to the sinful ways of the world."

Live a life characterized by "the putting off of your old self, which is being corrupted by its deceitful desires, and putting on the new self, created to be like God in true righteousness and holiness." Note the emphasis on the put-off and put-on that is explained in Ephesians 4:22-24. That is how we become more holy in our corrupt world.

Another reason to worship the holiness of God is this! *"But you are a chosen people, a royal priesthood, a holy nation, a people belonging to God, that you may declare the praises of Him who called you out of darkness into His wonderful light,"* 1 Peter 2:9. Peter's instruction in this verse reminds me of a great children's song that says, "You are the temple of the living God." Let us then look like a holy temple.

Prayer: Holy and loving Lord, You remind us that we each have a personal responsibility to be holy. We need Your strength to live in such a way. Lord help us, for we are weak but You are strong. In Jesus' name we pray. Amen.

Psalm 96:13b

"He will judge the world in righteousness and the peoples in His truth."

He will judge the peoples *"in His truth"*

From our text we can see that some people think that there are various versions of truth in the world. There really isn't. There is one truth and the rest are all just lies. People have their own opinion about what is true, yet God alone has revealed *"His truth"* to us in the Bible. Jesus Himself is the Way, the Truth and the Life. The world rejects God's truth and lives a lie for a lifetime. Why? So they can live their own selfish way. In The Judgment, their version of truth will be confronted by the holy God whose truth never changes.

We sinners sin because we are sinners. We naturally hate God and therefore we hate the truth of God. We make our own version of truth, to do as we please, not God's revealed will. Problem is, at death, our pattern of living will be in God's courtroom. Most people know that Jesus is the Way, the Truth and the Life. That is why they fight against Him so hard. <u>The atheist who says there is no God, hates God. How can anyone hate a God whom they say does not exist</u>? The truth remains: they selfishly want to live life, as they please, their own way. If they stay unrepentant, their end, has already been determined.

"He will judge the world in righteousness and the peoples in His truth." In one day, at death, there will already be a separation between those who loved God's truth and those who hated it. That is a type of judgment as God sends people to either Heaven or Hell. But at the end of the world there will be one final judgment.

Jesus warns us: *"Do not be amazed at this, for a time is coming when all who are in their graves will hear His voice and come out - those who have done good will rise to live, and those who have done evil will rise to be condemned. By Myself I can do nothing; I judge only as I hear, and My judgment is just,"* John 5:28-30a.

Prayer: Dear righteous Lord, even Pilate asked Jesus, "What is truth?" Pilate said this while looking right at Jesus who is the Way, the Truth, and the Life. O Lord, our world is in turmoil because it rejects Your eternal truth. Strengthen us to know Your truth and to live for it. In Jesus' name we pray. Amen.

Psalm 97:10

"Let those who love the LORD hate evil, for He guards the lives of His faithful ones and delivers them from the hand of the wicked."

"Let those who love the LORD hate evil"

To pursue a holy life, we need to hate evil. We need to hate sin, but love sinners. Jesus hated sin but loved sinners. Jesus separated the sin from the sinner. He loved them, healed them, and then told them to sin no more. What a great example for us!

In the last devotion, we said that the Biblical process by how we change is so little understood and practiced. Biblical change or repentance is when we stop doing what's wrong and replace it with doing what's right. The evil put-off must be done <u>before</u> the righteous put-on can happen. That's why the devil works hard to convince the world that nothing is sin and nothing needs to be put off. The devil laughs when we ignore the need to put off anything and merely try to "put on" a little perfume on the old garbage in our heart. He knows we still stink. Does this concern us personally?

"Those who love the LORD <u>hate evil</u>." Being <u>convicted</u> of evil thoughts, words or actions is required first, to put off any wrong living. In Ephesians 4, God tells us to put off bad words that come out of our mouth <u>before</u> we speak words that are a blessing to others. We must put off stealing <u>before</u> we can get a job and give to others. We must put off all bitterness towards others <u>before</u> we can forgive them. God's process of change is to put off and to put on, for a lifetime. Holiness is important to God, while Satan works to convince us that we are good the way we are.

God, *"guards the lives of His faithful."* Elijah hated the evil practices of the priest on Mount Carmel. God *"guarded"* his life and does so for us also. Those who courageously stand with God are protected by Him. God does more than just guard the faithful, *"He delivers them from the hand of the wicked."* God delivered Elijah from the hand of wicked queen Jezebel who wanted to kill him. This is important for us because, *"Elijah was a man just like us,"* James 5:17a.

Prayer: Lord, we see that You are a holy God and we are called to hate what Your holiness hates. Convict us to love what is good by Your good Holy Spirit. In Jesus' name we pray. Amen.

Psalm 98:9

"Sing before the LORD, for He comes to judge the earth. He will judge the world in righteousness and the peoples with equity."

"Sing," the holy Judge is coming

We have seen the holiness of God in the past two devotions and our personal responsibility to put off evil thoughts, words and actions that are not pleasing to God. Now we are told to, *"sing before the LORD."* We, along with all of creation are given a reason. *"Sing,"* for *"He will judge the world in righteousness and the peoples with equity."* *"Sing"* because, in verse 2a, *"He has made His salvation known."* *"Sing,"* because in 3b, *"all the ends of the earth have seen the salvation of our God."* *"Sing,"* because we do not need to judge anyone except our own heart. *"Sing,"* because God will judge true believers as righteous. Amazing grace how sweet the song that saved a wretch like me.

It is also quite amazing how so many people see our God as a grandfather sitting on a cloud waiting to bless them. God is surely gracious, but He is also a strict judge. He will not bend His law or take a bribe. God offers Jesus to every sinner, on *"the earth."* God gave His Son to stand in our place. However, many sinners mock the only Chosen Sacrifice for their sin. Our eternal problem is that if our sins are not on Christ, then they are on our own head. We must be judged for them for God in His perfect holiness must judge them!

"Sing" because the Righteous Judge, <u>as our friend,</u> is completely for us. God literally fights our bullies for us. He tells us, *"Do not take revenge, my friends, but leave room for God's wrath, for it is written: 'It is mine to avenge; I will repay,' says the Lord,"* Romans 12:19. We must *"Sing."* All we have to do is *"overcome evil with good,"* Romans 12:21b. We only have to be faithful. After that, <u>the results are up to God</u>! Hope you got that last point. We have so many personal problems because we worry about the results after we are faithful. An attitude of faith *"sings"* because God is so completely for us.

Prayer: O righteous Lord we are called to *"sing"* while You do all the judging. Forgive us for when we are judging instead of singing! How we trouble ourselves, over that which is not our responsibility. Lord, put a song, even many songs, in our hearts. In Jesus' name we pray. Amen.

Psalm 99:1

"The LORD reigns, let the nations tremble; He sits enthroned between the cherubim, let the earth shake."

"The LORD reigns, let the nations tremble"

Our eternal Lord lives and *"reigns"* supreme over Heaven and Earth. The Lord our God sits, *"enthroned between the cherubim."* We first see the cherubim after man's fall from holiness in the Garden of Eden. God put the cherubim at the entrance to the Garden to guard it, to stop all from entering it. In Exodus 25, God put the cherubim on the cover of the Ark of the Covenant. These two cherub angels are a sign of God's holiness, guarding and preventing anyone from entering it!

The cherubim's purpose on earth is much like that of Lucifer, Satan's name before he fell from glory in Heaven. In Ezekiel 28:12b-14a, God says about Lucifer, *"This is what the Sovereign LORD says: "You <u>were</u> the model of perfection, full of wisdom and perfect in beauty. You were in Eden, the garden of God;... Your settings and mountings were made of gold...You were anointed as a guardian cherub; for so I ordained you."* While in Heaven, the perfect guardian cherub Lucifer, protected the most holy place. Now fallen to Earth, Satan does the opposite. He works to prevent our holiness.

"Tremble" as we think about how Lucifer was judged when he sinned. *"Tremble"* as we think about how he was cast out of Heaven. *"Tremble"* for there remains no mercy for Satan. *"Tremble,"* because Satan wants to take us to Hell forever. *"Tremble,"* God presently *"sits enthroned between the cherubim."* See the cherubim sitting on that mercy seat of the Ark, with God between them. In the Ark is the perfect Law of God, the Ten Commandments. We must all keep the commandments perfectly to be holy, thus able to go to Heaven. But we can't do it perfectly! The One who will judge us is sitting on the mercy seat, offering us mercy and forgiveness! Will we do as the Psalm 99:5 says? *"Exalt the LORD our God and worship at His footstool; He is holy."* If we humble ourself before God, He will cover our sin.

Prayer: O holy Lord, You sit on the mercy seat offering us Jesus. You are willing to cover our sins with Your perfect Son's blood. Lord, how we need Your mercy! In Jesus' name we pray. Amen.

Psalm 99:5

"Exalt the LORD our God and worship at His footstool; He is holy."

"Worship at His footstool; He is holy"

We have a serious problem! Even as Christians, we still have a great deal of selfishness in our heart. By nature we want to exalt self, not God! We want to worship self, not God, the One who sits glorified in Heaven. We want to tell others what we have done, not what God has done and continues to do. We are so selfish, so in love with self since the day we were born!

Little children are often loud, busy exalting themselves, going on and on. "Watch me, mom!" "Watch me, dad!" Look what I can do! I am quite something! If the children were not so small, such talk would be so irritating to listen to. The sad part is, we all sound like this sometimes. As we get older, we know better to say words like, "watch me," and "look at me," but we do want people to watch us and look at us!

The point of this psalm is: see God! Look at His perfect holiness. Worship His holiness, for that is His incredible beauty. God's holiness is so awesome to behold that Isaiah cried, "Woe *is me I am undone.*" Why would Isaiah tremble so before God? Why did Adam hide from God when he had just one sin. Because God is perfectly holy, completely unlike anything we have ever seen. Just think, God is holy, sitting on a holy throne with a holy scepter in His hand, reaching out to us ugly sinners. Wow!

We worship at God's footstool humbly. We are literally begging for grace at the feet of God, totally undeserving of any part of His holiness. Mary washing Jesus' feet with her tears and wiping them with her hair is a picture of heartfelt worship of the holiness of God. She did this because she was overwhelmed that a holy God would touch her with His scepter of grace and pardon her.

Prayer: Majestic Lord, You are so amazing. Even though You are a holy God, far above us, You are willing to forgive our sins if we will just worship at Your footstool. Amazingly, it is only we who have been forgiven that can cry out in thanksgiving, Holy is the Lord. We worship You, our Lord and Savior. In Jesus' name we pray. Amen.

Psalm 100:1-2

"Shout for joy to the LORD, all the earth. Worship the LORD with gladness; come before Him with joyful songs."

"Worship the LORD with gladness"

What form of worship can be acceptable to God, if it is not given with *"gladness"*? The word *"Worship"* here in the NIV is translated *"Serve"* in the NKJV. The words serve and worship in the original Hebrew carry the same meaning. God commands our service and worship of Him be done with *"joy"* and *"gladness."* We so often fall short of keeping it. What is the problem? Is it God's fault we have so little gladness? Or, is it our fault? Are we secretly thinking that somehow God is not giving us His blessings or goodness in great enough measure?

It is our duty as created beings, to worship and serve God. Can we do our duty well, without *"gladness"*? No, not really, for then there is not sufficient love in our service! What if on a spouse's birthday we say, "Here, I brought you these flowers because it was my duty to do so." Our spouse should say, "Don't bother!" Duty without love has no real appreciation, no gladness in it.

Is our theology of God's grace missing something? Do we have the common problem that so many Christians still have? Are we doing our service and worship to God to try earn His favor? If we are, that is so backwards. Gladness flows from gratefulness. How grateful are we for the amazing grace and mercy of God? Have we really received it? If we have a shortage of gladness, it may be possible we think that God owes us something.

Redeemed Christians are legitimate sons and daughters of the living God, joint heirs with Jesus Christ! Let us then act like sons and daughters of God in worship and not go back to the misery we had before we were changed by God.

Prayer: Dear Heavenly Father, we confess our sin of being such a sad Christian. At times, we are a poor testimony of Your amazing grace. Rip our ungratefulness from us and fill us with the right spirit, Your Spirit. May we love and worship You for what You have done, and for who You are. For You are a God who not only saves but also protects and guides us for life. We worship You with joy and gladness. In Jesus' name we pray. Amen.

Psalm 101:1-4

"I will sing of Your love and justice; to You, O LORD, I will sing praise. I will be careful to lead a blameless life... I will walk in my house with a blameless heart. I will set before my eyes no vile thing... I will have nothing to do with evil."

Living a holy life, Part 1

We have a personal responsibility to strive for holiness as God works in us. Holiness is not simply by faith alone as many claim. If there is no faithfulness or personal responsibility on man's part, then why did the psalmist say, *"I will"* six times already in the first four verses?

Paul wrote to Timothy, *"Train yourself to be godly,"* 1 Timothy 4:7b. The word translated *"train"* is the same word that gymnasium comes from. Athletes must train regularly, daily, day after day. Believers must also discipline themselves to be godly. It will not be easy, but will require sustained effort. There is no such thing as instant holiness! We cannot expect that God will mold and shape us without us disciplining ourselves towards holiness.

God said to Cain, *"If you do what is right, will you not be accepted? But if you do not do what is right, sin is crouching at your door; it desires to have you, but you must master it,"* Genesis 4:7. Jesus said, *"If anyone would come after Me, he must deny himself and take up his cross daily and follow Me,"* Luke 9:23b.

Jerry Bridges gives three reasons why holiness is not sought after.

1. Our attitude toward sin is more self-centered than God-centered. We are more concerned about our own victory over sin than we are about the fact that our sin grieves the heart of God. Our holy God wants us to walk in obedience, not in victory.

2. Our second problem is that we have misunderstood living by faith to mean that no effort at holiness is required on our part.

3. Our third problem is that we do not take sin seriously. It is compromise on the little issues that lead to greater downfalls. Are we willing to agree with God on what is sinful, big or little? We must be serious about all sin if we are to live a life of holiness. God will not be glorified with any other attitude.

Prayer: Most Holy God, may we strive for holiness, for not much else really matters. Help us Lord. In Jesus' name we pray. Amen.

Psalm 101:2a

"I will be careful to lead a blameless life."

Living a holy life, Part 2

Jerry Bridges explains how "the pursuit of holiness," is like a "joint venture" with God, like a partnership. Holiness is not man alone nor is it God alone! The Holy Spirit makes us holy. But as we have seen yesterday, we still have a personal responsibility to pursue holiness. Jerry Bridges shows how holiness is much like how a farmer and God work together to finally harvest a crop in the field.

If a farmer wants a crop, he must first purchase the seed. He must get his machinery "field ready." He must go out into the field to till the soil. He can't just stay in the house and pray! He must break up the clods to make a good seed bed. He must plant the seed, even at the right time! He must eliminate the weeds in the field. He must put on fertilizer. All of these duties are his personal responsibility. God will not purchase the seed for the farmer. God will not till up the field or fix the farmer's equipment. God will not put the seeds in the ground at the right rate for that particular crop. God will not pull the weeds! It would be one very foolish and starving farmer that said it was God's responsibility to do what man must do.

God in His sovereignty makes the sun to shine and the rain to fall. God makes the seed germinate. God is always faithful to do His part and He always will. God, in covenant, made a promise to the farmer right after the worldwide flood. *"As long as the earth endures, seedtime and harvest, cold and heat, summer and winter, day and night will never cease,"* Genesis 8:22. In the end, the farmer cannot do what God must do, and God will not do what the farmer should do. Just like farming, there is a necessary partnership with God in holiness.

Ephesians has six chapters. In the first three, we see the sovereign grace of God calling a believer, giving them a new heart. Then in chapter four to six, we see man's responsibility to walk in holy living. The Spirit gives us joy when we walk God's way, guilt when we don't.

Prayer: Sovereign Lord, thank You for teaching us to be responsible in pursuing holiness. Convict us of this more and more because by nature we pursue other things more! In Jesus' name we pray. Amen.

Psalm 101:3b

"The deeds of faithless men I hate."

What is wrong with quitters?

God wants His people to stand out as being good workers. God is insulted when His people would rather quit and give up in their faithful living. God shows us many faithful workers. Joseph and Daniel are two good examples. Jesus is the perfect example. What then is wrong with lazy people.

A lazy person lacks integrity. A quitter's moral make-up or character is the real problem. A quitter will be quick to lie, cheat, or steal. What we are in our heart will show, for it leads to what we do! A person without integrity has no inner conviction, no moral compass, no desire to do what is right. They will always act according to their selfish interest. So integrity is far more than knowing what is right. A person with integrity, does what's right! *"The integrity of the upright guides them,"* Proverbs 11:3a.

A lazy person is not faithful. A faithful worker is a loyal worker. A faithful worker is a flexible worker, willing to adjust their efforts to the changing needs. A flexible worker is able to meet the needs of those they are responsible to disciple. A faithful worker is humble and very easy to work with. God notices the faithful. *"He guards the lives of His faithful ones,"* Psalm 97:10b.

The lazy have a bad attitude. Whereas, a person with a good attitude is teachable. In life, we will always be required to learn new things. We must be able to be corrected without getting angry or bitter. A good attitude keeps us productive and a team player, especially when times are difficult. A person with a bad attitude is quick to respond poorly when someone does them wrong. The problem is, there is no grace in a person with a bad attitude. A person with a bad attitude is lacking in gratitude. Such a person is destructive. *"An angry man stirs up dissension,"* Proverbs 29:22a.

Prayer: Dear Lord, You know that we live in a corrupt and cheating world. As Your children, we want to stand out as being faithful. May Your name and those we work for be lifted up by how we faithfully do our daily work. In Jesus' name we pray. Amen.

Psalm 102:1-2

"Hear my prayer, O LORD; let my cry for help come to you. Do not hide Your face from me when I am in distress. Turn Your ear to me; when I call, answer me quickly."

In distress again, I cry to God

Why are there so many psalms and other parts of the Bible where we cry out to God? It is because that is so often our distressed condition. In this psalm, we read the words and thoughts of an afflicted man. The writer is hurting and in much pain. He is weak and pours out his heart to God, not to others, who cannot really help him.

Contrast the concerns of the psalmist here, to how we commonly handle our trials and tribulations. Too often we complain the most to others who cannot help! How many men and women go to bars to try drown their sorrows. Does self-pity ever solve a person's problems? Is not our self-pity more in love with self, than looking to the One in Heaven who can help? Does it ever occur to us that God in His wisdom allows us to have problems, so that we will come to the end of our self-sufficiency and turn to Him?

Jesus said, *"Come to Me, all you who are weary and burdened, and I will give you rest,"* Matthew 11:28. He knew we would have burdens, even *"heavy burdens."* Too often we stop here and do not read further. In Matthew 11:29, Jesus continued, *"Take My yoke upon you and learn from Me, for I am gentle and humble in heart, and you will find rest for your souls."* What is Jesus' yoke? It is simply following the commandments of loving God first and others second. Our problem is we must deny our self-first living, to love God and others more. *"Gentle and humble"* living is having our love life in God's perfect order. Then we *"will find rest"* for our souls.

We were not meant to carry a heavy burden. Our Creator God wants us to depend on Him in faith. Will we then, take our concerns to God? Or, will we try carry them and then give in to fear and worry and even depression? Faith begins where fear and worry ends.

Prayer: Dear gracious Lord, we are stubborn and filled with pride. We so often do not look to You to be our help and strength. Our faith is too small. O Lord, help us to see that You are able and willing to carry our burdens. In Jesus' name we pray. Amen.

Psalm 103:1-2

"Praise the LORD, O my soul; all my inmost being, praise His holy name. Praise the LORD, O my soul, and forget not all His benefits."

"Forget not all His benefits"

When a lawyer asked Jesus what was most important in the Bible, *"Jesus replied: 'Love the Lord your God with all your heart and with all your soul and with all your mind,'"* Matthew 22:37. God created us for the purpose of having a love relationship with Him! This is also David's concern in Psalm 103. David's words show us that we need to be consumed with God, to know Him and enjoy Him! If we are not aware of what God has done for us, we cannot love, appreciate, or praise Him as we should. So then, let us meditate on what He has done.

"Forget not all His benefits." Remember in worship what God has done for you personally. Never think that God has only blessed the people in the Bible. He has also blessed you in the very same ways! Think of how He has.

God, *"forgives all your sins."* Nothing in the world is more important than this. Every Christian has every sin forgiven. The guilt of every past sin, every present sin and every future sin is totally gone. You too, are that holy and spotless before God. Through God's Son, every single sin is covered and removed. *"As far as the east is from the west, so far has He removed our transgressions from us,"* Psalm 103:12. We must never forget to praise Him every day for this great deliverance that we did not deserve and could never work for!

God made us His precious children. He is not just our Father, He is our Heavenly Father. With His powerful attributes, He is now and will be, forever for us.

God *"satisfies your desires with good things,"* Psalm 103:5a. Praise God He knows what is *"good"* for us and guides our heart to what is really important. We thank and worship Him for His good and tender care of our body and soul.

Prayer: Dear Heavenly Father, we so quickly forget Your benefits. We selfishly want more from You and are not thankful for what You have already given us. Lord, make us more satisfied with You, for we desire a deeper relationship with You. In Jesus' name we pray. Amen.

Psalm 103:2, 5

"Praise the LORD, O my soul, and forget not all His benefits ...who satisfies your desires with good things so that your youth is renewed like the eagle's."

My God keeps me young!

There are interpretations of this verse that mostly focus on what the eagle does in the renewal process, keeping it young. But the point is: God does this for us. It's not really about what we do! Let us do what the psalm tells us, *"Praise the LORD"* and *"forget not all His benefits."*

We may be in a difficult situation now, but, *"Praise the LORD,"* His eye is on us. Don't *"Forget all His benefits."* Be patient and trusting, for the only other option we have, is to fear and worry. That will make us old instead of young! Another passage concerning eagles says, *"Those who hope in the LORD will renew their strength,"* Isaiah 40:31. *"Hope in the LORD,"* is healthy living!

When God changes our hearts, it follows that our thoughts, words and actions will also change. Then our feelings and emotions change. The heart change that God does in us changes our physical bodies as well as our spiritual soul. A smiling heart becomes a smiling face. He takes our guilt and gives us His righteousness. He takes our anxiety and gives us peace. He takes our weakness and gives us His strength. Then we do look and feel younger. One lady in counseling said, "God recreated me, and I have received comments of my face glowing and that I look many years younger."

As the eagle grows older, its damaged and dirty feathers are continually being replaced with new ones, renewing the eagle. The bird plucks out the old and the new ones grow back. Our Biblical change process is like that according to Ephesians 4:22-24 NKJV. When we *"put off"* our old and dirty sin habits, see what comes next. *"Be renewed in the spirit of your mind and that you put on the new man, which after God is created in righteousness and true holiness."* That renewal process is God working in us. *"Praise the LORD."* God Himself renews our mind when we repent of our old sins.

Prayer: We praise You Lord for renewing our hearts and making us ever clean, all because of Your ongoing grace and mercy. In Jesus' name we pray. Amen.

Psalm 103:13-14 NKJV

"As a father pities his children, so the LORD pities those who fear Him.
for He knows our frame; He remembers that we are dust."

God's divine pity

Pity is a most awesome attribute of our Heavenly Father. Pity is also a great character point in an earthly father. Pity understands the need of justice but willingly gives grace instead. Pity then is all about compassion. It is where grace and justice meet. Notice what was previously said in our text. *"He (God) has not dealt with us according to our sins, nor punished us according to our iniquities,"* Psalm 103:10. His justice was not given, but His mercy was, all because of God's pity for our dying souls. In fact God's pity is so powerful that there is now, *"no condemnation in us."* Our sins are removed from us as far as the east is from the west!

Pity has everything to do with excellent parenting skills. God's laws are to guide the home. That again is the "justice" part. But His grace is to govern it! That is pity or mercy in action and it is all about compassion. The question is: "Do we as fathers and leaders in the home abound in pity?" Such compassion takes time and is void of having anger or any lingering bitterness over offenses. Justice can be quick and to the point. Pity takes much time in its application. A true father, *"pities his children."*

A man hurt me bad. I was angry with him and that anger moved into bitterness for years. God made me forgive him. I still understood that he was wrong, but began to pity him that he was so lost. In a much larger way, God *"knows our frame."* He who made us knows we are dust. He knows we need His divine pity. God also knows we deserve His just wrath! Since we are weak and He loves us, we are given pity. Without God's pity on us, we are lost for all eternity. Without our pity, our family hurts. When pity finds us, we find love.

God's pity moves us to compassion and thankfulness. How great it is to receive what we need instead of what we deserve! May our gratitude express itself in praise and worship to our beautiful God.

Prayer: O merciful Lord, we are so thankful that You took pity on our lost souls. You not only gave us what we needed in salvation but in our daily living also. We worship You. In Jesus' name we pray. Amen.

Psalm 103:17-18

"But from everlasting to everlasting the LORD's love is with those who fear Him, and His righteousness with their children's children — with those who keep His covenant and remember to obey His precepts."

God's everlasting love to our grandchildren

"From everlasting to everlasting," is a most important truth that covers the spiritual life of every child of God. From everlasting, beginning with the very first children in the world, with Cain, Abel and Seth, we see this truth that the *"LORD's love,"* is essential to have a meaningful life. Dear believer, here is both your warning and encouragement. Cain did not fear God or love God. He hated his brother. Cain killed his brother for he was not interested in God's *"precepts"* or commands to love! How loving are we?

We know that Cain became a restless wanderer. He got married and had lots of children. His children were so talented and brilliant. They invented things and made things. They carried on with their day to day living and in turn had children of their own. They were so busy living life. But nowhere is there any mention that they loved God or feared Him. Instead, the opposite was true. One son of Cain had two wives, the first to do so, against God's will.

Contrast this to Seth, the son that replaced Abel, the one Cain killed. We read very little about Seth, just one verse. *"Seth also had a son, and he named him Enosh. At that time men began to call on the name of the LORD,"* Genesis 4:26. Seth's descendants called on the name of the Lord. Cain's children ran from God's presence. The Lord's love was with which child and their children? It was the one who feared God and was interested in a relationship with Him! The proof is, *"They called on the name of the LORD."* The proof of God's favor and blessing was that God blessed Seth's line, so much so, that Jesus came from the line of Seth.

Prayer: Dear covenant-keeping Lord, how true it is, from the beginning, with the very first children, You loved those who called on Your name. You loved those who sought a relationship with You. But then, You promised that You would always love those who obeyed You. We know that we cannot obey You if we do not first love You. Lord, bless our relationship with You. In Jesus' name we pray. Amen.

Psalm 104:1

"Praise the LORD, O my soul. O LORD my God, You are very great;
You are clothed with splendor and majesty."

Talking to your soul

David is talking to his soul yet again. He is teaching his soul to do what is right, to *"Praise the LORD."* Why would David do this? It is likely that David is talking to his soul because he cannot understand why he sometimes does what he does. We too, do not completely understand our own heart, nor do we understand the hearts of others.

Jeremiah sheds some light on our souls/hearts, what is so true. *"The heart is deceitful above all things and beyond cure. Who can understand it?"* Jeremiah 17:9. God understands our heart. He says, *"I the LORD search the heart and examine the mind, to reward a man according to his conduct, according to what his deeds deserve,"* Jeremiah 17:10.

Julian of Norwich wrote, "It is easier for us to get to know God than it is to know our own soul. God is nearer to us than our own soul, for God is the ground in which our soul stands. So if we want to know our own soul and enjoy its fellowship, it is necessary to seek it in our Lord God." Now that is practical wisdom, and also what David is trying to teach us in this psalm.

Even though we do not understand our hearts, we are aware of our thoughts, words and actions. These all come from the condition of our heart or soul. A soul that is wicked and unconverted will have thoughts, words and actions that are consistently wicked. A soul that is transformed by Christ will have good thoughts, words and actions. *"The good man brings good things out of the good stored up in his heart, and the evil man brings evil things out of the evil stored up in his heart. For out of the overflow of his heart his mouth speaks,"* Luke 6:45.

Does my mouth speak *"good things"*? If not, then my heart or soul needs some changing. May we all then, speak to our souls about the need to praise God and to be a blessing to others who are created in God's image.

Prayer: Almighty Lord, what a profound statement of faith when we reverently *"Praise the LORD."* Yes Lord, it is You who deserve our praise. Work in us by Your Spirit to change our hearts so that our whole beings, every day, praise You! In Jesus' name we pray. Amen.

Psalm 105:1-4 NKJV

"Oh, give thanks to the LORD! Call upon His name; Make known His deeds among the peoples! Sing to Him, sing psalms to Him; talk of all His wondrous works! Glory in His holy name; let the hearts of those rejoice who seek the LORD!" Seek the LORD and His strength; seek His face evermore!"

Our covenant responsibility to God

God's covenants are a binding agreement where the stronger party, which is God, promises to bless us if we are faithful in our part. Every covenant has conditions. None are unconditional! Psalm 105 spells out man's responsibility to God's covenant in the first five verses. In verses 8-44, we see how God faithfully *"remembers His covenant forever!"* We need that reminder to have a visible and audible response to God's covenant faithfulness to us!

"Give thanks to the LORD." "Call upon His name!" Our gratefulness to Him, shows our appreciation for salvation and a relationship that is eternally wonderful! We thank people when they bless us. We must thank God much more than that.

"Make known His deeds." If we won a wonderful prize, we would tell our friends about our good fortune. Well, God has given us the best prize of all, Jesus. If we don't tell others, we place little value on the greatest gift ever! No gratitude = bad attitude.

"Sing to Him." "Sing psalms." The Psalms were written to be sung to God. *"Glory in His holy name."* Treasure the relationship that no one can take from us and from God. What a priceless treasure it is, that our holy God also makes us holy!

"Rejoice." Meditate on what we have in Christ not on what we do not have of the world's goods. Urgently, *"Seek the LORD and His strength"* Plead, *"seek"* search, ask fervently for God's help. We can't do life alone. Our strength is in Him. *"Observe His statutes and keep His laws,"* is the way the Psalm ends. Jesus said it so well. *"You are my friends if you do whatever I command you,"* John 15:14.

Prayer: Powerful and holy Lord, forgive our ungrateful, wandering hearts. We need and want a closer walk with You. We praise You for what You promise and provide in covenant for us, sealed in Your Son's precious blood. In His name we pray. Amen.

Psalm 105:13-15

"They wandered from nation to nation, from one kingdom to another. He allowed no one to oppress them; for their sake He rebuked kings: Do not touch My anointed ones; do My prophets no harm."

"Do not touch My anointed ones"

This verse is a comfort to believers and a warning to unbelievers. *"They (Israel) wandered from nation to nation."* God will protect His people from those who are more powerful. God rescued Israel when they were slaves of Pharaoh. When Pharaoh tried to stop God, he suffered greatly and died! In many events, God acted for His people. We see David who was rescued from Goliath and then from King Saul. We see Esther spared from Haman and those who wanted to kill the Jews. We see Elijah protected from Queen Jezebel.

What about you and I? By God's grace, we are also His chosen children. Paul said about God in Romans 8:31b: *"If God is for you, who can be against you?"* Paul's personal testimony is ours yet today. *"And the Lord will deliver me from every evil work, and preserve me for His Heavenly Kingdom,"* 2 Timothy 4:18a NKJV.

However, by nature we have crippling fear problems. God wants us to trust in Him. He will show us that He will protect us for our good and for His kingdom's sake. Last week, I went to the Philippines to teach church leaders and government workers how to help the many drug users. God prepared or *"anointed"* me to do that for Him. Part of the proof is what God did to protect me.

After landing in the Philippines, I found a hotel to get some sleep. In bed, I prayed and tried to sleep. But as I lay there it was like a hand came down upon me, fighting with me. I am sure it was demonic, trying to stop God's mission. I believe one of God's angels (Psalm 91) reached down and pulled that demon off from me! My body jerked upwards, after that, I slept soundly. I saw it all, while in prayer. *"Do not touch My anointed ones; do my prophets no harm."* This verse and truth includes demonic activity. Believers still wrestle with angels and principalities. Praise God, that our God and His angels are stronger.

Prayer: O Sovereign Lord, we are so blessed that You have not changed. You still protect Your people. How grateful we are that we belong to You. In Jesus' name we pray. Amen.

Psalm 106:35-37

"They mingled with the nations and adopted their customs. They worshiped their idols, which became a snare to them. They sacrificed their sons and daughters to demons."

Sons and daughters, sacrificed to demons

Israel was warned before entering Canaan. God told them they would see demons and spirits that were not God's Holy Spirit. God's exact words were, *"Give no regard to mediums and <u>familiar spirits</u>; do not seek after them, to be defiled by them: I am the LORD your God,"* Leviticus 19:31 NKJV. Israel then did what God told them not to do. We so quickly follow in their paths. How do we reverse it?

A sacrifice is an act of worship to seek and please the one we love. The *"familiar spirits,"* in Leviticus refer to Satan and his demons. They have power. In fact, they have *"spirit"* power. If we seek after them, they will quickly control our spirit. We now give our spiritual *"rights"* to them. We now live for them. How does it happen?

Through demons and demonic deception we can easily become addicted to idols. The demons get us to hold something in our hearts, other than God. These demons are mediums to Satan, just as Jesus is a mediator to God. The demons deceive us to fall for an idol that promises fun, fulfillment and peace. Of course, demons lie. But then we become hooked and a slave to that idol. That is why we read in our text, *"They worshiped their idols, which became a snare to them."*

Addicted and ensnared, what now do idol worshipers do? *"They sacrificed their sons and daughters to demons."* The next generations love demons even more. That is what we are seeing. When anyone leaves God for idols, they are *"defiled by them."* With the love of idols in their hearts, the idol becomes a *"snare."* The idol worshiper is now a slave to that idol, a slave to sin, addicted.

What can we do? Turn to the only One who can set us free. Jesus alone takes addicts of all kinds who are ensnared and brings them to total freedom. God's Spirit is stronger that Satan's demon spirit. God's followers become slaves to righteousness. Let us pray to Him.

Prayer: Righteous Lord, what a serious subject. Open our spiritual eyes. Rescue us from demonic powers. Your Spirit is stronger. Your Spirit makes us holy. We need You. In Jesus' name we pray. Amen.

Psalm 107:10-13

"Some sat in darkness and the deepest gloom, prisoners suffering in iron chains, <u>for they had rebelled against the words of God and despised the counsel of the Most High</u>. So He subjected them to bitter labor; they stumbled, and there was no one to help. Then they cried to the LORD in their trouble, and He saved them from their distress."

An addict's only hope

Four different times in Psalm 107, the people were in serious trouble. Four times they cried to God in prayer. Four times God answered them. Four times God saved them from their distress. Why or what was their problem? Broken people have the habit of living their lives doing what seems good and enjoyable to them. However, that does not fulfill them or bring them contentment in life.

Prisoners are addicted to the <u>ability</u> to do what they want, until, <u>disability</u> comes. They are now caught and very distraught. Prisoners now have but two possible responses. They will either become bitter and more independent. Or, they will become better and dependent on God's mercy to change them.

Every addict should know that it is never God's goal to punish sin but to cure it, now, and for all eternity. Jesus is that one cure. He is the addicted prisoner's only hope. No program will change anyone. It is impossible to have a change of heart unless Jesus cures it. A prisoner's actions cannot change either until the heart changes. There will be no change in a prisoner's feelings or emotions until their actions change. Jesus is the Way, the Truth, and the Life, the Master Changer.

Many prisoners I meet with in jail have left the path that their parents or grandparents walked. Many are now experiencing what our text is talking about. Those who cry out to God will be saved from their distress. They still have to do their time, but the distress is gone! Praise God who alone changes our hearts!

Prayer: Dear Merciful Lord, You give us hope and a new purpose. The old is gone, and a new life in Christ replaces it. You are now with us, instead of against us. How true it now is: Those whom You save, You continue to hear their cries for mercy, for they are now Your children. We praise You O God. In Jesus' name we pray. Amen.

Psalm 107:23-26

"Others went out on the sea in ships; they were merchants on the mighty waters. They saw the works of the LORD, His wonderful deeds in the deep. For He spoke and stirred up a tempest that lifted high the waves. They mounted up to the heavens and went down to the depths; in their peril their courage melted away."

When our courage melts away, then what?

This psalm in the NKJV begins, *"Oh give thanks to the LORD, for He is good!"* The exclamation point is included because our serious trials in life are temptations by Satan to doubt God's goodness. In the same trial, God wants to show us that He will care for us, as He tests us. God wants to get us through the storm, to grow our faith and dependence on Him. Our verses above describe a sailor's temptation to fear when the big storms come. God here purposely *"stirred up a tempest that lifted up high the waves."* Why? The difficult storm is a test to trust in God. Yes, God designs difficult trials to test our faith in Him. Faith must be tested to see if it is real. Will we pray and keep our eyes on the One who is bigger than the storm. Or will Satan convince us to give in to worthless and paralyzing fear?

This message from God to not be afraid or do not fear, is repeated 300 times in one way or another in the Bible. God wants His children to trust Him, rely on Him, look to Him, to have confidence in Him. Jesus said, to be afraid was both *"wicked and lazy,"* in Matthew 25:26. Jesus also said worry was *"little faith."* It is my experience that like many Bible characters, God Himself will teach us not to fear or worry. Why? Our giving in to the devil and doubting the goodness of God, is not faith in God. Job's wife did that and it was not righteous.

In verses 8, 15, 21 and 31, the exact same words plead: *"Oh, that men would give thanks to the LORD for His goodness, and for His wonderful works to the children of men!"* A right attitude is gratitude! God wants us to understand something about how He works faith in us. A song of faith comes to mind and this is our prayer.

Prayer: "Jesus Savior, pilot me over life's tempestuous sea; unknown waves before me roll, hiding rock and treacherous shoal: chart and compass come from Thee; Jesus Savior, pilot me." God is so good! In Jesus' good name we pray. Amen.

Psalm 108:12-13

"Give us aid against the enemy, for the help of man is worthless. With God we will gain the victory, and He will trample down our enemies."

"With God we will gain the victory"

Do we really believe that *"with God we will gain the victory"*? God will allow events in our lives to prove that He is always there to *"give us aid against the enemy."* Let me give you a very personal example.

It was summertime in South India. I had to go on a fourteen hour trip to teach. It was very hot, so I asked a staff member to get me a air-conditioned ticket on the train. At the train station, I noticed my ticket was not an A/C one. How could the staff make such a mistake in this heat? As I began the overnight journey I was feeling very sorry for myself. I did not sleep because I had a top bunk that was so hot, about 120 degrees. For 6 hours I swam in my own sweat!

At four in the morning, in the middle of a dense forest, the train came to a sudden stop! The number one air-conditioned coach had just been robbed. The terrorists took all the money, gold, jewels and watches, then hit the emergency stop, and escaped into the jungle. One hour later, again the train stopped quickly! A/C coach number two was robbed! Grateful, is not nearly a strong enough word to express my thanksgiving to God! And this is where David is at in our text. The king of Israel could not catch David, even in his own country! Our God is so awesome. *"With God we will gain the victory."*

God *"will trample our enemies."* We are oppressed on every side. We feel the pressure of demonic activity. The dark powers in the spirit world will try to frustrate the Lord's work. Satan does not want us satisfied with God or in close fellowship with Him. Satan does not want us working for the Lord. For when the Lord's kingdom advances, Satan loses. Our great God will, *"Give us aid against the enemy"*?

Prayer: Dear loving and protecting Lord, we will always win because the battle is Yours! Like sheep we are dependent on You our Good Shepherd. How thankful we are that You not only have the willingness to help us, but the ability to do so. We worship You. In Jesus' name we pray. Amen.

Psalm 108:12-13

"Give us aid against the enemy, for the help of man is worthless. With God we will gain the victory, and He will trample down our enemies."

"With God" demons become beggars

I am in the Philippines. It is 6:45 in the morning. I am in McDonald's eating breakfast. At 7:00, Pastor Buddy is going to pick me up to start teaching at a government venue. There, I will begin teaching workers and pastors how to Biblically reach addicts and their families.

One minute before Pastor Buddy picks me up, a demon-possessed man makes one last try to stop me. Demons tried a day earlier to stop me, when I arrived in Manila. God's angels pulled a demon off from me as my body jerked violently off the bed. God handled it, as He said He would in Psalm 91:11-12. Now, in McDonald's, a demon-possessed man comes up behind me. I didn't see him coming. He started stroking my shoulder, pleading like a beggar, calling me pastor. How does he know that I am a pastor type? His eyes are rolled back in his head. Only the white of his eyes is showing. He is crazy, and fully demon-possessed. The security guard grabs him and puts him out the door. I follow, as Pastor Buddy now enters the open door.

I tell the Pastor this demon-possessed man is pleading, "don"t go to the government hall to teach." This demon-filled guy is quoting Scripture, his face distorted, looking wild. There is a war going on. *"For we do not wrestle against flesh and blood, but against principalities, against powers, against the rulers of the darkness of this age, against spiritual host of wickedness in the heavenly places,"* Ephesians 6:12.

Note that this was the first of 125 conferences we have now done in the Philippines. Many hearts have been changed. Demons know what is going on as they try to stop God's work! God cared that there were four million drug addicts and their family members who needed to be ministered to. God even moved the president of the country to ask pastors and government workers to help addicts using the Gospel. All we need to do is pray and be faithful, as God works.

Prayer: O Powerful Lord, thank You for Your *"aid against the enemy."* In the Great Commission, You promised to be with us, even to the end of the age! You are! With You as our God, *"we will gain the victory."* We worship You and in Jesus' name, we pray. Amen!

Psalm 109:30-31

"With my mouth I will greatly extol the LORD; in the great throng I will praise Him. For He stands at the right hand of the needy one, to save his life from those who condemn him."

Looking to God when unjustly accused

We have those who unjustly hate us. That is David's concern throughout the psalm. This has to be people within the covenant "church" family, or David would have eliminated them. The psalm opens with someone giving false accusations. David summarizes his pain by saying, *"In return for my friendship they accuse me, but I am a man of prayer,"* Psalm 109:4. Notice how David takes his burden to the Lord in prayer. He does not carry it alone.

David does more than pray. He praises God's power, wisdom and mercy to act on his behalf. That is quite the opposite of our anger, bitterness and complaining! David fully believed what is written in Psalm 91. *"'Because he loves Me,' says the LORD, 'I will rescue him; I will protect him, for he acknowledges My Name. He will call upon Me, and I will answer him; I will be with him in trouble, I will deliver him and honor him,'"* Psalm 91:14-15.

Like David, we need to exercise our faith with a right attitude. Even Peter, after many trials in his life, finally understood his trials. He wrote, *"Dear friends, do not be surprised at the painful trial you are suffering, as though something strange were happening to you. But rejoice that you participate in the sufferings of Christ, so that you may be overjoyed when His glory is revealed. If you are insulted because of the name of Christ, you are blessed, for the Spirit of glory and of God rests on you,"* 1 Peter 4:12-14.

We not only have God's wisdom in His Word, we also have His Spirit in abundance. *"The Spirit helps us in our weakness. We do not know what we ought to pray for, but the Spirit Himself intercedes for us with groans that words cannot express,"* Romans 8:26b. Why would we want to carry our heavy burdens alone? God is so willing and able to help us, always.

Prayer: Dear loving Lord, forgive us for our weak faith that does not yet fully trust You. May we submit to You, our faithful Creator and continue to do good. In Jesus' name we pray. Amen.

Psalm 110:1-2

"The LORD says to my Lord: 'Sit at My right hand until I make Your enemies a footstool for Your feet. The LORD will extend Your mighty scepter from Zion; You will rule in the midst of Your enemies.'"

The reason there is a New Testament

This is David's messianic psalm, written for the crowning of Jesus. When Jesus rode into town on a donkey on Palm Sunday, the crowds applied this very psalm to their joyful praise. *"Hosanna to the Son of David!" "Blessed is he who comes in the name of the Lord!" "Hosanna in the highest!"* Matthew 21:9. The people knew what the Pharisees were unwilling to admit, that King David spoke about this Jesus who was coming down the road. They knew, as we must know, that Jesus was both divine and human. Why was it necessary for Jesus to be human, to be the son of David, his descendant?

Adam, in the book of Genesis, did not do something that he had to do in order to live forever. Adam did not keep the covenant of works, a binding agreement with God. *"And the LORD God commanded the man, 'You are free to eat from any tree in the garden; but you must not eat from the tree of the knowledge of good and evil, for when you eat of it you will surely die,'"* Genesis 2:16-17.

Adam and all who came after him until Jesus was born, were sinners who did not and could not keep the covenant of works. So, the holiness of God provided the blood of innocent animals to be shed, paying for their sins. Blood, *"because the life of the flesh is in the blood,"* Leviticus 17:11. Innocent blood paid for guilty sinners.

After 4000 years of blood sacrifices, God sent His own Son who was fully God, yet also man. Jesus was born of a woman, totally innocent because His father was not Adam, but was of the Holy Spirit. Then Jesus lived a perfect life. When He was killed on the cross, His innocent blood replaced the innocent blood of animals. The covenant of works was kept by Jesus. Now we have been given a new covenant, the covenant of grace, also called the New Testament.

Prayer: My Lord and my God, how privileged we are to have a new covenant of grace. You graciously hold out Your scepter of peace and forgiveness to all who believe. You make us Your holy children for all eternity. We worship You. In Jesus' name we pray. Amen.

Psalm 111:10

"The fear of the LORD is the beginning of wisdom; all who follow His precepts have good understanding. To Him belongs eternal praise."

The fear of the LORD, the beginning of wisdom

The *"fear"* of the Lord here is having respect and admiration for who God is, for His Word, and for what He does. If we have no fear of God, then we will live to do what we want, ignoring Him. .

Do not think it is only those who have drug, alcohol and sex type problems are those who do not fear God. Some sit in church almost every Sunday, but their body language shouts, 'I do not want to be here." Others willingly go to church on Sunday, but live far from God the rest of the week, and then, think that they know God. There is a big difference between knowing the Word God, than knowing the God of the Word! God must be our best friend. A letter I recently received from a man in prison tells what happened in his life.

"I've been a so called Christian all of my life. But I always had doubts and finally convinced myself that until I see something real or experience something for myself, I am going to live for me. Well, the eight straight months of delusional thoughts I had, pulled me in the direction of the Lord. It was God letting me know that He alone is the only one to be feared. And as long as I wanted to run around acting like a terrorist, instilling fear in people, He was going to be there instilling the fear of Him into me. It was a very scary yet humbling experience. God's presence was what I was looking for to erase all of my doubts. Now I need to grow in my faith. Will you help me learn how to live the Christian life?" Yes, for *"to Him belongs eternal praise."*

This man was educated, but not wise! True faith does not come by education any more than wisdom does. Faith is something we live and daily practice in our relationship with God and others. God Himself moved this man who had so little fear of God, to where he is now. The fear of the Lord truly is the beginning of wisdom! This young man is now walking with God. It took prison to get him to fear God. What will it take for you? Do pray for your own walk with God.

Prayer: Merciful Lord, You are the Way, the Truth and the Life. You alone are the Author and Finisher of our faith. We need You in so many ways. Fill us with Yourself. In Jesus' name we pray. Amen.

Psalm 112:1b & 7

"Blessed is the man who fears the LORD, who finds great delight in His commands." "He will have no fear of bad news; his heart is steadfast, trusting in the LORD."

Like Father, like son!

God will bless us if it is safe to do so, if we humbly find *"great delight in His commands."* God's *"great"* blessings are conditional to our *"great"* love for His Word and His will. What a man sows, he will reap. What goes around, comes around, is true! In Matthew 7:12, Jesus said, *"so in everything, do to others what you would have them do to you, for this sums up the Law and the Prophets."* What is true with others is true with God. If we want His great blessings, we need to love what He loves and that is His perfect Word, the Bible. There are four blessings that will follow us when we *"delight"* in God.

First blessing, <u>we will become righteous like the Father</u>. We see in Psalm 112:3 that His *"righteousness endures forever."* We praise God for His righteousness because in Christ, it is freely given to us!

Second blessing, <u>we will become gracious like the Father</u>. When we love God with a *"great delight,"* we love what He loves, making us gracious also, for the heart of our God is gracious.

Third blessing, <u>we will become steadfast like the Father</u>. *"His heart is steadfast, trusting in the LORD,"* Psalm 112:7. True faith trusts! The heart that fully trusts in God will not quickly experience fear, worry or become depressed. Our God has all things under His control. May we trust Him so that the blessing of steadfastness increasingly defines who we are!

Fourth blessing, <u>we will become honored like the Father</u>. *"His horn will be lifted high in honor,"* Psalm 112:9b. We all want respect and honor. The way to get honor, is to honor and respect what God does. God's will for us is to love Him and others, in that order. We, who are selfish, need a changed heart to be honored by God and others. May we go to prayer and thank Him for His many blessings!

Prayer: O gracious Lord, Your Word is so clear. If we love You, it will not only honor You, but will in turn be a blessing to us. If we neglect You, we will forfeit many of Your beautiful blessings. Lord, thank You for being so loving and faithful! In Jesus' name we pray. Amen.

Psalm 113:5

"Who is like the LORD our God, the One who sits enthroned on high?"

"Who is like the LORD our God?"

What a beautiful praise psalm! The children of Israel, and we too, are called to praise God in song and in joyful meditation. Already in the first verse we are called to praise God three times. *"Praise the LORD. Praise, O servants of the LORD, praise the name of the LORD. Let the name of the LORD be praised, both now and forevermore,"* Psalm 113:1-2. We, who are His chosen children, are the ones called to praise Him. Who else will do it? Unbelievers are busy cursing God. As God's children, we know how to cry out when we need deliverance and blessings. How quickly we can then lift our hands to Heaven, pleading for God to act on our behalf. Do we then thank Him after His mercy has been given?

In verse five, we are prompted to meditate on all the amazing attributes or the character qualities that our God has. We are called to compare who our God is to the other gods. The psalm closes with how God *"raises the poor from the dust."* 'He also, *"settles the barren woman in her home as a happy mother of children."* No other god can do that!

What other god is eternal? What other god is all wise and all powerful? What other god never changes so that we may know he is forever the same? What other god can see everything? What other god is present everywhere? What other god loves and forgives like our God? At the same time, what other god is so full of holy wrath that he can send someone to Hell forever? What other god is so faithful, patient and good as our God?

"Who is like the LORD our God, the One who sits enthroned on high?" The answer is, "None in the present;" nor will there be one like our God in the future. He alone is God! Let us praise Him!

Prayer: O majestic Lord, there is no one like You, who created the whole world and everything in it. You keep the entire world running. You know every person. We know that You put us here to seek You and to find You and to worship You. Thank You for this psalm that helps us meditate on Your greatness. In Jesus' name we pray. Amen.

Psalm 114:5-6

"Why was it, O sea, that you fled, O Jordan, that you turned back, you mountains, that you skipped like rams, you hills, like lambs?"

Why does the creation obey God?

The short answer to our text is, the creation has to. Psalm 114, is a beautiful song, a psalm of praise to God's creative power. This song was sung in the temple, looking back at God's deliverance *"out of Egypt,"* Psalm 114:1b. In Egypt, they were slaves, unable to deliver themselves. God took mercy on them. As a result, the people of Israel now had a new relationship with God. *"Judah became God's sanctuary, Israel His dominion,"* Psalm 114:2. God lived in them literally, and then He lived through them.

Why should we sing this song? Egypt is symbolic of our slavery to sin also. That was our exact problem before God saved us. We believers are present day Israel, God's chosen people. Peter wrote about how we are living stones that are being built by Him (God's creative power) into a spiritual house. Peter adds, *"You are a chosen people, a royal priesthood, a holy nation, a people belonging to God, that you may declare the praises of Him who called you out of darkness, into His wonderful light,"* 1 Peter 2:9. That is something to sing about!

We have a great privilege of being one of God's children, just like God's creative power in the formation of the world. This is what Israel is singing about in Psalm 114. They remembered how, *"the sea looked and fled, the Jordan turned back,"* Psalm 114:3a. Again, why? He who made the sea flee, also makes His people flee sin. God spoke, and Egypt let them go. God spoke to the sea, and the sea let them go. The first creative miracle *"out of Egypt"* is a symbol of our salvation. The second is our baptism as we passed through the water. Canaan or Heaven is our destination. Psalm 114 praises God for His creative power in us and in the physical world.

Prayer: Dear Creator and Heavenly Father, we too worship You for continuing to turn our darkness into light. You move us from lost to found. You place us in Your love instead of being under Your wrath. You alone deserve our worship and song of praise. In Jesus' name we pray. Amen.

Psalm 115:8-9

"Those who make them (idols) will be like them, and so will all who trust in them. O house of Israel, trust in the LORD — He is their help and shield."

Idols deceive us!

Idols deceive us, but how? The great deceiver, Satan, still works to deceive us spiritually, so he can take us to hell with him. Satan hates God with a passion! Satan was originally the number one guardian angel in Heaven, guarding the Holy of Holies. Now fallen, he does not want us to be holy. That is why Satan deceives us to worship or love and trust him through idols.

Satan wants to give us experiences through idols, that will enslave us physically and spiritually. Jesus told the enslaved Pharisees, *"You belong to your father, the devil, and you want to carry out your father's desire. He was a murderer from the beginning, not holding to the truth, for there is no truth in him. When he lies, he speaks his native language, for he is a liar and the father of lies,"* John 8:44.

What are some of the lies of Satan and his demons concerning idols? The alcohol idol promises to relax you and give you a good time. It promises to help you forget your problems. All lies! God's warning is: *"Do not gaze at wine when it is red, when it sparkles in the cup, when it goes down smoothly! In the end it bites like a snake and poisons like a viper,"* Proverbs 23:31-32. Does our health or marriage improve if we are enslaved to alcohol? Do our problems go away if we abuse alcohol? Or do we have more problems?

Another lie Satan and his demons deceive us with is the adultery idol. A great time is promised! *"The lips of an adulteress drip honey, and her speech is smoother than oil,"* Proverbs 5:3. She seems so sweet! *"But in the end she is bitter as gall, sharp as a double-edged sword. Her feet go down to death; her steps lead straight to the grave,"* Proverbs 5:4-5. And what about the man who follows after her? *"He will die for the lack of discipline, led astray by his own great folly,"* Proverbs 5:23. How idols deceive us!

Prayer: Most holy Lord, You are the One who sanctifies us. Lord, You are the only Way, the only Truth and the only Life. Strengthen us to flee from Satan's demonic deceptions. In Jesus' name we pray. Amen.

Psalm 115:11

"You who fear Him, trust in the LORD — He is their help and shield."

No help from idols; big help from God

The big question is: do we have idols? What is the number one thing in life that we cannot do without? What is more important to us than anything else? Is it our Lord and Savior or is it something else?

Only God is our *"help and shield."* What a beautiful truth no idol could ever give! Three times the psalmist repeats these words so that we will absorb its truth. We are reminded that idols can't see, hear, smell, or ever come to our aid. In fact, we will be just like them if we cling to them. Everyone soon becomes what his idol or god is like!

What does our text mean for us as Christians? It means that our God sees us! He who never slumbers or sleeps hears us, even if we lose our voice. Our great God is everywhere, with all wisdom and all power. He has the biggest storehouse of blessings, with the willingness to bless and protect us. The Psalm doesn't say, He <u>might</u> be our help and shield! It says, *"He <u>is</u> their help and shield."* This is both a present reality and a future promise! Why then do we fear our enemies? Why do we fall to pieces when we read of economic disaster? Why do we wonder what will happen to our loved ones? Why do we give in to senseless self-pity that kills us physically, mentally and spiritually? Why do we even plead with God to be with us when he has already promised that He will never leave us or forsake us?

This Psalm is for today! God is our *"help and shield."* God is on the offensive for us, even as He defends us. God will give us what we need exactly when we need it, just as Hebrews 4:16 teaches. Our comfort is in the fact that God knows what we need. He knows whether the medicine of pain or the medicine of pleasure is needed!

Who else can do what our God does? James 5:17 says the prophet Elisha was just like us. Elijah tells us about our enemies, *"Don't be afraid,... those who are with us are more than those who are with them,"* 2 Kings 6:16! God has twice as many good angels to defend us, than Satan has demonic angels to hurt us. And, God is more powerful.

Prayer: O God, our *"help and shield,"* open our eyes that we may see how awesome You are. What a blessing You are to us, Your adopted children. We thank You! In Jesus' name we pray. Amen.

Psalm 116:1-2

"I love the LORD, for He heard my voice; He heard my cry for mercy. Because He turned His ear to me, I will call on Him as long as I live."

"He has turned His ear to me"

"I love the LORD" is a very personal statement of faith. Saying, *"I love the LORD"* is also a Biblical creed and a moving testimony. If we can truly say to God, *"I love you,"* it is proof that God has been working in our hearts! Think of how precious to our ears it is when a child or grandchild says to us, *"I love you."* It is sure proof that we have first loved them and moved them to say such sweet words. Saying, *"I love the LORD,"* is praise and worship to God's ears. He, too, is moved!

One reason we love God so much is because He hears us when we speak. He is never too busy reading a newspaper. Our Lord is not too busy watching world events on His big screen TV. The Lord's mind is engaged on our every word. He is actively listening for our cries for mercy. That brings up a good point concerning our own ears. Do we hear our spouse or children when they cry for mercy?

If we have communication problems in our homes, it's guaranteed, someone is not listening! Is that someone me or you? Think of the how, God hears. *"He turned His ear to me."* If we turn to others when they speak, it is visible proof that we are carefully listening to them. If we are too busy to listen, then we are too busy! Our Lord is our perfect example of active listening! *"He turned His ear to me."*

There is one grace point that must be clear. God does not turn His ear to everyone. In Psalm 66:18, the writer admits, *"If I had cherished sin in my heart, the LORD would not have listened."* Is any sin safe in our heart's, like a ship is safe in a harbor? If so, then our text is not for us personally. God needs to hear our confessing cries for mercy and we need His forgiveness.

As a tender shepherd himself, David could say, *"My sheep hear my voice."* That is why the psalmist so boldly proclaims about God, *"He heard my voice."* More than that! God delights to hear the voice of one of His beloved children. Praise the Lord.

Prayer: Dear loving Lord, we take great delight in You. We love You. Lord, build our relationship with You even more! May we listen to You, even as You listen to us. In Jesus' name we pray. Amen.

Psalm 116:7-9

"Be at rest once more, O my soul, for the LORD has been good to you. For You, O LORD, have delivered my soul from death, my eye from tears, my feet from stumbling, that I may walk before the LORD in the land of the living."

Rest in the Lord, *"once more"*

David was a passionate man and was also called a man after God's own heart. He had great victories in life. But at the same time David had great trials. The Psalms are full of David's seemingly impossible situations. He had no choice but to cry out to God because what he was facing was beyond his own power to correct or control. David knew how to grab God by faith and not let go. He teaches us in this psalm to do the same.

David admits, *"I was overcome by trouble and sorrow,"* in Psalm 116:3. When he knew he was in over his head, in verse four, he said *"Then I called on the name of the LORD: 'O LORD, save me!'"* His prayer is just four words! This was not a whispered prayer, but a loud cry of desperation, like that of a drowning man. David confesses, in verse six, *"When I was in great need, He saved me."*

"Be at rest once more," Psalm 116:7. Two words really stand out because the *"once more"* comes often in our lives too. We beg for the Lord's help and He revives our weak spirits! How do we get into such a state of unrest? We take our eyes off from God and our devotion to Him weakens. Then a trial comes and the *"once more"* kicks in. God has our attention again. He shows us *"once more"* of our need of Him. How He builds our faith in every trial. Every deliverance by God refreshes our soul again! Like David and like Peter too, when we take our eyes off the Lord, we begin to sink. What a psalm of hope as we realize that God will lift us up *"once more"* until our life is over and we are forever with Him in Heaven. God alone preserves us in the faith. Glory to God in the highest.

Prayer: O God of our salvation, how excellent is Your name in all the earth. You are amazing and we love You so much for Your amazing grace, *"once more."* With David we can truly say, *"I love the LORD, for he heard my voice."* In Jesus' name we pray. Amen.

Psalm 116:15

"Precious in the sight of the LORD is the death of His saints."

We die in order to live forever!

Did you ever think of what the death of one of God's children means <u>to Him</u>? He is finally going to see another child, face to face. What God planned in eternity past, is now happening. God will welcome each of His children at Heaven's door. God will greet His children by name. He will eagerly show His people His house of many mansions prepared for them.

In Heaven, the saints are so amazed at the glory of God and how beautiful He and His eternal Heavenly kingdom really are. What a sad truth it is that some foolishly choose to believe like the *"rich man"* in Luke 16. What a shock he had when he died and found himself in Hell. He begged God to let him warn his family about a real life after death. But God did not allow that because earth's people were told already by Moses and the prophets, the whole Old Testament.

Jesus told the thief on the cross about life after death. *"I tell you the truth, today you will be with Me in Paradise,"* Luke 23:43. Jesus also said about the resurrection at the end of the world, *"Do not be amazed at this, for a time is coming when all who are in their graves will hear His voice and come out — those who have done good will rise to live, and those who have done evil will rise to be condemned,"* John 5:28-29. All die in order to live on, eternally!

The only question that will be known on the Day of Judgment is: Have we been redeemed by the blood of Jesus? Believers know this, *"Precious in the sight of the LORD is the death of His saints."* Today, do we live in the light of eternity? The day of our physical death is coming soon. Our soul will separate from our body. And if our spiritual soul belongs to God today, it will not matter where the physical body goes temporarily. But if our spiritual soul belongs to Satan, our eternity will be with him and it will not be precious! May we live in the light of eternity!

Prayer: O Sovereign Lord, You lovingly warn us so many times that life is short on this earth. You tell us that our souls will live on. Lord, cover our sin so we can be precious in Your sight today and forever. In Jesus' name we pray. Amen.

Psalm 117:1-2 KJV

"O praise the LORD, all ye nations: Praise Him, all ye people. For His merciful kindness is great towards us; and the truth of the LORD endureth forever. Praise ye the LORD."

Radical Christianity from a radical Savior

Jesus came to earth as *"LORD,"* yet He was in a body, fully man. Jesus showed us clearly what a perfect life should look like. He was radical, in that He was refreshingly different. He had the power of God, yet was the humblest man alive! What a contrast to our sinful world.

"His merciful kindness is great towards us." Who can fully understand His amazing mercy? The more we study it the more we see His mercy is far deeper than what we can grasp! He alone, who has the power to send us to Hell for eternity, offers us mercy and pardon! We sinners love His mercy, because we are in such a mess, without hope. Jesus loves sinners so much that, in Him, we can start over again with a totally clean slate. Every single sin we have ever committed is mercifully forgiven. His mercy makes a sinner cleaner than a newborn baby that is born already sinful. *"His merciful kindness,"* willingly forgives every future sin we will ever commit. His mercy endures forever!

Equally true is: *"the truth of the LORD endureth forever."* Even though Jesus loves sinners, He does not love their sin. That is why once a sinner is forgiven, God gives His new creation, His redeemed sinners, the power to stop sinning. He expects it. He demands it. He longs for it. Paul talked for three chapters in Ephesians about the grace and mercy of God in salvation. Then, he pleads this "truth" with us, *"I urge you to live a life worthy of the calling you have received. Be completely humble and gentle; be patient, bearing with one another in love,"* Ephesians 4:1b-2. We can't live like we used to live!

These two verses in Psalm 117, make up the shortest chapter in the Bible. They are also the very center of the Bible, for it is the very heart of Christianity also. God's merciful kindness gives us new life and His truth changes us for all eternity. How can we not *"Praise the LORD."*

Prayer: O merciful Lord, You changed our hearts to endure forever in Your presence. We praise You for giving us a life in Heaven that is already sure, when we are in Christ. With You for us, who can really be against us? *"Praise the LORD."* In Jesus' name we pray. Amen.

Psalm 118:4

"Let those who fear the LORD say: "His love endures forever."

Do we believe His love endures forever?

We doubt God's love at times. The truth is: we are not perfect in our love for God. One way we doubt God's love, is when we give in to fear. Both fear and its sister, worry, ultimately doubt the goodness of God. In our "fears," we find God guilty of not being as good to us as we think He should be. There are millions of other people, all trying to determine what is good. We all have a faith problem that begs to be corrected. God wants us to trust that He is good and that *"His love endures forever."* When we trust God, we depend on Him. That is what faith is.

How do we doubt God's love? Something difficult happens to us. We lose a loved one or have a terminal disease. We have a trial that seems likely to derail us. We focus intently on what may happen. We often live too much in the future, fearing what the future holds. In our great concern about the future, is God, Jesus or the Holy Spirit there in our thoughts? No, not really! We try to figure how we are going to navigate life on our own. We are way too independent, rather than dependent on God.

Yesterday, I met a man on the street, who came to Christ in jail, through a book I wrote. Yet as a new Christian, he was still weak. Through tears he told me how his wife does not want to be around him and has left him. He loves her, but she won't come back. He was mostly trusting in himself to bring her back. He was not leaning on God in faith like he should. If his wife smiled at him, his hope soared. When she cursed him, he went into depressed thoughts. Like all of us, he needed to learn that <u>God's love will never bring us where His grace will not be there to reach us</u>. He too must learn by faith that when he cannot trace God's hands, he must trust God's loving heart. God gives us all trials, bigger than we are, to teach us to trust Him. Why? To teach us that, *"His love endures forever."* It really does!

Prayer: O faithful and loving Father, we still have so much to learn. Our faith is still weak, so teach us to trust You; delight in You; commit our way to You, and then rest in Your love that endures forever! In Jesus' name we pray. Amen.

Psalm 118:8 NKJV

"It is better to trust in the LORD than to put confidence in man."

Self-confidence or God-confidence?

Confidence is good, if it's based on God's truth and righteousness. There is such a huge difference between self-confidence, compared to confidence in God and in His Word. Self-esteem and Christ-esteem, are complete opposites. Today we hear so much about how people need to have more self-confidence and self-esteem. The Bible says nothing positive about having confidence in yourself.

Self-confidence is pride in our ability, in our wisdom and in our possessions, to guide us and deliver us from the problems in this world. When we think that we can make it in our own strength, some serious trial will come that will put us in our proper place! Peter walked on water, until that is, he took his overconfident eyes off from Jesus. As Christians, we are not our own: we were bought with a price. Our self-confidence is that "I" in the middle of "sin" that will kill us!

Can a child make it on his or her own in this cruel world? No, they will be so lost and hurting without wise direction. But what if that child has tons of confidence and is "street smart"? Can they make it then? God answers the question. *"There is a way that seems right to a man but in the end it leads to death,"* Proverbs 14:12. We are to live dependent on God, as His children.

God was the saints' confidence in the past. He delivered Noah, Moses, Esther, David, Daniel, Peter, Paul and so many more. The Lord has not changed. The Lord is still our confidence in the present and in the future also. *"By awesome deeds in righteousness You will answer us, O God of our salvation, You who are the confidence of all the ends of the earth,"* Psalm 65:5 NKJV. *"The LORD will be your confidence,"* Proverbs 3:26a. Let us not be like Israel, who so often neglected to put their confidence in God.

Prayer: Dear Almighty Lord, forgive our self-centered, self-focused and self-exalting life. Help us to die to self. *"O LORD, not to us but to Your name be the glory, because of Your love and faithfulness."* Lord, You deserve the praise and glory. In Jesus' name we pray. Amen.

Psalm 119:1-2

"Blessed are they whose ways are blameless, who walk according to the law of the LORD. Blessed are they who keep His statutes and seek Him with all their heart."

Introduction to the longest Bible chapter

Only the Spirit of God could write this masterpiece! But then, we know that all the Bible is inspired. *"For prophesy never had its origin in the will of man, but men spoke from God as they were carried along by the Holy Spirit,"* 2 Peter 1:21b. The main emphasis of the psalm is the practical usefulness of the holy Word of God for our lives. And the man who was moved by God to write it, did not even have a full Bible!

The 119th psalm clearly shows the amazing order of our God. Satan by comparison, is a master of disorder! The Old Testament was written in Hebrew, which has 22 letters in its alphabet. The first Hebrew letter is Aleph and amazingly, the first 8 verses all start with Aleph. The psalm continues in this same pattern. Each of the 22 sections then start with the next letter in the alphabet, as do all 8 verses, ending with Tau, the last letter.

By contrast, six is commonly the number of man, with 666 being the Antichrist. Seven in the Bible is the number for the completeness of God, or God at rest. The number 8, is the number for the one and only perfect Man, Jesus Christ. The number 8 is an important part of the meaning of Psalm 119. The New Testament was written in Koine Greek and that alphabet begins with alpha and ends with omega. Jesus identified Himself to John in the giving of the book of Revelation. He said, *"'I am the Alpha and the Omega,' says the Lord God, 'who is, and who was, and who is to come, the Almighty,'"* Revelation 1:8. It is significant then that eight is the number for what is eternal and for the resurrection.

Prayer: Amazing Lord, Your order and creativity is so clear in creation and all through the Bible. How wonderful to have this psalm that points to the tremendous importance of Your holy, inspired Word. May Your Word live in us more and more! You are the Aleph and the Tou, the Alpha and the Omega, the author and the perfecter of our faith. We worship You. In Jesus' name we pray. Amen.

Psalm 119:9

"How can a young man keep his way pure? By living according to Your Word."

A young man can keep his way pure!

What an important question our text asks! What a great answer is given. What a deep spiritual and physical truth is expressed in such simple language. All of Psalm 119 directs us to God's Word and the great value there is in it. Our text is one of many verses in this lengthy psalm that show us how to live God's way, the only pure and right way. It stands to reason then, that there is an impure way to live that God does not approve of. Purity is most important to God because God's character is perfectly pure.

Purity is much about a relationship with God and a waiting by faith, on God's Word and will. Purity calls for an intimate relationship with God first, and then with others. Elizabeth Elliot said about purity, "I realized that the deepest spiritual lessons are not learned by God letting us have our way, but by His making us wait, bearing with us in love and patience until we are able to honestly pray what He taught His disciples to pray: *'Thy will be done.'"* Well said. It is God's will that we need, not our own selfish will.

Purity is a great treasure for young people to seek. The Apostle Paul spoke out openly on purity saying, *"It is God's will that you should be sanctified: that you should avoid sexual immorality,"* 1 Thessalonians 4:3. He is showing us that a relationship with God drives or guides our other relationships. How opposite this is to how the world thinks. Their finding fulfillment everywhere is a main goal in life. <u>He or she who seeks fulfillment everywhere will find it nowhere</u>! How empty is a life when purity is not protected and prized.

Prayer: Most holy Lord, Your Word shows us that only Jesus was born pure. We are born impure. We all have Adam's blood in us. And our father Adam lost his purity in the Garden of Eden. Through Your grace, Adam regained his purity when You clothed him through that first blood sacrifice in Genesis 3:21. How too, we need to regain our purity through Christ. *"Living according to Your Word,"* directs us to Christ who takes our impurity and gives us His purity. We praise You for pure Jesus. In His name we pray. Amen.

Psalm 119:11

*"I have hidden Your Word in my heart that I might not
sin against You."*

Are our devotions a delight?

I recently met an older teenager who claimed to be Christian. She could proudly tell me the characters and details of countless, worthless movies! Yet she asked, "Who was Thomas in the Bible?" And she thought "Ecclesiastes" was a Tamil word. Her problem is our problem. We have the written Word of the living and eternal God, infallible, forever true, forever relevant, yet we read it so little!

What if a loved one overseas wrote us a personal letter? Would we open it? Would we not read every word carefully, over and over? Yet God our Creator, King, Redeemer and Friend wrote us a letter. The dust on the cover of our Bibles shouts at us, "You hypocrite!"

If we have any hope to know the true God, any hope to know of His power and purposes, then we must know His Word. David was said to be a man after God's own heart. Why? David was delighted to be devoted to God. The Psalms that David wrote were meditations of David's devotion as he recounted his experiences and how God's holy attributes gave him strength.

What can we say about David's devotion? Where did it come from? There is only one answer: God. "Now the LORD said to Samuel... 'Fill your horn with oil, and go; I am sending you to Jesse the Bethlehemite. For I have provided Myself a king among his sons,'" 1 Samuel 16:1 NKJV. See the big difference between David and Saul. When God chose Saul, He said, "Make them a king," 1 Samuel 8:22b. Why? The people did not want God. They rejected Him. If we want to be devoted to God, we have to want God. We have to get serious, kneel down and pray and pour out our heart to God. Has God ever refused a beggar? No. He says, "Come to Me, all you who are weary and burdened, and I will give you rest," Matthew 11:28.

Prayer: Dear gracious Lord, we desire a deeper relationship with You. We want to be devoted to You, yet we know that You must also draw us to Yourself. Lord, we can only humble ourselves in prayer and beg for more of Your mercy and grace! In Jesus' name we pray. Amen.

Psalm 119:33-34

"Teach me, O LORD, to follow Your decrees; then I will keep them to the end. Give me understanding, and I will keep Your law and obey it with all my heart."

Obedience, God's responsibility or ours?

Today there are those who are endlessly searching for a victory in their walk with God. But, is victory a right pursuit? In this psalm and throughout the Bible, it is obedience, not victory, that we so need! If we have obedience, we will have a victory over sin for sure. Then whose responsibility is it for a Christian to become obedient? Is it God's responsibility? Note what God said to Cain, *"If you do what is right, will you not be accepted?"* Genesis 4:7b.

Like many others, too often I have said that our sanctification, our growing in obedience is God's responsibility! I pointed to Philippians 2:13 as my proof text. *"For it is God who works in you to will and to act according to His good pleasure."* I was missing something. The verse starts with *"For."* That little word connects verse 13 to what comes before. We do need the context to see the whole truth.

"Therefore, my dear friends, as you have always obeyed — not only in my presence, but now much more in my absence — continue to work out your salvation with fear and trembling," Philippians 2:12. In other words, you're saved, now continue to obey. Verses 12 and 13 are connected because it is our responsibility to be obedient. In salvation, God gave us the knowledge and the power to obey. That is why the psalmist says to God, *"teach me,"* and *"give me understanding."*

Paul taught, *"Put to death, therefore, whatever belongs to your earthly nature,"* Colossians 3:5a. He lists many sins in the next verses and how we need to replace them with godly living. It is our sole responsibility to repent. When we do, the Holy Spirit fills us with joy. When we do not change and sin, the Holy Spirit gives us pain and grief. Why then do we struggle in life? Our victory is missing. Our struggling, is still two words, delayed obedience.

Prayer: O Lord of lords, forgive our struggling and disobedient hearts! The psalmist prayer and petition is ours. Teach us to follow Your decrees. Give us understanding to obey Your laws with all our heart. In Jesus' name we pray. Amen.

Psalm 119:67

"Before I was afflicted I went astray, but now I obey Your Word."

Affliction, God's way of teaching us

How difficult it is for us to have prosperity and good health for a length of time, without getting lazy spiritually. God mercifully allows us to go through affliction to put our eyes back on Him again. It was Spurgeon who said, "We should be every now and then salted with affliction, lest we putrefy with sin."

Disciple Peter once cared more for himself than for his bloody and beaten Lord. He denied the Savior's claim on his life. He was then in deep despair for his foolish pride. The loving eye of Jesus remained on Peter and he learned a big lesson that day! Later on, Peter could boldly write to us about why he had to learn what he did.

"In this you greatly rejoice, though now for a little while you may have had to suffer grief in all kinds of trials. These have come so that your faith – of greater worth than gold, which perishes even though refined by fire – may be proved genuine and may result in praise, glory and honor when Jesus Christ is revealed," 1 Peter 1:6-7.

My experience is like that of Peter and David. At times, the joys and pleasures of this present world make it more difficult to think of the world to come. We love our easy chairs! We so easily leave the Lord's battles to others. We have already fought the good fight. And then God corrects us, to keep us fresh, spiritually speaking.

The truth is: sometimes affliction for a believer may be a sign of God's displeasure, but it's also proof of His love. With David we must say, *"It was good for me to be afflicted so that I might learn Your decrees,"* Psalm 119:71. Our God never gives up on those He has called to Himself. When afflictions come, grace is right there to make us more courageous for serving our God. Healed, we are far more motivated by the hope of the Heaven, filled still more with zeal for God. We learn freshly again, that it is our relationship to God and His work that is the most important passion of our life.

Prayer: O loving Lord, we thank You for not allowing us to sleep spiritually! Help us to appreciate Your rod of affliction! We want to be more faithful for You, Lord! In Jesus' name we pray. Amen.

Psalm 119:116-117

"Sustain me according to Your promise, and I will live; do not let my hopes be dashed. Uphold me, and I will be delivered; I will always have regard for Your decrees."

"Do not let my hopes be dashed"

Five years ago I was rushed to the hospital with severe chest pain from what turned out to be an artery, 95% blocked. With God's help and the prayers of many, I was at peace and at the right place. I was certain of one thing. God was not finished with my service to His kingdom. My prayer mirrored the words in our text.

"Uphold me and I will be delivered." Through God's strength we have the strength to carry on. We are His. God lovingly warned me right into the hospital. He protected me, body and soul. He has put all of us here to serve Him. By His grace, that is the desire of my heart. Even two nurses were interested in the Gospel.

"Do not let my hopes be dashed." Among other things in various countries, I am also teaching in the prison system here. Most of the men I teach are going to be in prison for a long time. After many months we have become good friends. We pray for each other and care about each other. In fact, they were praying for me when I went into the hospital, even as I was praying for them.

My prayer to God was to allow these men to be missionaries wherever they are in the prison system. It's all about discipleship. I see many of the 1500 in this jail. Many of the men are already reaching out to others who are without direction. They promise to do more.

"I will always have regard for Your decrees." God's Word is still changing many people. We must not back down in the battle for truth. The world is like Pilate who said to Jesus, *"What is truth?"* Please pray for His Word to continue to go out through us, His children.

Prayer: Dear gracious Lord, You are good! What a privilege to be Your ambassadors of reconciliation to many around the world. Use each one of us more and more for Your eternal kingdom. In Jesus' name we pray. Amen.

Psalm 119:165

"Great peace have they who love Your law, and nothing can make them stumble."

God's secret to peace

We may say and sing that we love God's law, but do we? Most of us know there are ten commandments, but few know that the first four commandments are to love God and the next six are to love others. It is rare for people to know that there are no commandments to love yourself. Is it any wonder then, that so many people lack peace in their life? We do not even know what the law teaches about love.

I heard a "reformed" professor say millions of young people are depressed because they hate themselves. He said that if they loved themselves more, they would not be depressed. God says, *"No one ever hated his own body,"* in Ephesians 5:29a. This professor turned the Bible upside down! How can such a person help people with a spiritual problem? God promises peace when we *"love His law,"* which is loving God and then others in that order. So many have personal problems because that order is not right. The "self-first" idea of peace is another religion. Their peace is temporary because it is dependent on circumstances, possessions or people, not on God.

We lack peace because God is not the most important relationship in our life, and others are not second. When this happens the Holy Spirit gives frustration, not peace. Prisons all over the world would be empty, and churches would be full, if the Biblical order of love was just lived out. The letters J.O.Y. spell joy. The "J" stands for Jesus, the "O" for others, and the "Y" stands for yourself. To experience joy and peace in our life, the order must be 1. Jesus 2. Others 3. Yourself. That is peace! If we put the O before the J, we look for peace in others changing. God can give us peace, even if others do not change.

A man in prison said that all he ever wanted was for his father to love him. He put his earthly father before his Heavenly Father, and had no peace. Tomorrows lesson begins with another J.O.Y. example.

Prayer: O Lord, we blame little money, difficult circumstances, and unloving spouses and wayward children for our lack of peace. Forgive us for our out of order "love life." We praise You for giving us a peace the world cannot give. In Christ's name we pray. Amen.

Psalm 120:6-7 NKJV

"My soul has dwelt too long with one who hates peace. I am for peace; but when I speak, they are for war."

When others treat us badly, then what?

A truck driver came into the chapel crying. His wife just left him. Tears of repentance over his mistakes poured from his eyes. God did His work on this man. I only had a few minutes with him. He said that he would do many "good things" to get his wife back. I warned him. Do your "good things," <u>for God</u> (JOY) as worship first! Only God can change your wife's heart. If you don't do this, what will happen when she does not quickly come back? You will be tempted to give in to anger, bitterness, fear and worry. You will not look like a new Christian. Wait for God to change your wife, even as you stay faithful.

We recognize that others are not what they should be to us. But what are we to them? Do we have a new spirit? Do we confess their sins or ours? Does our faithful "church-going" match the way we live each day? Are the deeds of the flesh in Galatians 5:19-21 still in us?

Just like in our text, we too are persecuted. We too are tempted to hate back. God says, *"Vengeance in Mine, I will repay."* What can we do but keep a sound mind and not give in to a spirit of fear. As Christians, we have the fruit of the Spirit woven into the very fiber of our being. It needs to show. Galatians 5:22-23 describes how we as Christians have a God-given, Spirit-filled, personality. The old fighting spirit of anger and bitterness has gone. A new spirit has come. *"The fruit of the Spirit is love, joy, peace, longsuffering, kindness, goodness, faithfulness, gentleness and self-control,"* <u>to others</u>.

So then, what can we do when seemingly "good people" want to fight with us? God's good answer is in 1 Peter 2:15, *"For it is God's will that by doing good you should silence the ignorant talk of foolish men."* May we concentrate on being in the center of God's will. That is where peace really is, not in what others say or don't say.

Prayer: Loving Father, we too cry out to You as the psalmist does here. Protect us from those who attack us. Help us not to get discouraged, but to peacefully press on for You. For You alone are the Prince of peace. Lord, turn our hearts to You so that Your kingdom may advance in us and through us. In Jesus' name we pray. Amen.

Psalm 121:2-4

"My help comes from the LORD, the Maker of Heaven and Earth. He will not let your foot slip — He who watches over you will not slumber; indeed, He who watches over Israel will neither slumber nor sleep."

More than a traveling Psalm

We often read this Psalm when we go on a journey. We want God's protection and blessing. This psalm is a major source of hope and encouragement from the Lord. Our God is so faithful, all the time!

He who is the Creator and sustainer of everything is our personal help. He who sees all and knows all is our God. He who has infinite mercy and unlimited wisdom is our advocate. He who has thousands of angels to dispatch at His command is our Commander. So when God says, *"He will not let your foot slip."* It is not an empty promise.

Dare we ask a personal question? Why then do we still worry way too often? Why do we still have some seeds of doubt concerning the goodness of God in our difficult times? We know in our head that He works all things for our good and His glory. We have a trust sickness.

Part of our problem is that His ways are so much higher than our ways. His thoughts are so far superior to ours. Our hearts are inferior to God's heart. *"The heart is deceitful above all things and beyond cure. Who can understand it?"* Jeremiah 17:9. God who is far greater than us, does have everything figured out for our good and for His glory.

This we know for sure about God. *"He who watches over you will not slumber; indeed, He who watches over Israel will neither slumber nor sleep."* No matter what happens, God is there! There is no watchman like God. He not only watches over us continually, He is also willing to help us, any time. God has everything in our little world under His control. Can anything happen that God does not know about or see? Can anything surprise our God? Even though we do not fully understand how and when God moves in   mysterious ways, it is right here that we need to trust Him. True faith is all about a sincere trust in God.

Prayer: O Creator of all, we thank You that Your Holy Spirit prays for us even as You watch over us. Truly our help comes from You who alone are Lord. May our eyes never leave You, who will never forsake us. May Your kingdom come, not ours. In Jesus' name we pray. Amen.

Psalm 122:6-9

"Pray for the peace of Jerusalem: 'May those who love you be secure. May there be peace within your walls and security within your citadels.' For the sake of my brothers and friends, I will say, 'Peace be within you.' For the sake of the house of the LORD our God, I will seek your prosperity."

Peace, security and prosperity in the church

God wants peace, security, and prosperity in the church. Christianity is a love affair with the Lord Jesus Christ. Those who love each other, love to look at each other. The "church" is the body of Christ, the bride of Christ. Our Bridegroom Christ, grooms the church like a master gardener grooms a garden. Such gardens bear much fruit. Groomed by Christ, the church must be at peace, must be secure, and will prosper.

Jesus is our friend in our "need." We need Jesus more than anything. His church is made up of sinners who had a sin debt problem that they could not pay. When Adam sinned he lost his and our righteous standing with God. He lost his peace and eternal security. With him we fell spiritually, socially, materially, eternally and more. We have a friend in Jesus who restores us to God. *"God made Him who had no sin to be sin for us, so that in Him we might become the righteousness of God,"* 2 Corinthians 5:21. Jesus meets our deepest needs, willingly and lovingly. The church prospers when our love for Him is real.

Jesus is our friend in "deed." *"For you know the grace of our Lord Jesus Christ; that though He was rich, yet for your sakes He became poor, so that you through His poverty might become rich,"* 2 Corinthians 8:9. "What a friend we have in Jesus, all our sins and griefs to bear! What a privilege to carry everything to God in prayer. O what peace we often forfeit, O what needless pain we bear; all because we do not carry everything to God in prayer."

Friends of Christ will befriend others. Together we walk in and out of many lives. True friends leave footprints on many hearts.

Prayer: O loving Lord, You show us that true peace is not what we buy, but who bought us. The Apostle Paul finally had peace, not because he found something, but because Jesus found him. Lord fill us with Your presence so there can be peace, security, and prosperity in the church. In Jesus' name we pray. Amen.

Psalm 123:1-2

"I will lift up my eyes to You, to You whose throne is in Heaven. As the eyes of slaves look to the hand of their master, as the eyes of a maid look to the hand of her mistress, so our eyes look to the LORD our God, till He shows us His mercy."

We are totally dependent on God

We are given two examples to help us see how reliant we are on God. A slave is dependent on his master for everything. A maid waits on her mistress to see what needs to be done in her service. A slave or maid is not independent in any way and neither are we. We live in a world that stresses independence, but we are dependent on God.

"I will lift up my eyes to You." Why? We are children of father Adam. When Adam fell into sin, we fell with him. We are guilty, God is now our judge. When God remakes us in Christ, as Christians, He is now our Father. What a relationship change! We now depend on Him to complete the work He is doing in us. God alone directs us to be pleasing to Him, useful on this Earth. We look to Him for direction and protection. May His will be done in our lives, for our natural will still strays from Him and from His loving commands. We now say, *"I will lift up my eyes to You, to You whose throne is in Heaven."* Authorities on this Earth do not have a throne in Heaven. Our God, who sits on a throne in Heaven, is also in control on this Earth, ruling all things. What a comfort. Nothing is too hard for our Lord!

Slaves and maids, *"look to the hand of their master.* May *"our eyes look to the LORD our God, till He shows us His mercy."* May we not get tired of "looking to" the Lord. Because of His great love, we are not consumed. His power is infinite. His wisdom is beyond searching out. He always sees us. He is everywhere present. Mercy is His divine specialty and He loves to give it to His children. By giving us mercy, God is bringing glory to Himself even as He builds our faith in Him. May we approach His throne boldly, *"till He shows us His mercy."*

Prayer: Dear Merciful Lord, we are totally dependent on Your mercy. Satan says don't go to You, for we don't deserve to go. True. But Lord, that is why we beg You for Your mercy! We come in Christ's name, as joint heirs with Your Son. Fill our cup, Lord. Accomplish Your purposes in us. In Jesus' name we pray. Amen.

Psalm 124:8

"Our help is in the name of the LORD, the Maker of Heaven and Earth."

"Our help is in the name of the LORD"

This is a song of ascents the people of Israel sang as they went up to Jerusalem to worship God. The psalm opens with praising God for protecting them from their enemies. Even today, little Israel is still surrounded by enemies. But what about our enemies? Do we not also have the name of the LORD as our own personal help?

Since our help is in *"the name"* of the LORD, what is in *"the name"*? Each of the many names of our one God, describes a different part of His character. EL, ELOAH: means God is mighty. ELOHIM: shows that God is the Creator and strong. EL SHADDAI: means "God Almighty." "The Mighty One of Jacob" in Genesis 49:24 speaks of God's power over all. ADONAI: means "Lord" in the New Testament. The name, YHWH or JEHOVAH is "LORD," (all capitals), given to Moses in Exodus 3:14. The meaning is that God is accessible, near to those who call on Him for deliverance in Psalm 107:13. We ask Him for forgiveness in Psalm 107:13, and for guidance in Psalm 31:3.

The name YAHWEH-JIREH: means "The LORD will provide," used by Abraham when God provided the ram to be sacrificed in place of Isaac. The name, YAHWEH-RAPHA means "The LORD who heals" is found in Exodus 15:26. Jehovah is the One who heals us in body, by preserving us and by curing diseases. He cures our soul, by pardoning iniquities. The name, YAHWEH-NISSI: means "The Lord our Banner," used in Exodus 17:15, in a victory over the Amalekites. The name, YAHWEH-M'KADDESH: means "The Lord who sanctifies and makes Holy." God alone makes us holy. The name, YAHWEH-SHALOM: means "The Lord our Peace." The name, YAHWEH-ROHI: means "The Lord is our Shepherd." Used by David as he realized his relationship as a shepherd to sheep, was his relationship with God.

Prayer: Lord, the meaning of Your name shows us how complete You are! You alone are our everything, our all. You, who sees and knows everything is our everlasting and eternal God. With You, we lack nothing. *"Our help is in the name of the LORD."* Accept our praise and worship. In Jesus' name we pray, Amen.

Psalm 125:1

"Those who trust in the LORD are like Mount Zion, which cannot be shaken but endures forever."

Difficult trials are the food of faith

Kings have a covenant responsibility to protect their people. Various threats will come to threaten the welfare of the citizens. When the hand of the king demonstrates his ability to protect them, the hearts of the people rejoice. They now trust in that king even more. As His believers, we have much more than a powerful earthly king. We have a Heavenly King. Our God King is also an eternal One. He is not in power and authority for a week or month, but forever. *"As the mountains surround Jerusalem, so the LORD surrounds His people both now and forevermore,"* Psalm 125:2.

God promises us in His Word that He will bless us. The question is, how strong is our faith in God? The strength of our faith is the size of our love and hope in God. Will God do as He has promised? Faith has little to do with feelings. It is rooted in our hope, our love for Him, even as we trust in Him. Faith is dependent on the character of our God to do as He says He will do. Faith is resting on and in His Holy Word.

God is delighted when we exercise our faith. He has great joy in His heart when He protects and directs His children in their daily trials. In fact, our trials are the very food of faith. Trials cause us to trust in God more. Yet in the same trials, Satan wants us to doubt in God's ability to care for us. How we respond in our trials each day, demonstrates our level of faith.

When we read the Word of God, we must be captivated by how God exercised His sovereign love to all those who trusted in Him. We are no different than David who could slay a giant in God's strength. The mighty God who shut the mouths of hungry lions for Daniel is our God. The God who opened the sea for Israel to walk across on dry ground, is still the One who opens our way to the promised land. What have we to fear leaning on the everlasting arms?

Prayer: Dear powerful and loving Lord, how great You are. We are privileged way beyond what we can understand. Help us to trust You more and more. We worship You. In Jesus' name we pray. Amen.

Psalm 126:5-6

"Those who sow in tears will reap with songs of joy. He who goes out weeping, carrying seed to sow, will return with songs of joy, carrying sheaves with him."

"Go"

I was ready to walk out the door of McDonald's to teach in the government offices in the Philippines. These meetings were to teach various church leaders how to reach those with addictions. Suddenly, a demon-possessed man came up from behind me and started pleading, "Don't Go!" "Don't Go!" How interesting! If demons don't want us to *"Go,"* then we should know that God does. I was beginning to appreciate the urgency of God's *"Go."*

Weeks later, the pastor who arranged the training sessions was saying, "We need to study this counseling book and then go." Since he had seen the demon-possessed man in McDonald's, I walked up behind him and pleaded, "Don't Go!" "Don't go!" Then I turned to Luke 10 where Jesus sent out disciples. Who were these 70? Surely they had not known Jesus for a long time. Jesus said to them, *"Go! I am sending you out like lambs among wolves,"* Luke 10:3. I added, "What do you think would happen if they studied for a year or so?" Nothing. Who wins? Satan. What part of God's *"Go"* don't we understand?

God commanded the church to go to sinners. John Wesley said, "The church must go to sinners or go to oblivion. A church that merely teaches its own is already in the cemetery." Why don't we "Go"? Is it unbelief? Is it a lack of faith? Are we too comfortable? God told Moses to *"Go"* to Pharaoh. Moses said, "No, not qualified." God said, "I just qualified you." Jesus said in Luke 19:10, *"The Son of Man came to seek and to save what was lost."* The seeking comes first.

Jesus said to His disciples, *"All authority in Heaven and Earth has been given to Me. Therefore go and make disciples,"* Matthew 28:19-20. God said to Isaiah, *"Whom shall I send?"* Who will go for us?" Isaiah replied, *"Here am I. Send me!"* The farmer that does not go and sow will have no harvest.

Prayer: Dear Lord, we are thankful to be on Your team, going under Your authority, in Your power, equipped by You. In Jesus' name we pray. Amen.

Psalm 126:6

"He who goes out weeping, carrying seed to sow, will return with songs of joy, carrying sheaves with him."

Sow the seeds, return with joy

Life is difficult. Pain, doubt, some anger, anxiety and a lot of confusion can overwhelm us. Even though God allows heavy trials, He is always there to rescue us. And then, our faith grows! God is seldom early with His blessings, but never late. Examples from history will help us see *"songs of joy"* if believers stay faithful in the trials of life.

Joseph was sold as a slave by his brothers. Surely many tears were shed. Years later, Joseph was second in command in Egypt. God had his life under control the whole time. And then there was rejoicing.

In the book of Esther, God's enemies seem to be in total control. The wicked Haman even had a date fixed, to eliminate the Jews. In the last hours, just in time, God intervened. He saved Esther and her people and destroyed Haman. After weeping for days, *"songs of joy"* broke forth.

Job lost his children, his servants, his possessions and his health in just one day. After a time of suffering, God restored Job and he regained his health and possessions. After sadness, came joy.

August 2, 1492, was the last day the Jews were allowed in Spain. There was so much weeping. Many people were killed, possessions were confiscated and the people were kicked out. On August 3, 1492, Columbus sailed and ended up in America. In the USA, the Jews were to continue to prosper.

Are you now going through a time of trial, pain and turmoil? Then put your hope in God. He promises every believer something special! *"No temptation has seized you except what is common to man. And God is faithful; He will not let you be tempted beyond what you can bear. But when you are tempted, He will also provide a way out so that you can stand up under it,"* 1 Corinthians 10:13.

Prayer: Gracious Lord, may our weeping never keep us from sowing! May we be faithful for You, no matter what comes our way. For You are God, able to do above what we imagine or think. Lord, we look to You, to work all things for our good. In Jesus' name we pray. Amen.

Psalm 127:1-2a

"Unless the LORD builds the house, its builders labor in vain. Unless the LORD watches over the city, the watchmen stand guard in vain. In vain you rise up early and stay up late, toiling for food to eat."

Over commitment brings down the house

Over commitment is the ruin of many homes. Our God cares about commitment, but He is not a God of over commitment! Granted there are many committed to nothing and to no one. They wait for people, the church or the government to help them. That is under commitment.

God created man to work, even to enjoy work! But working 12 or more hours a day and then crawling in bed and doing it again the next day, week in week out without a break, is called over commitment. What kind of house is being built? Even a pastor can be over committed. He may go out to every invitation, yet leave his family without his attention. If he prays in a thousand houses but not in his own, whose house is he building? Our work or our ministry can so easily become our idol. *"Unless the LORD builds the house, its builders labor in vain."*

God is far more interested in what we are becoming, than what we are doing! We have the responsibility to be a Christ-like husband or father, wife or mother. More than money is needed to build a home. Children understand the need to work, but they also need a relationship, and that takes time.

James Dobson wrote, "At one point I remember being scheduled seventeen straight nights away from home at a time when we had a little toddler who loved to play with her daddy. Gradually, I came to understand that the Lord wanted me to use good judgment and common sense in the things I agreed to do — even if they involved very worthwhile causes. There will always be more good things to do than one man or woman can get done! I realized I needed to maintain a healthy balance between Christian duty, work responsibilities, recreation, and meaningful family life."

Prayer: Loving Lord, we want You to build our houses. We do not want to spend any part of our life, *"in vain."* Help us "good workers" to see the need to spend our time building relationships with You and with others. In Jesus' name we pray. Amen.

Psalm 128:1

"Blessed are all who fear the LORD, who walk in His ways."

When God is your walking friend

In this psalm, God promises blessings for *"all who fear the LORD, who walk in His ways."* God loves those who are devoted to Him. This does not say that God blesses those who go to church. He blesses those whose *"walk"* is with Him. He blesses those who are doers of the Word. *"Blessings and prosperity will be yours,"* Psalm 128:2b.

In Proverbs 31, a Biblical wife and her family are blessed when she *"walks"* with God. Proverbs describes what a godly wife looks like, as she *"walks"* with God. She shapes the next generation to love the Lord. She encourages her husband to do many things to build God's kingdom. When two people *"walk"* with God in marriage, they serve others and each other too. <u>Good theology is caught as children are taught by the example of their parents</u>.

God promises those who love Him, *"Your sons will be like olive shoots around your table,"* Psalm 128:3b. Your children will be content, at peace, growing spiritually, flourishing, as they sit in your home. They will not be wandering the streets, lonely for love, looking for attention. Children who are lonely for love quickly fall into the arms of predators, who will make children slaves to serve their own purposes. Such children are not flourishing.

In this psalm, God gives His sure and powerful benediction or blessing on God-fearing families. It says, *"May the LORD bless you from Zion all the days of your life; may you see the prosperity of Jerusalem, may you live to see your children's children,"* Psalm 128:5a. In other words, may you have spiritual blessings in abundance, and may God give you the physical strength for many more years to build His precious kingdom!

It is so sad that many people walk in and out of this world without God and without His blessings. God blesses families whose walk is with Him, causing them to leave footprints of their goodness in our world. May God bless your home and family life.

Prayer: Dear Heavenly Father, You are a faithful God who truly loves Your children. You even give them Christ's precious name, Christian. We praise and worship You. In Jesus' name we pray. Amen.

Psalm 129:2-3

"They have greatly oppressed me from my youth, but they have not gained the victory over me. Plowmen have plowed my back and made their furrows long."

The church family, abusive or loving?

How do we respond to abuse? On her sixteenth birthday there was a party for this girl at church. They had a good time playing games, beautiful innocent fun. She returned home at 11:00 that night, a half hour later than promised. Her dad was furious. He beat her so bad that he left welts on her back. Her mother, afraid, did not say a word. This man prided himself in his "good doctrine," but knew nothing about love. He drank too much to go along with his daily anger. And he was an elder in the church. This scene is all too familiar.

After her horrible beating, the young lady escaped through her bedroom window. She ran crying to the bus stop three miles away. She stopped five hundred miles later. Those who prey on beautiful, young girls spotted her first. They forced her into a life of drugs and prostitution. She sank lower into the depths of despair. She ran again ,but ended up in the same situation. She was used and abused again and again by those who love wickedness. Again, she ran.

A loving, married couple picked her up and began to help her heal. She was given new clothes and a clean bed. She experienced love and compassion. Instead of being used and abused, she was gently led into a life of peace and full acceptance. She found out that what God said was so true! *"But the LORD is righteous; He has cut me free from the cords of the wicked,"* Psalm 129:4. There is a God and He is very loving! He sends out His angels to help. Pray for them.

One church member abused her. Another church member loved her. Are we the abusive type, or the loving type?

Prayer: Loving Lord, what a beautiful Savior You are. You truly do deliver us. You truly are a God of mercy and grace. When we are so down and so lost, it is You who rescues us. You are the one who re-stores us. You forgive and protect us. "What a fellowship, what a joy divine leaning on Your everlasting arms." We worship and praise You for reaching out to us who are without hope in a wicked and perverse generation. In Jesus' name we pray. Amen.

Psalm 130:7

"O Israel, put your hope in the LORD, for with the LORD is unfailing love and with Him is full redemption."

Hope in the LORD's *"full redemption"*

We lose hope in God through our doubt, fear, worry, and even in our anger and bitterness. We call these kind of responses, "anxiety," which can lead to depression. We then struggle because our lack of hope doubts God's ability to care for us. *"Faith is the assurance of things hoped for,"* Hebrews 11:1a. Satan through his demonic helpers cannot take our salvation from us. But if they can get us to doubt God and His ability to care for us, then we will be a poor witness to those around us. How do we maintain our hope in God? That is the question that needs an answer.

We keep our hope in God through the testimony of the Bible, by the Holy Spirit, and through prayer. Our weak faith needs to read the Bible. We may have the Bible in our house, but is it in our hearts? That is the house that really matters. The Bible speaks to our souls, our spirits, calming us and redirecting our hearts to trust in God's ability and willingness to care for us. We will be tempted, at times, to serious anxiety when a difficulty presents itself. It is then, that we must put our hope in the LORD's unfailing love for us personally.

God's Spirit gives us eternal hope. We are made of two parts, body and spirit. We are more spirit than we are body because our spirit is eternal. Our body dies. Until it does, our spirit tells our body what to do. God ministers mainly to our spirit or soul. *"The Spirit Himself testifies with our spirit that we are God's children,"* Romans 8:16. The same Holy Spirit who wrote the Bible, writes on our hearts.

"With Him is full redemption." We must be filled with hope, assured of God's complete salvation! John wrote, *"I write these things to you who believe in the name of the Son of God so that you may know that you have eternal life,"* 1 John 5:13. As Christians, we already have eternal life, today. God is so good!

Prayer: O Lord, what a complete and full salvation You give to us. Fill us with Your Spirit, so that our hope in You flows in and out of us. Use us to give others hope. In Jesus' name we pray. Amen.

Psalm 131:1-2a

"My heart is not proud, O LORD, my eyes are not haughty; I do not concern myself with great matters or things too wonderful for me. But I have stilled and quieted my soul."

Have I *"stilled"* my soul?

David is sincere in worship to God as he travels up the mountain to Jerusalem. His short song of ascents is only three verses. But there is a wealth of knowledge in this psalm. The worship of God, the well-being of others, and even myself, is at stake.

Have I stilled my soul is a good question. Am I anxious? Am I too tense, too stressed out, too often? Why are my muscles so tight? Am I getting too much exercise or am I filled with soul tension? What is going on? Do I bring this on myself? Are the pressures of life too great? The truth is that I still have some wrong responses to people and events. There are some things that are not the way they should be, yet my worry, according to Jesus, is little faith.

David makes a beautiful observation that explains why his soul is *"stilled."* He tells us why he is not anxious, but content with God. David fully trusts that God, with all of His powerful attributes, will surely direct him and completely care for him. He has learned from his "faith experience," that God is trustworthy and will not disappoint him.

David learned that he is personally responsible to be faithful. After that, it is God's responsibility to take care of the results. This is why David could say that he was content and at peace.

David knew for sure that God and all of His powerful attributes were always for him. David learned that going into God's own area of responsibility was foolish and a lack of faith. *"I do not concern myself with great matters or things too wonderful for me."* Why? Because God was completely able and willing to care for David. He alone completely handled the results of David's faithful living.

David is now gone. Jesus has come. God has not changed in His willingness and ability to personally care for every believer. Jesus still says in Matthew 11:28, *"Come to Me, all you who are weary and burdened, and I will give you rest."*

Prayer: O loving Lord, may we cast all our cares on You because You care for us. We worship You. In Jesus' name we pray. Amen.

Psalm 132:15

"I will bless her (Zion's children) with abundant provisions; her poor I will satisfy with food."

Blessings to those who trust in the LORD

Psalm 132 begins, "O LORD, *remember David and all the hardships he endured.*" David was in distress often. At times he was in a *"horrible pit"* and in *"miry clay."* His problem is ours. We are in and out of trusting in God. It is an important faith lesson for us that David did not cry for the help of man! He trusted God to deliver him. God heard David and did what no man could possibly do, He rescued him. David records the greatness of God's mercy that was always, just in time. He writes to us so that we will turn to God for help.

If we go to man and sound off our complaints, we are basically saying that God is not fair. In love, God allows affliction to teach us what we would never learn any other way. God will remove whatever stands in our way in our relationship with Him. Peter tenderly said, *"Beloved, do not think it strange concerning the fiery trial which is to try you, as though something strange happened to you,"* 1 Peter 4:12 NKJV.

In our trials, it is difficult to live by faith. Yet it is through our trials that God builds our faith and dependence in Him. Notice what David by faith learned. *"I waited patiently for the LORD; and He inclined to me, and heard my cry,"* Psalm 40:1 NKJV. Our afflictions by God's hand, make His mercy necessary, all to build up our small faith. God delights in us coming to Him for His mercy and grace! Then we will be able to say with David, *"He also brought me up out of a horrible pit, out of the miry clay, and set my feet upon a rock, and established my steps,"* Psalm 40:2 NKJV.

God humbles us in our afflictions so He can bless us! As Zion's children, God rescues us for His own glory and praise. He also delivers us and provides for us so that we will encourage others to trust in Him also. He continues to bless us with *"abundant provisions"* for His glory and our good. He is so worthy of our trust and worship!

Prayer: Dear most gracious Lord, we thank You for Your beautiful promises in this psalm. May we never forget Your tender mercies to us. We praise You for them! In Jesus' name we pray. Amen.

Psalm 133:1

"How good and pleasant it is when brothers live together in unity!"

Relationships, the spice of life

No one will be able to stand before God in The Judgment and say, "I was a great worker but I was not good at my relationships with others." God gave us ten commands, to help us in our relationships. We have four commands to have a relationship with God and six to form relationships with others, *"in unity."*

If we are not interested in better relationships with God and man, we are in rebellion to God. Our relationships either get better or they get worse. There is no neutral in the transmission of love. We must constantly build relationships, not take them for granted. That was Israel's big mistake. Today, husbands and wives still make the same mistake with each other and with their children. Building relationships takes time and energy, just like building a house does. Even after the house is built, we still need to maintain it!

Jesus came into this world to have a close relationship with us. He speaks to us as a bridegroom does to the bride, *"Arise, My darling, My beautiful one, and come with Me,"* Song of Songs 2:10b. How can there possibly be unity in the church without a close relationship between Christ and the church, which is the body of Christ?

The Lord Jesus Christ is so fully committed to us. In the Song of Songs 2:9, Christ is outside our house. He is *"gazing through the windows."* He is peering into the hearts of His believers, looking to bless them all, abundantly. Christ is not *"gazing,"* looking to find fault. He already took away the sins of every believer by saving us. He was already fully committed to us, even before the creation of the world. Why then are we looking for fault in the church instead of pursuing love? Fighting is wicked, lazy, selfish, and arrogant. Can we believe in an eternal relationship with God and yet want to end our relationship with others in the church. Something is wrong with our love, faith and obedience.

Prayer: O loving Lord, Your commitment to us is so loving. When we are committed to others we will love them much also. Examine our hearts. Make us love You and others more and more. In Jesus' name we pray. Amen.

Psalm 134:3

"May the LORD, the Maker of Heaven and Earth, bless you from Zion."

God's benediction, receive it with joy

In most churches, the worship service ends with the pastor giving a benediction. This is commanded by God, for His personal, promised blessing. Recently in my church the pastor gave the usual blessing. A visitor had his right hand out reaching for the blessing. That is the right idea. Where did this command of God's blessing come from?

"*The LORD said to Moses, Tell Aaron and his sons, 'This is how you are to bless the Israelites. Say to them: " 'The LORD bless you and keep you; the LORD make His face shine upon you and be gracious to you; the LORD turn His face toward you and give you peace,'"* Numbers 6:22-26.

In the history of the church since Moses, there has been a form of this high priestly blessing. God wants to bless His people. God wants to show a believer and the world, that He can make a difference in a believer's life. If people assemble to worship God, He blesses them. He must bless them and He will, for that is the very character of God. We do worship God for who He is, and for what He continues to do. When we go to "church" we give worship and honor to God, but we also receive a blessing from Him.

What do we receive in "blessings" from God in His benediction? We receive undeserved, grace and peace. We all deserve death and misery for our sin. "*For the wages of sin is death, but the gift of God is eternal life in Christ Jesus our Lord,*" Romans 6:23. Salvation is grace. We cannot work for it or buy it. It is a eternal blessing from God.

We receive the blessings of mercy from God. Jesus said, "*Blessed are the merciful, for they shall obtain mercy,*" Matthew 5:7.

God's benediction is in Trinity to you personally. Receive it with joy! "*May the grace of the Lord Jesus Christ, and the love of God, and the fellowship of the Holy Spirit be with you all,*" 2 Corinthians 13:14.

Prayer: Gracious Lord, we love and appreciate You even more than Your blessings! Yet Your blessings are so many, we could never list them all. We deserve none of them. Lord, You are so precious to us! Accept our worship. In Jesus' name we pray. Amen.

Psalm 135:5

"I know that the LORD is great, that our LORD is greater than all gods."

Self-confidence or God-confidence?

A great song is, *"How Great Thou Art."* God is far greater than we will ever understand. Faith demands we must have complete confidence in Him. Wisdom shouts, *"Trust in the LORD with all your heart and lean not on your own understanding; in all your ways acknowledge Him, and He will make your paths straight." "For the LORD will be your confidence and will keep your foot from being snared,"* Proverbs 3:5-6 & 26. Foolishness shouts, "be self-confident."

Ask Naaman, the former leper, about God's seemingly crazy command, *"Go, wash yourself seven times in the Jordan, and your flesh will be restored and you will be cleansed,"* 2 Kings 5:10. Naaman was not confident in that dirty river healing him. His pagan advisers said, *"If the prophet had told you to do some great thing, would you not have done it?"* When Naaman finally trusted in God, he was healed!

We don't need to wash in that dirty Jordan River. We are washed in Christ's pure blood. Our new faith will be constantly tested! Do we now have confidence in God? Will we trust God when a difficult trial comes? Or will we trust self and our own strength? True faith and the Bible shouts to us, *"I know that the LORD is great."*

"Now faith is being sure of what we hope for and certain of what we do not see. This is what the ancients were commended for," Hebrews 11:1-2. A true faith must see the invisible, believe in the incredible and receive the impossible. Did Israel's walking around Jericho seven times without a weapon and then shouting for the walls to come down, make sense? What a crazy, military strategy from man's view. Joshua had "God-confidence" and received the impossible, a huge victory!

When we can't understand what God is doing, we especially need to trust Him. In the end, our self-confidence gets shattered. That's good, *"The LORD will be your confidence."* It is a good thing that God builds our faith for we naturally live by sight, by our own self-confidence, not by faith or trusting in God.

Prayer: Almighty God, we often lack confidence in You. We thank You for teaching us what faith is all about. In Jesus' name we pray. Amen.

Psalm 136:1 NKJV

"Oh, give thanks to the LORD, for He is good! For His mercy endures forever."

God's mercy to us is personal

The mercy of God is different than His providence and love. God's providence is His inexhaustible and eternal storehouse of everything a believer needs both spiritual and physical. His love is why He gives the storehouse to us. God's mercy is His covenant giving of His huge, inexhaustible supply to us, even though we do not deserve it.

God's "mercy" is eternal. If God's *"mercy endures forever,"* it has to be eternal. There never was a time when God was not merciful. There never will be a time when God will fail to be merciful. God cannot help but be merciful because that is His character. Our text gives thanks for God's never-ending mercy to His true believers.

God's "mercy" is judicial. God the Eternal Judge gives mercy to people by taking away their death sentence. Mercy is a judicial term for when a judge gives a guilty offender a lesser sentence than what is deserved. So when God gives us eternal life instead of eternal death, that is judicial mercy to the greatest possible degree!

God's "mercy" is limited. That is what makes it very personal. God's mercy is not for everyone! What if an earthly judge pardoned everyone? Would not his mercy then cease to be mercy? By its very definition, the word mercy has to be limited and personal!

God put Esau and King Pharaoh in the world not to bless them, but to use them for His glory. God's perfect holiness was glorified by doing that. Why do we have a problem with this? God tells us why He did this: *"that He might make known the riches of His glory on the vessels of mercy, which He had prepared beforehand for glory, even us whom He called,"* Romans 9:23-24a NKJV. God saves some of every tribe, tongue and nation in the world, but not every single person in the world. The Lord's salvation to us is very personal.

Prayer: O Lord, we praise You for giving us Your judicial mercy when we deserved spiritual death! We stand in awe of Your tender mercy that was given simply because of Your good pleasure and nothing in us. That is why we will lovingly sing for all eternity, *"Worthy is the Lamb."* In Jesus' merciful name we pray. Amen.

Psalm 137:1

"By the rivers of Babylon we sat and wept when we remembered Zion."

Why do we hurt the ones we love?

Our text fits what I saw in jail this week. As I went to teach a pod of 30 men, a new man was waiting outside the pod. He wanted to talk about the difficulty of becoming a member of this "God Pod," where I daily teach how to live God's way. Through tears, this man said that he could not face the men in the pod because of what he had done. He told me that he has now ruined three important relationships in his life. The day before, he tried to strangle his girlfriend to death. He was completely without hope, without God.

After praying to start our two hour class, the new man asked if he could address the pod. Through tears he sobbed, "Why do we hurt the ones we love? If you see me weeping, it's because yesterday I had my hands around my girlfriend's neck. I choked her so bad that she has a black ring around her neck and has a severe concussion." The other guys in the pod said, "at least you admit it."

Why do we hurt the ones we love, is a great question! We turned to Jeremiah 17:9-10. We read that our hearts are deceitful above all things and desperately wicked. God tells us that He alone knows our hearts. In Matthew 15:18-19, we see that out of the heart flows all the wicked things we do. There is little grace, love and mercy flowing out of us because there is so little of the grace of God in us. That is why we hurt the ones we love. Our problem is: we need to grow in grace.

Israel was taken captive, prisoners for 70 years. God severely disciplined them for loving evil instead of loving Him who is good. They had a bad attitude. Even though they loved God a little, they loved their ugly sin habits more. Are we following the same course? Are we angry and bitter? Is our daily worship and our Sabbath day observance going well? Are we headed away from God or to God? After being disciplined by God and sent to the Babylon prison, Israel longed for the good old days back at home.

Prayer: Gracious Lord, fill us with Your love, grace and mercy so that we can love You and others. Our hearts need to be softened and changed for Your glory. As we receive grace from You, may we now extend grace to others. We ask this in Jesus' name. Amen.

Psalm 138:8a

"The LORD will fulfill His purpose for me; Your love, O LORD endures forever."

"The LORD will fulfill His purpose for me"

This psalm is very personal, and true for every believer that ever lived. David here testifies that God fulfilled His purpose throughout David's whole life. We know that David was chosen by God to be a relative of Jesus Christ. But is our text also a personal promise to us? Will the Lord *"fulfill His purpose for me"*? Yes, in two ways. First, God has also made us His relative through Christ. Secondly, God planned ahead, exactly what His children would do for Him, even before the world was made. *"For we are God's workmanship, created in Christ Jesus to do good works, <u>which God prepared in advance for us to do</u>,"* Ephesians 2:10b. Can you then see from our text, why *"The LORD will fulfill His purpose for me"*? It is all part of His eternal plan. Can anyone change God's eternal plan? No. What God opens, no one can shut. What God shuts, no one can open. We are by grace, God's workmanship. That must humble us as we do His will.

As Christians then, we are God's privileged children. Paul reasons with us to think Biblically concerning our new relationship with God. *"Now if we are children, then we are heirs - heirs of God and co-heirs with Christ,"* Romans 8:17a. What present and future blessings we have in Christ. Paul writes to the Galatians to remind them and us of Jesus' perfect humanity. *"God sent His Son, born of a woman, born under the law, to redeem those under the law that we might receive the full rights of sons. Because you are sons, God sent the Spirit of His Son into our hearts, the Spirit who calls out, 'Abba, Father.' <u>So you are no longer a slave, but a son</u>, and since you are a son, God has made you also an heir,"* Galatians 4:4b-7. How great is our God.

How must a son or daughter then respond to the love of a Father in Heaven who specifically adopted them? The answer is: with worship and faithful living.

Prayer: Beautiful Lord, what a blessed truth that *"Your love, O LORD endures forever."* We, the objects of Your grace are so privileged! You are the Author of our faith. You perfect our faith. We worship You for Your undeserved favor. In Jesus' name we pray. Amen.

Psalm 139:1-3

"O LORD, You have searched me and You know me. You know when I sit and when I rise; You perceive my thoughts from afar. You discern my going out and my lying down; You are familiar with all my ways."

Searching for a Biblical spouse

Are you looking for a spouse who loves the Lord, one with good, moral principles? You are picky and you should be. But if you are still waiting, God knows your thoughts. The verses above show that God knows everything about you, so much so, that David could say, *"All the days ordained for me were written in Your book before one of them came to be,"* Psalm 139:16. The Apostle Paul takes this even further. As God's Christians, *"We are God's workmanship, created in Christ Jesus to do good works, which God prepared in advance for us to do,"* Ephesians 2:10. Let's apply these verses to a Biblical marriage.

God knows your every thought and what kingdom work He has prepared for you! It stands to reason then, God also knows whom He has prepared to partner with you, to encourage you and to love you. Being single is fine, but not all have that gift. What is most common, God made clear to the first man, *"It is not good for the man to be alone. I will make a helper suitable for him,"* Genesis 2:18b.

Pray, "Lord show me the person You have prepared for me to help in Your service." God honors such a prayer for His name's sake. It is normal then, that we may be personally prepared spiritually for a Biblical spouse. Yet God may have some special work in mind that needs additional training. What better thing can we do in the meantime as we wait on God than to just be faithful?

We must eliminate our selfish behavior. That is a command for everyone in Philippians 2:3-4. A selfish person never makes a good spouse! We must be focused on others. We must go to work, with the right attitude, understanding that all work is ministry and service to God. Praying for a spouse is not enough. When we pray for our daily bread, we do not stay in bed. We must go and look for work. It is in the faithful going that God will supply our needs.

Prayer: Matchmaker Lord, we so appreciate Your Word. We need Your direction, Your grace and Your selection. Unite those who need a Biblical spouse to do Your work. In Jesus' name we pray. Amen.

Psalm 139:7-10

"Where can I go from Your Spirit? Where can I flee from Your presence? If I go up to the Heavens, You are there; if I make my bed in the depths, You are there. If I rise on the wings of dawn, if I settle on the far side of the sea, even there Your hand will guide me, Your right hand will hold me fast."

God is always everywhere present

The words of our text are beautiful. May the truth sink to the depths of our soul. In Trinity, God fills all parts of the universe, everywhere at once. That is called God's omnipresence. God is near us, all the time. No one can hide from God or be any place where God cannot reach them. David adds, *"'Surely the darkness will hide me and the light become night around me,' even the darkness will not be dark to You; the night will shine like the day, for darkness is as light to You,"* Psalm 139:11-12. From these verses, we can see how God's presence and eyes are everywhere, working together for our good and His glory.

The omnipresence of God should cause us to fear sin! Since God always sees our sin. We cannot hide it from Him. God's presence that is everywhere, is also eternal. His holy wrath will always be present in Hell. His love will always be present in Heaven.

God's omnipresence must move us to trust Him. If God had all power and wisdom but was not everywhere, He might still miss us. But our God is everywhere, thus He is trustworthy. *"'Can anyone hide in secret places so that I cannot see him?' declares the LORD. 'Do I not fill Heaven and Earth?' declares the LORD,"* Jeremiah 23:24.

What other god is like our God? What other god placed us in this world to watch us, to love us dearly and to protect us eternally? What other god will we stand before in the Judgment? The answer is none except our God! He is the God of gods.

Prayer: O Lord of lords, how thankful we are that You are always everywhere present in the universe. No matter where we are, You are there. What a comfort and benefit this is for us. And then to think, You are our Father in Jesus Christ also. Even when we sin You are always there to convict us by Your Holy Spirit, drawing us back into Your holy presence. Our words cannot express our gratitude clearly enough. May Your most holy name be praised. In Jesus' name we pray. Amen.

Psalm 139:23-24

"Search me, O God, and know my heart; test me and know my anxious thoughts. See if there is any offensive way in me, and lead me in the way everlasting."

Search my heart, Lord

This is one of the most beautiful prayers in the entire Bible. It begins with the personal request, *"search me."* It says, "Look at my life, God. Am I living as I should? Are there adjustments I need to make in my relationship with You or with others?" The words, *"search me,"* plead with my Creator and Redeemer to examine my life today. Therein is the beauty of this prayer. My spiritual life is ultimately between God and *"me."* Today, I am calling on my God to draw closer to *"me,"* and for *"me"* to be closer to God. I dare not wait until tomorrow, for that is the devil's day. If Satan can get me to put off doing something about my relationships today, he has won a small battle. Tomorrow he will try to get me to wait another day to be more serious with God. *"Seek the LORD while He may be found; call on Him while He is near,"* Isaiah 55:6.

"Know my heart; test me and know my anxious thoughts." That's also, a wise request. God says, *"the heart is deceitful above all things and beyond cure. Who can understand it? I the LORD search the heart and examine the mind, to reward a man according to his conduct, according to what his deeds deserve,"* Jeremiah 17:9-10. The text above moves me to ask God, *"is there is any offensive way in me?"* God is the only One who truly understands my heart. Lord examine it, according to Your righteous standards.

My soul knows, there is a judgment coming. What I do today will be judged someday soon. Therefore, I pause in life's journey to ask God, "How am I doing? Am I living in the light of eternity? Does my heart care about what is near and dear to You, Lord?" *"Lead me in the way everlasting."* Lead me to those things that really matter!

Prayer: Eternal Father, apart from Your holy Word and Will, I do not know what is *"everlasting."* Search me and test my heart today. Lord, lead me ever closer to You. Prepare my heart and use all of my life for eternal things. Prepare me for an eternity with You. Make me love what You love. In Jesus' name I pray. Amen.

Psalm 140:1-2

"Rescue me, O LORD, from evil men; protect me from men of violence, who devise evil plans in their hearts and stir up war every day."

Moving with the wicked is ugly

This note is to our grandsons and granddaughters. Your dad and mom and your grandpa and grandma are getting older. Someday soon, we will not be here with you. God will take us to Himself. We have something important to say to you. These words are also a loving warning from God to get your attention.

There are other children who will come along and encourage you to do what is wrong. That is negative peer pressure. Will you listen to them if they want you to do something that sounds fun, but is wrong? Or, will you do what is right? We also pray that you do not encourage others to do what they should not do. God always hates sin because He is a holy God. And God wants you to be holy too and so does your grandpa and grandma, and your dad and mom.

Whose approval is it that you seek the most? That is a key question in life. The condition of your heart is shown by whose approval you are seeking. You will seek that which you love the most. In school, do you want the approval of others more than the approval of God? Wisdom shouts, *"My son, if sinners entice you, do not give in to them."* Your actions show the condition of your heart. You will have a pattern of obedience or one of disobedience? You are either a slave to sin, or you are a slave to do what is right.

You surely want God's blessings in life. But know this: God does not so quickly bless proud sinners. You cannot live a good life without God's blessings and protection. The more you love God, the more He blesses you. We have seen that for a lifetime. Love obedience, not disobedience. *"Honor your father and your mother, as the LORD your God has commanded you, so that you may live long and that it may go well with you,"* Deuteronomy 5:16a. Don't move with the wicked. That's ugly!

Prayer: Dear Heavenly Father, help our children and grandchildren to be obedient to You and Your Word. Bring them all to Heaven. In Jesus' name we pray. Amen.

Psalm 141:1

"O LORD, I call to you; come quickly to me. Hear my voice when I call to You."

Moving with God is beautiful

Christianity is an intimate love relationship with God. We can see this relationship in the Song of Solomon. *"Let Him kiss me with the kisses of his mouth — for your love is more delightful than wine,"* Song of Solomon 1:2. Solomon's book is also called the Song of Songs because this song was the best of the 1005 songs that Solomon wrote, according to 1 Kings 4:32. The song is an allegory. The same words express the love of Christ and the Church, and that of a close marriage relationship.

The Gospel of grace is the Father, Son and Spirit kissing a sinner and then the new believer responding to that love. We see a picture of that throughout the song. Also in the parable of the prodigal son, we see the father kissing the son, even before the wayward son makes his confession to the father. The Christian life is an intimate relationship with God, a true beauty treatment.

Jesus' electing grace "kissed" every believer before the world was even made. Before we were even born, He was already holding us. Then at some point in our lives, He kissed us with His salvation. He took our sin and gave us His perfect righteousness! Jesus is the bride-groom of the Church and we are the bride. Our God kisses believers all the way into eternity, forever and ever. Truly the intimate love of God meets the deepest need we will ever have! The love of others will fail us at times, but God's love never fails.

In the Song of Solomon, the Shulamite bride greatly desires to be intimate with her husband. Believers greatly desire to be intimate with God. See the beautiful love words, *"Let the king bring me into his chambers. We rejoice and delight in you; we will praise your love,"* Song of Sol. 1:4b & 5a. Moving closely with God is a beauty treatment at its best. He puts a smile in our hearts that fills our whole being. May we then pray and seek God in this loving, intimate relationship.

Prayer: O most beautiful and loving Lord, when we don't desire You, humble us. For we can't live without Your divine kisses. Help us to learn and experience more about Your beautifying love so that we may love You more. In Jesus' name we pray. Amen.

Psalm 142:1-2

"I cry aloud to the LORD; I lift up my voice to the LORD for mercy. I pour out my complaint before Him; before Him I tell my trouble."

David's cave experience

David wrote this Psalm from a cave in Adullam when King Saul and the whole army were after him. David is in deep distress. He sees no way out of the situation he is in. David's eyes are glued on God. God has David's full attention. God is about to use this serious trial to deepen David's faith and show him another great deliverance! We have here an excellent worship scene. We also have a deep theological truth that can better be experienced, than understood by reading about it.

David does not utter a mind-wandering prayer. He does not give God a weather report or a history lesson in prayer. David is right to the point. He says, *"I cry aloud."* *"I lift up my voice."* David is not silent as he prays to God and as he also teaches us here about serious prayer.

David brings his *"complaint"* to God <u>alone</u>! This point is given to us four times in just two verses. For us to complain about God in our heart, would be foolish and prideful. David goes straight to his God in his difficult situation. God knew what David needed to prepare him for what he will soon experience as a leader. I know some pastors and counselors who were wrongly hurt in a significant way at a young age. They knew the pain of rejection and jealousy. God used that pain to train them to have compassion on the hurting. That is evangelism and discipleship training at its best. God rescued them when they cried for mercy. God is a Master at rescuing His children.

By this time of our text verse, God had already delivered David from the lion, from the bear and from Goliath. Not for one second was God unaware or unwilling to give David the needed protection. Our God is never too weak to deliver us. Even as a maturing believer, David still needed God's daily protection and so do we. Let us ask God for it right now.

Prayer: Almighty Lord, how great You were in delivering David. How great You are in delivering us. We worship You and are so grateful for Your amazing, timely protection. In Jesus' name we pray. Amen.

Psalm 142:3-4

"When my spirit grows faint within me, it is You who know my way. In the path where I walk men have hidden a snare for me. Look to my right and see; no one is concerned for me. I have no refuge; no one cares for my life."

When my spirit grows faint, God knows

How vulnerable and fragile we really are. It is a fact of life that our spirits will grow weak at times. God knows that and even allows a physical or mental weakness to get our eyes more focused on our need for Him. David said, *"When my spirit grows faint within me, it is You who know my way."* David did not say, "if my spirit grows weak," he said "*when*." We all have doubts and fears. These times are a test from God to prove the reality of our faith and trust Him. Satan will also use our time of weakness to try get us to doubt God. Understand the very real, spiritual war that we are in. It is a sign of strength when in our weakness, we turn to God. Paul said, *"when I am weak then I am strong!"* We are strong when we ask God for His mercy.

When David's trials suddenly confronted him, he was confident that God could and would help him. Think back to when David faced the giant Goliath. David immediately said to Saul, "Let no one *lose heart on account of this Philistine; your servant will go and fight him,"* 1 Samuel 17:32. David said to the giant, *"I come against you in the name of the LORD Almighty,"* 1 Samuel 17:45b. David knew that the battle is God's. He just had to be faithful, and so do we.

We need David's kind of faith in the ability of God to help us. If we do not have a living faith in God, we will doubt Him in our serious trials. God not only knows our way in our great trials, He also has a serious concern for us. God asked the hurting Job a great question. *"Do you watch when the doe bears her fawn? Do you count the months till they bear?"* Job 39:1b-2a. If God cares so much about when a deer is going to give birth, will He not care for us? Let us look to our great God in prayer.

Prayer. Dear Creator and Lord, You are far bigger than any trial we will ever face. You alone are the Author and Perfecter of our faith. Our eyes are on You to deliver us and give us more mercy. In Jesus' name we pray. Amen.

Psalm 142:5-6

"I cry to You, O LORD; I say, "You are my refuge, my portion in the land of the living. Listen to my cry, for I am in desperate need; rescue me from those who pursue me, for they are too strong for me."

In our desperation, may our faith look up!

In this psalm David is in serious prayer! He is hurting and desperate! David is fearful and worried as he looks around. We too are this desperate at times! Do we by faith look up? God is not only David's *"refuge,"* He is ours also. Far more than that, God is also David's and our *"portion,"* our exact need, just in time.

The mercy of God is never early. Nor is it ever late. God's mercy is designed to be a just-in-time faith builder. God knows we need to experience His mercy to better understand the depths of it. Think of how David looked back at the mercy of God with the bear and the lion, before he offered to fight the giant Goliath. May we also look back to what God has done and apply it to our present trials.

God has His sovereign all-powerful mercy waiting for us by the boatload. We need to seriously ask for it. We need to cry for it prayerfully, as David does in this Psalm. David knew what the writer of Hebrews later wrote. *"Let us then approach the throne of grace <u>with confidence</u>, so that we may receive mercy and find grace to help us in our time of need,"* Hebrews 4:16.

God has His endless supply of mercy, but we do need to humbly ask for it. David understands his personal responsibility to cry out to God. Do we? God's sovereignty is over everything. It's man's responsibility to ask, seek and knock at Heaven's door. God's sovereignty and man's responsibility are the best of friends! See how they meet here.

David is in a trap and needs out, now, before the one who set the snare can wring his neck and pluck his feathers. God rescued the needy Esther just in time from the hands of the wicked Haman. God rescued David just in time. The point is: God will rescue us! Will we cry to Him for mercy to free us from people and situations that are too strong for us?

Prayer: O sovereign Lord, too often we look around in worry and lose the battle. Forgive us for not looking up to You who take great joy in being merciful to Your children. In Jesus' name we pray. Amen.

Psalm 142:7

"Set me free from my prison, that I may praise Your name. Then the righteous will gather about me because of Your goodness to me."

Set free, to witness

Remember the context here. David is alone. He is on the run from Saul. The pagan countries will not shelter him. David is hiding in a cave, afraid and pleading with God to save him. David has a strong desire to survive this serious trial and then show his gratitude to God for His deliverance. David vows to broadcast the goodness of God to others in great need. God delivered David so wonderfully. God basically resurrected David from the cave, much like Jesus rose from the grave years later. What happened next to David is a great lesson for us in evangelism.

"All those who were in distress or in debt or discontented gathered around him, and he became their leader," 1 Samuel 22:2a. God used David's serious trial to launch a ministry to others. God does that for us too! Look up 2 Corinthians 1:3-4. See how God wants to use our trials to help others. Hurting people are hungry for real spiritual help. I see guys in jail who are so eager to learn how to straighten their lives out. So often in the "church," we are too comfortable.

Years ago a pastor asked me, "Are you satisfied with where you are at spiritually?" I said, Yes. What a horrible answer. Now I also can see that many in our churches are too comfortable spiritually.

Who were these four hundred men? They were the debt-ridden, the discontented, the outcast in society, those who were *"heavy laden."* Jesus also said, *"Come unto Me, all you who are weary and burdened, and I will give you rest,"* Matthew 11:28. Those who came to Adullam Cave were drawn, pulled, by the mercy of God. It's so amazing! The hand of evil Saul could not find David, but the hurting were led to David by God Himself. Wow! This is exactly how we are led to our Savior. Praise God.

Prayer: Dear most merciful Lord, forgive us. So often our evangelism efforts welcome those who are well off, not the needy and the hurting. May we see that it is the sick of heart that need help and deliverance through Jesus Christ. Help us to be more effective in evangelism for Your name's sake. In Jesus' name we pray. Amen.

Psalm 143:3-5

"The enemy pursues me, he crushes me to the ground; he makes me dwell in darkness like those long dead. So my spirit grows faint within me; my heart within me is dismayed. I remember the days of long ago; I meditate on all Your works and consider what Your hands have done."

"I remember the days of long ago"

<u>Our main problem in life is not what will happen to us, but how we will respond to what happens to us</u>. David said, *"the enemy pursues me."* He is under attack. *"My heart within me is dismayed."* David is feeling demonic pressure. How wonderfully David responds. *"I remember the days of long ago; I meditate on all of Your works and consider what Your hands have done."* David knew that God's faithfulness over the years was constant. The size of his God was much larger than the size of his current problem. That is the key!

David does not stare endlessly, at the *"enemy."* David thinks of God's character or His attributes down through history. He *"remembers"* God's deliverance to Abraham, Joseph, Moses and Joshua. As he *"remembers,"* and *"meditates,"* his focus shifts from his *"enemy,"* to God's merciful providence. David *"remembers"* how God protected him in the fight with the bear, the lion and Goliath. David's hope soars, as his trust in God goes up. The same will be true for us.

Jesus knew *"remembering"* was important when He corrected the Ephesian church for their cold hearts. *"Remembering"* is important to our repentance (Biblical change) process. *"Remembering"* helps us put off the old wrong thinking and replace it with right thinking. Jesus said to the Ephesians, *"Yet I hold this against you: You have forsaken your first love. <u>Remember</u> the height from which you have fallen! Repent and do the things you did at first,"* Revelation 2:4-5a. That is Biblical counsel from the world's best counselor. Members of this Ephesian church started out strong and then their love for God cooled off. They were struggling and needed to "remember."

Prayer: O Lord, may we *"remember"* how those saints from *"long ago"* were protected by Your powerful hand! May we then be faithful in the present, always keeping our eyes on You. For You are our great and compassionate God! We worship You. In Jesus' name we pray. Amen.

Psalm 143:8

"Let the morning bring me word of Your unfailing love, for I have put my trust in You. Show me the way I should go, for to You I lift up my soul."

What' is the meaning, *"to You I lift up my soul"*?

David is pleading expectantly to God in prayer. He is sure of God's coming mercy. David needs relief, for once again he is pursued by the enemy. Those on the front lines get attacked often! Should we expect anything less? David realizes that he is not strong enough to defeat the enemy by himself, nor is he able to take the strain of it all. He admits in verse four, *"My spirit grows faint within me; my heart within me is dismayed."* That is exactly our emotional state as we too plead with God to act for us.

When we are in deep trouble, we must openly admit it to God, as David does. David literally reaches for God. *"I spread out my hands to You; my soul thirsts for You like a parched land,"* Psalm 143:6. Only God can fill our yearning. David places his soul in God's care, *"To You I lift up my soul."* Our soul belongs to God. He gave it as a gift to us. We belong to Him both body and soul. Why? He made us, body and soul. We are here by His design, in His timing, for His purposes.

Paul tells us, *"Set your minds on things above, not on earthly things,"* Colossians 3:2. The *"above"* is in Heaven, where God is and where Christ is seated on His throne by His Father. Angels are all around the throne, not governing, but are servants of God! Angels are ministering spirits, ready and able to do God's will. When we pray, our spirits are transported to this throne room in Heaven. Like the angels, we must be ready and willing to serve God, right where He has presently placed us on Earth! It is for this reason that we pray with David, *"Show me the way I should go, for to You I lift up my soul."*

Prayer: Dear Father, Son and Holy Spirit, we are like ships on the ocean. You are our Captain. You show us that the most dangerous place on earth is safe, if we are in the center of Your will. And the safest place on earth is the most dangerous, if we are outside of Your will. Show us the way Lord. Place us in the center of Your divine will. In Jesus' name we pray. Amen.

Psalm 143:10

"Teach me to do Your will, for You are my God; may Your good Spirit lead me on level ground."

Which Spirit/spirit is leading us?

What a great prayer our text is! Only God's Spirit leads us to Himself and to a life of devotion to Him. God's Spirit is the Holy Spirit, the third person in the Trinity, who was already visible in the Old Testament. In Genesis 1:2, *"the Spirit of God was hovering over the waters."* In Genesis 6:3, God's Spirit was already contending with man to change his wicked habits. When David said, *"May Your good Spirit lead me on level ground,"* David very clearly understood that there was another spirit, an evil one that also wanted to lead him away from God.

Years ago I witnessed another spirit working in some churches in India. Many people were falling down, acting strange. My spirit was telling me that this is not right. But why? God opened my eyes after months of pleading with Him to understand this. He used Leviticus 19:30-31 NKJV to help me see something important about the spirit/Spirit world. *"You shall keep my Sabbaths and reverence My sanctuary: I am the LORD. Give no regard to mediums and familiar spirits; do not seek after them, to be defiled by them: I am the LORD your God."* The Israelites were going into Canaan where evil spirits were the norm and God was warning them.

What I saw was a perversion of worship to a *"familiar spirit,"* not to God. The people emptied their mind of clear thought by jumping and dancing, working themselves into a hypnotic frenzy. Empty minds are quickly filled with the demonic. That is why drugs and drunkenness are so wrong. When the conscience is dulled, we are quick to do what is shameful. In this place, even the pastors were "sleeping around" and drinking. There was so much anger. What they did in church was wrong. But what was even worse was the rest of the week. The lying, cheating and stealing was epidemic.

David prayed for God's *"good Spirit"* to lead him. Which Spirit or spirit is leading us? Our actions all week will be the proof.

Prayer: Dear Lord, You tell us that there is a spirit/Spirit war for our souls. May Your good Spirit lead us to a close relationship with You. For You are the one who sanctifies us. In Jesus' name we pray. Amen.

Psalm 144:3

"O LORD, what is man that You care for him, the son of man that You think of him?"

God's care, gives us great wisdom

All through the Bible, the fear of the LORD and knowledge of God are directly linked together. Wisdom is the right knowledge of God applied in our daily living. Wisdom rewards us with a long and productive life. Both wisdom and knowledge are why we need the Bible. Consider how the knowledge of God profitably affects us.

"Every prudent man acts out of knowledge," Proverbs 13:16. A prudent man considers how people in the world live differently and is convinced God knows best and lives accordingly.

"The mocker seeks wisdom and finds none, but knowledge comes easily to the discerning," Proverbs 14:6. Wisdom is not possible without the knowledge of God because God is truth. A mocker has no desire for the truth. A mocker sees himself, not God.

"The lips of the wise spread knowledge," Proverbs 15:7. There is a big warning in this verse! It is one thing to acquire knowledge; many do in various schools. But then, after graduating from a good school, they fail to lead a productive life. Their lifestyle and their way of dealing with people does not fit knowledge and wisdom. They said that they were in school to learn how to serve. Truth is, they wanted to be a king or a queen. It takes a wise person, filled with knowledge of God, to be His ambassador in this world.

"Gold there is, and rubies in abundance, but lips that speak knowledge are a rare jewel," Proverbs 20:15. One simple example of this is the whole evolution versus creation debate. One is foolishness, and one is wisdom. The Old Testament genealogies point to a 4004 year time frame before Christ. That revealed wisdom of God makes so much sense in understanding His plan for this world and for us personally.

Prayer: O Lord, we praise You for Your great care of us by teaching us what the world does not, which is knowledge and wisdom. How true it is, when we esteem Your knowledge, You are glorified and we are truly blessed. We thank You for Your truth that never changes. In Jesus' name we pray. Amen.

Psalm 145: 7&9

"They will celebrate Your abundant goodness and joyfully sing of Your righteousness." "The LORD is good to all; He has compassion on all He has made."

"The LORD is good to all"

Because of God's "goodness" that even the worst sinner can approach Him without fear. It is in God's divine nature that He is approachable, welcoming us sinners to come to Him. God's "goodness" permits us to come to Him for forgiveness. Hebrews 4:14-15 shows us Jesus is our sympathetic High Priest, who loves to intercede for us. Understanding the goodness of God is important when we pray to God, through Jesus. In Psalm 86:5 we read, *"You are forgiving and good, O LORD, abounding in love to all who call to You."*

God is "good," so we must be "good." The author of Hebrews gives us great advise. *"Remember those in prison as if you were their fellow prisoners, and those who are mistreated as if you yourselves were suffering,"* Hebrews 13:3. The chapter continues, *"<u>And do not forget to do good</u> and to share with others, for with such sacrifices God is pleased,"* Hebrews 13:16.

Satan pressed Adam and Eve in the garden to doubt God's "goodness." Since then, it is also our natural tendency to doubt God's goodness. Questioning the goodness of God, implies we know more about what is good than God does. Lord, forgive such idolatry.

In our trials, it is especially important to think and pray about the goodness of God. For it is in our trials that we are tempted to doubt the goodness of God. If God is for us, who can be against us? Even when we sin, our good God forgives, cleanses, and restores us.

Prayer: Good and loving Lord, we thank You for Your goodness to us. We confess that we have been much like the prodigal son who proudly left his father, demanding his goodness. We have been like the Pharisees who self-righteously demanded Your good blessings. How often You have told us, if we will just humble ourselves and pray, You will give out of Your goodness. Lord, humble us to see that like the prodigal we are hungry, dirty, wretched and in need of Your divine goodness and mercy. In Jesus' name we pray. Amen.

Psalm 145:18-19 NKJV

"The LORD is near to all who call upon Him, to all who call upon Him in truth. He will fulfill the desire of those who fear Him; He also will hear their cry and save them."

God will hear our cry!

Did you ever wonder how near God is to us? It does not matter where we are in this world, God is near! But then our text adds, God is especially near to those who call upon him in *"truth."* Our great God who moves His dependent children to pray, also moves His own heart to hear us! He will hear us because we are His workmanship.

"He also will hear their cry and save them." John Calvin said that "oppressions and afflictions make man cry, and cries and supplications make God hear." When man works, man works. But when man prays, God works! Even in the worst of tragedies, we serve a God who cares and works on our behalf.

Sometimes the way God works will surprise us. Surely, Noah did not expect to build an ark in a desert. Daniel did not expect a lion's den. Moses did not expect a burning bush. Esther did not expect to be a queen. Saul did not expect to be blinded by Jesus Christ! Now you and I are on the world's stage. God will help us in our time of crisis! *"He also will hear their cry and save them!"*

Don Moen was right! "God will make a way where there seems to be no way. He works in ways we cannot see. He will make a way for me. He will be my guide. Hold me closely to His side. With love and strength for each new day, He will make a way!"

God meets each of His children in their need. He will not let one of His children go through more than they can bear. *"Those who fear Him,"* know His presence is what we need. What great strength we have in taking God at His word, that all things will work for our good even if we do not understand how. That is where faith comes in.

Prayer: Dear Lord, we take great comfort in knowing You, *"will hear our cry."* We treasure Your nearness! We take great comfort that You will never leave or forsake us even in times of trouble. You are precious. Your presence is so sweet. In Jesus' name we pray. Amen.

Psalm 146: 7b-8

"The LORD sets the prisoners free, the LORD gives sight to the blind,
the LORD lifts up those who are bowed down,
the LORD loves the righteous."

Jesus' missionary focus

The Great Commission is clear concerning missions. We learn from Jesus that we need to go. But to whom must we go? What must we do when we go? Make *"disciples"* is the emphasis. Yet in examining the evangelism efforts of many, we see more of a desire to reach out to those in other churches. Then we say our church is actively growing in numbers. But is God's church really growing? Truly, we must disciple all who come, but are we reaching out to the lost?

We are often told to bring people to church. Again that is good but something is somewhat wrong with that. It is a pastor's job to equip believers to go out and do evangelism. That is meeting people where they are at. For example, yesterday I was at a bank. A worker there asked me what I do. I told him, "Evangelism type work, especially to prisoners and drug addicts." He broke down, crying. He admitted that he got strung out on cocaine the past weekend. He needed to be pointed to Christ right then.

Jesus was and still is specifically interested in *"prisoners," "the blind,"* and *"those who are bowed down."* Jesus sought them out. That is part of the *"go"* in the Great Commission. He did not wait for them to come to Him. Jesus never had a sign in front of a building announcing the worship times. Did Jesus even have His own building? Truly our buildings are needed, but most of the lost are in the world.

We need to invite all people everywhere, to come to Jesus, the only Savior there is. Jesus said, *"Come to Me, all you who are weary and burdened, and I will give you rest,"* Matthew 11:28. Jesus built His church from the broken and hurting. We must become a servant to the hurting, pointing them to a spiritual life with Christ. *"The LORD loves the righteous."* Let us then, bring His love with us into missions.

Prayer: Dear loving Lord and Savior, You sought us when we were blind and broken, prisoners to sin. May we not forget what we once were and how You changed us. May we reach out in Christ's love to others who do not yet know You. In Jesus' name we pray. Amen.

Psalm 147:3-4

"He heals the brokenhearted and binds up their wounds. He determines the number of stars and calls them each by name."

Our God heals broken hearts

No one can live well without hope. With God, there is no such thing as a hopeless situation. There are only those who lose hope because their hope is misplaced. God *"heals the brokenhearted."* O that the hurting might meet our Lord who was broken for them, all so that they might be healed in every way. Brokenness does not need to define who we are. Scripture reaches out to all of us! God can redefine any life through a rebirth! *"He binds up their wounds."*

The Gospel good news is: It is not when we were born into the world that matters, but when we are reborn in Christ. God knows who we are and what our situation is. If God, *"determines the number of stars and calls them each by name,"* then that must shout to us that God knows every person also. He knows you too! We are much more precious to God than a star. God gave us a spirit, which is our soul. No star has a soul. His living and loving Spirit is the One who cries out to our spirit! God's Spirit is called the Comforter. As Comforter, He heals broken hearts and binds up their wounds.

That wounded man who lays on the roadside in Luke 10 is you and I. That "good Samaritan" in the parable is still Jesus. When all others passed us by, He did not. Jesus has the physical blood of many races flowing through His heart, is also God. He brings us to the inn and gives us new clothes, even robes of righteousness.

He heals broken hearts. He sets our life on a new road that leads to Heaven instead of that place of eternal torment. We are now His child for all eternity. What is to come is far more important than where we have been. If God is for us who can be against us? For, *"He heals the brokenhearted and binds up their wounds,"* forever!

Prayer: O merciful Lord, what a compassionate and most powerful counselor You are. We praise You Father, Son and Spirit. For we who deserve our brokenness, are made whole by Your grace and now fit for Heaven. We worship You. In Jesus' name we pray. Amen.

Psalm 147:11

"The LORD delights in those who fear Him, who put their hope in His unfailing love."

Christmas, and God's unfailing love!

In a few days, it will be Christmas. Of all days of the year, many are discouraged and depressed. These are wrong responses to past hurts. There are many relationships that need to be fixed. Relationship fixing begins with Jesus who was born *"LORD."* If we do not have *"hope in His unfailing love,"* we will easily become depressed. Listen to one man who found hope in the midst of great discouragement.

Almost 160 years ago, in 1863, the great poet Henry Wadsworth Longfellow was sad and depressed on Christmas Day. His wife had just died in a fire and his son left to join the army. On that Christmas morning, Longfellow heard the local church bells ring and then wrote the wonderful Christmas carol, "I Heard the Bells on Christmas Day." He expressed his discouragement but then he wisely focused on the *"unfailing love"* of God!

> And in despair, I bowed my head;
> there is no 'peace on earth,' I said;
> for hate is strong, and mocks the song
> of 'Peace on Earth, Goodwill to Men!'
>
> Then pealed the bells more loud and deep:
> 'God is not dead nor doth He sleep;
> the wrong shall fail, the right prevail,
> with Peace on Earth, Goodwill to Men.'

The angel's words to Mary about the Christ child within her, are our words of comfort also. *"The angel went to her and said, 'Greetings to you who are highly favored! The Lord is with you,'"* Luke 1:28. In Christ, we too are highly favored. That baby who was physically in Mary, is spiritually in every Christian heart! *"The LORD delights in those who fear Him, <u>who put their hope in His unfailing love.</u>"*

Prayer: Gracious Lord, our hope is in Your Son and in His unfailing love. We thank You for Jesus, who unites us to You. In His name, we pray. Amen.

Psalm 148:1

"Praise the LORD. Praise the LORD from the heavens, praise Him in the heights above."

How do I not praise the Lord?

Psalm 148 and Psalm 150 both tell us: *"Praise the LORD."* So what then is the opposite of praising God? It would be a life of sadness and complaining. That pretty much describes a depressed person who has little hope! Studies show that 25% of college students are depressed. God describes much about man's problem in Proverbs 12:25 NKJV. *"Anxiety in the heart of a man causes depression, but a good word makes it glad."* *"Praising the LORD,"* are good words.

A long and difficult pregnancy <u>tempts</u> a woman to be anxious. Jesus called such worry, *"little faith"* in Matthew 6:30. There is a great <u>temptation</u> to fear when a man's job is not going well. And Jesus calls our fear, *"wicked and lazy"* in Matthew 25:26. Wicked because we are not trusting in God. Lazy because our faithfulness is missing in our daily living. Such a living pattern does not, *"Praise the LORD."*

Last week a man in prison told me everyone in prison should read "Climbing Out of Depression," a book I wrote ten years ago. He passed it on to a depressed man in the next cell who had a big smile a week later. But in the church, it's embarrassing to admit that we are depressed. I was that way once. In the church, we want to believe that we are so sanctified that there cannot be wrong thoughts, words and actions that can lead to depression. God gave us David, Elijah and Peter who were once depressed. They changed, and so can we.

Even pastors are more likely to be depressed on Mondays, after their busy weekend. Self-pity is a huge temptation. A trusting faith must not go down that deadly road. All of life is about being faithful, and then leave the results of our service in God's hands. The results are His responsibility, not ours. We need to praise the Lord and in faith, wait expectantly on Him. Let us all then, stay faithful. Let us do everything for God and never stop praising His holy name.

Prayer: Loving and gracious Lord, lift up those who are so sad and anxious. Help them to see that You will never leave them or forsake them in life's journey. In Jesus' name, we pray. Amen.

Psalm 149:4-5

"For the LORD takes delight in His people; He crowns the humble with salvation. Let the saints rejoice in this honor and sing for joy on their beds."

Sing for joy on your bed

Are we discouraged? Is our head bowed down? Are we troubled? Martha from Bethany was like that. She was, *"worried about many things!"* Jesus said, *"Martha, sit at My feet."* It is only at Jesus' feet that we can make sense out of the trials in life.

The psalmist tells us to rejoice in the honor that God has placed on us, His people. Our Good Shepherd loves His sheep, and especially cares for the one that is cast down in Psalm 42. When Jesus was busy counting His sheep, He found only 99. He knew the missing one was *"cast down"* and hurting. Such a sheep was an easy target for the wolf. Jesus quickly rescued that lost one and helped it to walk again. That was me and it could be you.

"The LORD takes delight in His people." At the time of salvation, you are a prince or princess in the eyes of God! Redeemed, you are a relative, even a co-heir with Jesus Christ! You are fully adopted into His family. God bought you with His Son's blood. He paid a lot for you. He took great joy in delivering you from the clutches of Satan. God now *"takes delight"* in your relationship with Him.

"He crowns the humble with salvation." Great trials are part of the humbling process that God puts us through. Think of how Joseph, Moses and David were humbled through their trials. God's *"crowns"* can only fit on humble heads! God knows how to prepare and shape us as vessels for His noble service.

"Let the saints rejoice in this honor and sing for joy on their beds." How we need a right attitude while we are on our beds. Self-pity is self-love and it is killing many people. Instead of self-pity, we need to rejoice in the goodness of God. Satan wants us to doubt God's love for us. God wants us to sing. May our great God who works all things for His glory and our good, put a grateful song in our hearts!

Prayer: Dear gracious Lord, forgive us for doubting and questioning Your goodness. Like Paul and Silas in prison, may we sing on our beds as we hope in Your deliverance. In Jesus' name we pray. Amen.

Psalm 150:2

"Praise Him for His mighty acts; praise Him according to His excellent greatness!"

Praise God, through Jesus we win!

When Adam fell in the garden, perfect praise of God immediately ended. The human nature of man was permanently changed, and will be, until man is once again forgiven of his sin and is right with God. After salvation comes gratitude and praise to God for restoring us.

The road to Heaven is called *"narrow and difficult"* to all those God mercifully saves. Grace-filled Christians are called to praise God for His deliverance. Granted, we live in a very fallen world, one that grumbles, and not thankful. We who are Christian, must remember how God called the children of Israel out of Egypt, out of sin and slavery to it! Remember how a week after their deliverance, they were grumbling, not praising God, and God was not pleased with them.

God took care of Israel, in a desert. Will He not take care of us in today's desert? At one time, *"Moses answered the people, 'Do not be afraid. Stand firm and you will see the deliverance the LORD will bring you today... The LORD will fight for you; you need only to be still,"* Exodus 14:13-14.

God took care of Judah who was surrounded by three enemies. *"Listen, all you of Judah and you inhabitants of Jerusalem, and you, King Jehoshaphat! Thus says the LORD to you: 'Do not be afraid nor dismayed because of this great multitude, For the battle is not yours, but God's,"* 2 Chronicles 20:15 NKJV. How we must praise our great God who still owns the battle!

God said to Isaiah, *"So do not fear, for I am with you; do not be dismayed, for I am your God. I will strengthen you and help you; I will uphold you with My righteous right hand,"* Isaiah 41:10.

"The plans of the LORD stand firm forever, the purposes of His heart through all generations," Psalm 33:11. God said of Himself, *"I the LORD, do not change,"* Malachi 3:6a. Jesus said, *"Surely I am with you always, to the very end of the age,"* Matthew 28:20b.

Prayer: O Lord, the very last verse in the Psalms is still Your will for our lives. *"Let everything that has breath praise the LORD. Praise the LORD!"* Psalm 150:6. In Jesus' name, hear our prayer. Amen.